Men and the Classroom

The teaching of young children has long been dominated by women. This global phenomenon is firmly rooted in issues relating to economic development, urbanisation, the position of women in society, cultural definitions of masculinity and the value of children and childcare. Yet, despite media scare stories and moral panics about the underachievement of boys, there are surprisingly few empirically supported answers to vital questions such as:

- Is the feminisation of the profession really a problem?
- How is the relationship of gender and teaching considered within a framework of feminist theory?
- What are the perceptions of students of teaching, in comparison to other professions?
- Why are so few men attracted to teaching?
- Can more men be attracted into the classroom?

The authors of this ground-breaking book have undertaken the largest, most in-depth study ever carried out on this topic, assessing both teachers' and students' views on teaching. Radical change is inevitably called for in order to increase the proportion of men entering the primary teaching profession, but many short-term and more achievable strategies are also suggested here which could be implemented by policy makers and senior managers quickly and efficiently. Academics, students and researchers will find this a long overdue exposé of one of the most critical issues facing the teaching profession today.

Sheelagh Drudy is Professor of Education at University College Dublin. **Maeve Martin** is Senior Lecturer in Education at the National University of Ireland. **Máiríde Woods** is Advocacy Executive in Comhairle (the Information, Advice and Advocacy Agency), Dublin. **John O'Flynn** is Lecturer at Mary Immaculate College of Education, Limerick.

Men and the Classroom

Gender imbalances in teaching

Sheelagh Drudy, Maeve Martin,
Máiríde Woods and John O'Flynn

Routledge
Taylor & Francis Group

LONDON AND NEW YORK

First published 2005 by Routledge
2 Park Square, Milton Park, Abingdon, Oxon OX14 4RN

Simultaneously published in the USA and Canada
by Routledge
270 Madison Ave, New York, NY 10016

Routledge is an imprint of the Taylor & Francis Group

© 2005 Sheelagh Drudy, Maeve Martin, Máiríde Woods and John O'Flynn

Typeset in Galliard by Keystroke, Jacaranda Lodge, Wolverhampton
Printed and bound in Great Britain by TJ International Ltd, Padstow,
Cornwall

British Library Cataloguing in Publication Data
A catalogue record for this book is available from the British Library

Library of Congress Cataloging in Publication Data
A catalog record for this book has been requested

ISBN 0–415–33568–X (hbk)
ISBN 0–415–33569–8 (pbk)

Contents

Tables

Figures

Acknowledgements

The research reported in this project was supported by many individuals and institutions, to whom the authors are deeply indebted.

The funding for this project was provided by the Research and Development Committee of the Department of Education and Science in Ireland, and this is very gratefully acknowledged. Mr Gearóid Ó Conluain of the Department of Education and Science was most generous in his help and support, as was the Gender Equality Unit of the Department of Education and Science.

The project was greatly facilitated by the support of the Education Departments at the National University of Ireland, Maynooth and at University College Dublin. Professor John Coolahan, Head of Education at NUI Maynooth is owed a particular debt of gratitude for his unfailing support. The research benefited greatly from the advice and guidance of an expert Advisory Group at the design stage. The members of this group were most generous with their time and insights and their contribution is most gratefully acknowledged. The members of the Advisory Group were: Professor John Coolahan, Education Department, NUI Maynooth; Professor Patrick Clancy, Department of Sociology, University College Dublin; Professor Áine Hyland, Education Department, University College Cork; Dr Peadar Cremin, Mary Immaculate College Limerick; Ms Mary Dunne, Department of Education and Science.

The team was greatly helped and encouraged at an early stage of the project by Ms Caoimhe Máirtín, formerly of St Patrick's College Drumcondra and the Marino College of Education, who provided information and advice. The research was also greatly supported and encouraged throughout the project by the Irish National Teachers' Organisation which also generously provided advice and information.

The greatest debt is owed to those who provided the data on which the report is based. The pupils in the sample and pilot studies were generous with their time and with their willingness to allow researchers into their lives at a period in which they were involved with very serious decision-making for their futures. The student teachers in the colleges of education co-operated in a most helpful and constructive way and provided insights into their own professional choices and development. This report is dedicated to these pupils and student teachers in a very particular way.

The principals and staffs in the sample and pilot study schools were most accommodating and unfailingly co-operative during the fieldwork period. The guidance counsellors in the schools were very supportive both in the facilitation of the fieldwork and in providing their own very valuable insights. College of education administrators and academics were most helpful in facilitating the study and in providing their views on the issues. The researchers are very much indebted to them all. We are also very grateful to the practising primary teachers who participated in the focus-group study and to all of our research students who encouraged us during the research and who frequently provided their own insights.

Data collection was greatly helped by the ready and efficient provision of information on patterns of college entry by Dr Martin Newell and his staff at the Central Applications Office in Galway. We thank them for this. A particular debt of gratitude is owed to Ms Miriam Galvin of University College Dublin who provided sterling assistance at the editorial stage of the project and contributed greatly to its finalisation. Finally, sincere thanks are due to Ms Alison Foyle, Ms Jessica Simmons and Ms Anna Clarkson of RoutledgeFalmer for their advice and encouragement.

Chapter 1

Introduction: men, the classroom and feminisation

Gender differences in educational participation and achievement are a major subject of public policy concern internationally. International performance indicators routinely include data on gender differences. Each year, the publication of data such as those contained in the OECD annual publication, *Education at a Glance*, and the release of national statistics on examination performance, tend to generate 'moral panics' in the media about the underperformance of boys and what this might represent (Arnot and Weiner, 1999: 7). These debates are frequently followed by discussions in the media on the assumed impact on boys of the feminisation of teaching and the low number of males who choose the profession (and, in particular, primary/elementary teaching) as a career. The quality of the teaching workforce has been a central concern in the establishment of a major international review on the attraction, development and retention of teachers established under the auspices of the OECD (OECD, 2003b). As part of this international review, the decline of the proportion of males in teaching has been highlighted as an issue of concern to policy makers (OECD, 2004).

This book explores a number of themes relating to the choice of teaching as a career. It examines the existing balance of women and men in the teaching profession internationally; the patterns at entry to teaching; and, finally, some of the questions that are raised by these trends. The analysis of international trends forms an essential background to the study of gender differences in choice of teaching as a career.

The site chosen for the survey of school leavers and student teachers in order to explore the attitudes, values and trends underlying the choice of teaching, and the gender differences evident in these patterns, is the Republic of Ireland. Ireland represents an interesting case study in a number of respects. During the 1990s it experienced very rapid economic growth. In the 1980s the Irish economy was stagnant, with high unemployment and high emigration. In the 1990s Ireland became one of the new 'tiger' economies with increases in transnational corporation exports accounting for up to three-quarters of the economic growth, particularly in computer related industries (O'Hearn, 1999: 125). The remainder of the growth was in associated service and construction sectors, and in tourism. Ireland became a 'showpiece of globalization, a prime example of how a region could turn around from economic laggard to tiger in just a few years, by integrating itself maximally into the global division of labour' (ibid.). Ireland, at the beginning of the twenty-first century, is the most globally integrated country in the world due to its deep economic links and its high level of personal contact with the rest of the world as well as its technological/internet connectivity and its political engagement with international organisations (A.T. Kearney/*Foreign Policy*, 2004).

Ireland has been attractive to knowledge-based industries such as computers and telecommunications, not only because of its advantageous tax packages for foreign (especially US) investors and access to EU markets, but because of the relatively high rates of educational participation among its youth population. It is widely acknowledged that, in Ireland as well as internationally, the decade of the 1990s was a period of unprecedented change in education as well as in the economy.

While the very factors that underpinned Ireland's economic growth in the 1990s made it very vulnerable to the global economic downturn after September 11th 2001, its rates of educational participation and generally good performance on international testing measures (e.g. Shiel *et al.*, 2001; OECD, 2003a), together with a rolling programme of educational reform,[1] continue to prove attractive to foreign investors. As regards entry to the teaching profession, through the periods of rapid economic growth in the 1990s and through the subsequent economic downturn since 2001, the number of applicants for places on teacher education courses has demonstrated an overall increase, mainly accounted for by female applicants. The consequent decline in the proportion of males in teaching and the feminisation of the profession, especially at primary/elementary level, has become the focus of frequent expressions of alarm by journalists and teacher union representatives alike. This book begins by raising the question of whether the feminisation of teaching is a problem, and whether it should be a cause for alarm among policy makers. The book locates patterns of entry to teaching within the context of international research on gender and teaching. It utilises a study of the career choices of school leavers and student teachers, their values and attitudes to teaching, to explore the reasons for the low representation of men in teaching. The site for this case study is Ireland. While entry to teaching in Ireland demonstrates patterns that have a social and historical specificity, given Ireland's specific location as a country that has, in policy terms, embraced the global changes of late modernity, it is argued that the trends observable in this study of gender differences in choice of teaching in Ireland may be interpreted as an 'ideal type' in terms of the structuring of the profession.

Feminism and gender

In order to discuss men and teaching it is necessary to begin by considering feminist views on the issues. Given the brief of this study of men and teaching it could be argued that it might be more logical to have begun with gender studies or, more specifically, with men's studies. However, since these latter areas have arisen subsequent to and possibly as a response to feminism, the various perspectives within women's studies can be regarded as being historically and theoretically prior.

Feminism is a broad-based philosophical outlook that includes a variety of perspectives, theories and methodologies. Tong groups these into the categories of 'liberal', 'Marxist', 'radical', 'psychoanalytic', 'socialist', 'existentialist', and 'post-modern' (Tong, 1992: 1). Without wishing to reduce the complexity of her analysis, two of the main conclusions presented by Tong may be highlighted. First, she historicises and critiques liberal feminism, which had its origins in the late nineteenth century and was, among other matters, concerned with contemporaneous education policy (ibid.: 11–37). Some of the issues addressed and indeed framed by such liberal feminist perspectives will be discussed below. Second, from an objective and theoretical point of view, she regards socialist feminism as being the most sophisticated form of feminist analysis available in that it includes sociological categories other than gender[2] in its analysis (ibid.: 235–7). In a similar vein, Biklen and Pollard argue that 'we must speak of feminisms rather than feminism because of the many differences between perspectives on gender in feminist theoretical positions' (Biklen and Pollard, 1993: 3). They make a distinction between political categories of feminism, such as 'socialist', 'liberal' and 'radical', and those categories which refer to the theoretical orientations of feminists, namely, 'materialist', 'cultural' and 'post-modern' (ibid.). A second distinction made by Biklen and Pollard may be helpful in the interpretation of information arising from this research on teaching. They suggest that the various traditions and theories can be divided into two main areas, according to how these theories respond to and consider difference. They describe these perspectives thus:

> One perspective emphasizes commonalities among women and minimizes difference. Views which represent this perspective cluster around the understanding that gender links all women together. . . . Another group of feminist perspectives clusters around what we might call a multipositional or multilocational view. These perspectives represent a way of considering gender that argues that other identities (of race, class, ethnicity . . .) cannot be subsumed under the category 'woman'.
>
> (Biklen and Pollard, 1993: 3–4)

Tong (1992: 174–6) adumbrates the view that the latter approach represents a development from the former. It is this general approach which underpins much of the perspective and methodology of this research, insofar as the issues of career values, occupational choice and teacher recruitment are considered within an overall social and economic context, and not in relation to gender in isolation. It is recognised that factors other than gender may be related to the low numbers of males who elect to take up teaching as a profession.

Campbell and Greenberg (1993) note that studies which unquestioningly report their findings in terms of 'sex-differences' also tend to conflate the categories of 'sex' and 'gender' and in the process fail to distinguish between biological differences and culturally-acquired behaviours and/or norms. It is useful then, to make a clear distinction between what is understood by biological sex (male/female) and by gender (masculine/feminine). In practice, it is not always easy to separate these two categories and the 'grey area' in between is the focus of much debate. However, the theoretical view that 'sex' and 'gender' are discrete terms that describe very different aspects and conditions of human life informs the approach to this study of recruitment to teaching.

Campbell and Greenberg also argue that, very often, the differences within each sex are greater than the differences that exist between the sexes (1993: 76–8). To an extent, this observed tendency is borne out in empirical studies of school leavers' and college students' levels of attainment, career-related values, and perceptions of teaching as a career.

There are a number of terms that are common to all gender studies. Britzman states that causality and origin are the primary concerns of essentialist theories of gender, and that such views are intricately linked with common sense. In other words, essentialist theories suggest that masculinity and femininity are innate human characteristics acquired at birth. For example, from an essentialist perspective it would be regarded as natural that men should seek out technical careers in technology and science rather than careers in social services. She comments that:

> In this view, gender exists prior to the social meanings it generates: that is, gender is a function of nature and thus already contains particular qualities prior to how these qualities become reworked by social and historical meanings. For example, caring has come to be regarded as being a natural 'female' trait or type of occupation.
>
> (Britzman, 1993: 31)

Such a view of gender has much in common with theories of socialisation into sex-roles, such as that developed by Parsons in the mid-twentieth century. Parsons' theory of socialisation represents a modified form of essentialism in that, although it is assumed that males take on masculine identities and females take on feminine identities, they must learn to do so through the process of socialisation in the home and at school (Parsons, 1959). Thus, while it is acknowledged that social processes are involved, these are assumed to be natural and 'normal'.

Against this, theories of social constructivism, especially those developed by radical feminists, 'push at the boundaries of common sense and challenge the historicity of normative categories; how they become established, the languages that orient them, and the structures that maintain normality and abnormality' (Britzman, 1993: 32). Extreme versions of social constructivism are controversial because they 'decentre the subject'. An example of this would be the view that male and female identities are formed apart from any innate or biological traits (ibid.). This perspective has been challenged on two major grounds. First of all, it fails to accommodate the possibility that biochemical factors may influence the disposition and behaviour of men and women. Second, it is assumed that individual subjects are passively socialised into gendered roles as opposed to beingn active agents in the formation of their own identities.

Clearly, it is beyond the scope of this study to enter into any form of 'nature/ nurture' debate. However, it may be useful to bear in mind that, while in reality it is difficult to separate the two, the concepts of sex and gender are quite distinct. In some areas of human experience, for example, reproduction, the distinction is quite clear, yet in others, such as work and familial responsibilities, the boundaries are less clear. Within the biological category of 'sex', the distinction between 'male' and 'female' is generally unproblematic. The same cannot be said for 'gender', which differentiates between 'masculine' and 'feminine'. Ramsden describes the 'problem' of gender thus:

> That role and constellation of temperament, attitudes and behaviours – what our sexual definition requires of us – may be called our gender. What is expected to be appropriate to or typical of one or other sex is referred to as femininity or masculinity.
>
> (Ramsden, 1988: 22)

He argues that this process, by which biological sex is made to match the 'appropriate' gender identity leads to both sexism and sex-stereotyping (ibid.: 23–4). So, the designation of persons (or their occupations) as 'masculine' or 'feminine' may be viewed as either descriptive, prescriptive or both. Moreover, these identities are constructed in terms of polarities – i.e. one speaks of 'the opposite sex' (ibid.: 22). Biklen and Pollard put forward this definition:

> Gender is a category of analysis that refers to the social construction of sex. What we have come to identify as belonging to men's or women's behaviors, attitudes, presentation of self, and so on is produced by social relationships and continually negotiated and maintained within cultures.
>
> (Biklen and Pollard, 1993: 2)

Other problems emerge when the apparently objective, biological labels of 'male' and 'female' are used to describe and prescribe typical and appropriate behaviour for persons of either sex. That is, there is a conflation of the concepts of biological sex and gender. As Britzman had noted, this reflects the common sense view.

It might be concluded therefore that, while it is possible to make theoretical distinctions between sex/gender, male/masculine and female/feminine, in some theoretical positions and in everyday language, such terms tend to be regarded as synonymous. Moreover, even when a desire to delineate meanings exists, it is quite difficult to distinguish completely those qualities of women and men that are innately biological and psychological from those that are culturally acquired or socially constructed.

A third problem, and one which is most relevant to issues relating to recruitment into teaching, stems from the relational frame in which femininity and masculinity are inevitably located. The very confusion (and controversy) which surrounds the discourse on gender itself constitutes a part of social reality that is relevant to this research. As Christine Williams (1995: 49) states: 'Gender differences may be an ideological fiction but they have very real material consequences.'

Thus, feminist definitions of sex and gender make a clear distinction between the two concepts. This can best be summarised by using the distinction made by the anthropologist Ann Oakley. She used the term 'sex' to refer to the most basic physiological differences between women and men. 'Gender', on the other hand, refers to the culturally specific patterns of behaviour which may be attached to the sexes. It is, thus, culturally determined and highly variable (Oakley, 1972). Cultural definitions and perceptions of 'gender appropriate' behaviour patterns, choices and occupations are fundamental to understanding the levels of male/female representation in the teaching profession.

Current patterns in the teaching profession

When sociologists and educators refer to 'feminisation' they are referring to labour market changes where the participation of women in various occupations is increasing. The changes in gender composition at entry to teaching are the focus of our research and the trends are outlined below. The existing composition in the profession itself is first presented.

Female predominance in school teaching is to be found in most countries throughout the world. In all European member states, and indeed in former Eastern bloc satellite states for which figures are available, women are in the majority at primary level. In some countries they are greatly in the majority with the largest proportions found in Brazil, the Russian Federation, Italy and Slovakia where women form over 90 per cent of primary/elementary school teachers (UNESCO, 2003). In only a few countries are the number of women and men in primary/elementary teaching approximately equal. These are China, Indonesia and Tunisia, where women form between 49 and 54 per cent of the primary teaching force (ibid.). However, globally, the patterns in less developed countries present some variation. Females are in a minority in primary teaching in the least developed countries (UNESCO, 2003). While the proportion of women in primary teaching increased in all geographical regions worldwide in the latter part of the twentieth century (the period 1970–97), in the least developed countries they remained in a minority (see UNESCO, 2001, Appendix 1, Table 1). Indeed, examination of the proportions of women in teaching in the different regions worldwide suggests that the proportions could reasonably be taken as indicators of economic development in the various regions (ibid. and UNESCO, 2003).

At secondary level internationally, the percentage of women teachers is lower than at primary level. For example, in OECD countries the United States, the United Kingdom and Ireland are among those with higher proportions of women teachers at second level, the US having 56 per cent at lower and upper secondary/ high school, the UK with 59 per cent and Ireland with 58 per cent at lower and upper secondary combined (UNESCO, 2003). However, a number of countries have higher proportions of women teachers in secondary/high school. For example, Italy (73 per cent at lower, and 59 per cent at upper secondary) Canada, with 67 per cent at lower and upper secondary combined, Finland (71 per cent at lower, and 57 per cent at higher secondary), the Czech Republic (81 per cent at lower, 56 per cent at upper secondary) all have overall higher proportions of women teachers in secondary/high schools. At the other end of the spectrum there are some countries with very low proportions of female teachers at secondary level. Exact comparisons are difficult as many of these countries, unlike Ireland, combine their figures for primary and lower secondary and provide upper secondary separately. There are also slight variations according to the different compilations of databases (e.g. as between OECD and UNESCO figures, and sometimes even between different tables produced by each of these organisations). The proportions for women in upper secondary are particularly low in the following countries: the Netherlands (40 per cent), Germany (39 per cent), Switzerland (32 per cent) and Korea (28 per cent) (UNESCO, 2003). As for less developed countries, the proportion of women in second level teaching is even smaller than that in primary teaching (see Appendix 1, Table 1).

No discussion on the feminisation of teaching can ignore management structures. The management of teaching is one area where there is little evidence of feminisation. While teaching is a predominantly female profession, it is largely administered and managed by men (Acker 1989, 1994; Lynch, 1994; Griffin, 1997; Warren, 1997). In all countries for which figures are available, women are under-represented in educational management. For example, although women are in the majority in primary teaching they hold under half of the primary headships in Italy, Ireland and Austria. They represent a little more than half in Sweden and the United Kingdom. The highest percentage is found in France (65 per cent), while in Denmark barely 17 per cent of *folkeskole* headships are occupied by women (European Commission, 1997: 115). In secondary education, in most of the countries for which data are available, only between 21 and 30 per cent of school principals are women. This rate is, however, very much higher in Sweden (over 40 per cent), while in Luxembourg and Austria it scarcely reaches 19 and 18 per cent respectively (ibid.).

However under-represented women are in principals' posts, it remains the case that men are under-represented in the classroom, but especially at primary/ elementary school level. To what extent a pattern which is almost universal throughout the developed world could be considered problematic merits some exploration.

So, is there a problem?

It would appear that the issue of whether the high proportion of women in, and entering, the teaching profession (and its corollary, the small proportion of men – in primary/elementary teaching especially) is perceived as a problem very much depends on the perspective of the commentator. Certainly, the expression of concern is not new. There is evidence of the expression of fears arising from the increasing feminisation of teaching as early as the end of the nineteenth century in the United States (Hansot, 1993) and in the 1950s and 1960s in the United Kingdom (Acker, 1994). Recently, in the United Kingdom the problem of teacher recruitment has become the direct concern of policy makers (House of Commons Education and Employment Committee, 1997–8). Many of the types of concerns that have been expressed about the feminisation of teaching may be grouped under the following headings: (a) male role models; (b) levels of competence of female teachers; (c) the professional status of teaching.

Male role models

One strand of commentary relates to concerns that boys require male teachers in schools if they are to develop properly both academically and personally. This expression of concern focuses in particular on male underachievement in relation to their female counterparts. Recent research and public examination results in many countries have tended to confirm patterns of gender differences in academic achievement – i.e. on average, in the last decade and a half of the twentieth century in most of the developed world girls perform better. Girls learn to read earlier, obtain higher grades and co-operate more with their teachers. The tendency among journalists, policy makers and other social commentators to connect the issues of boys' performance in schools with the feminisation of teaching has been observed by Miller. In some cases, she observes, the latter is used as a scapegoat for the former and she rejects any interpretation of the situation in purely causal terms, pointing out that the values and mechanisms of the wider society need to be included in any such analysis (Miller, 1996: 157–8). Gender differences in performance are not necessarily associated with the feminisation of teaching. When looking at academic achievement and performance, it is also very important to consider factors other than the sex of students – such as social class and locality. In particular, social class has proved to be a major factor in school retention for both boys and girls (Epstein et al., 1998; Lynch, 1999).

Without doubt, data on gender differences in performance in public examinations in Ireland and many other countries indicate that girls' performance is better overall (Drudy and Lynch, 1993; OECD, 2003a; OFSTED, 2003). However, there is no evidence that this is necessarily correlated with the feminisation of teaching. International studies on performance in mathematics at age fifteen indicate that boys outperform girls in these tests (although these differences could be associated with the tests themselves – Drudy, 1996). Whatever the reason for these gender differences in mathematics test results, there is no evidence that boys underperform in mathematics in countries in which the teaching forces have very high proportions of women. While boys' scores are significantly higher than those of girls in many countries in maths, the gender differences are uneven in science and girls' scores are significantly better in reading literacy (Shiel *et al.*, 2001: 92–3; OECD, 2003a: 127).

In recent times much concern has been expressed in the media about the lack of 'male role models' in teaching, especially in the primary/elementary sector. It might, perhaps, be more productive to think of this issue in broader terms – i.e. in terms of socialisation and the hidden curriculum of schooling. The presence or absence of male primary/elementary teachers is an issue that has been argued to be relevant to all gender and education concerns. While there is widespread commentary and opinion on the assumed need for male role models, there is relatively little systematic research on this matter. Such research as has been conducted raises interesting questions. For example, Mancus (1992) found that boys and girls were less rigid in their gender-role classifications when they had both male and female teachers. Compared with boys who experienced no male teachers, boys in mixed-staff schools were more likely to view both males and females as nurturing and as having authority. These perceptions, she argues, gave them a wider range of behavioural choices. They were more likely to see themselves as academically competent and thus more motivated towards achievement. In addition, 'they will be more likely to share authority and express nurturing behaviour when they see male teachers doing so' (1992: 126–7). This area merits further research so that the fears and assertions expressed in the media can be replaced with comment and analysis based on systematic observations.

Levels of competence

Questions such as those raised above indicate certain assumptions about the relative competence of men and women teachers. Acker's examination of debates on teachers (of either sex) indicates that much of it reflects a lack of respect for their intellectual abilities (Acker, 1994: 81). In particular, there is evidence of a low regard for women teachers (ibid.). Issues have also been raised about the stressful impact on women teachers arising from teacher accountability procedures in the UK which, it is argued, move practices away from humanistic, wholistic and child-centred pedagogy (Raphael Reed, 1998: 66–7) and towards more 'phallo-centric' school cultures based on practices invoked by total quality management. Recent research (Mahony *et al.*, 2004) suggests that performance management systems now being introduced into what is ostensibly a feminised profession represent a move towards the masculinisation of teaching as both an activity and as an organisational structure.

Internationally, there are little robust data on the comparative competence of men and women teachers already in the profession. There is some information on this issue at point of entry to the profession in the form of gender differences in awards made to graduates of primary and post-primary initial teacher education programmes, and also from skills tests administered to newly qualified teachers. For example, in the United Kingdom the Teacher Training Agency has conducted skills tests in the areas of numeracy, literacy and information and communications technology. These tests provided little evidence of superior competence for either gender. While men passed the numeracy test with fewer attempts than women, the reverse was true for literacy. There was no significant difference between the performance of men and women on the ICT test (TTA, 2003). Other research has suggested a somewhat greater tendency for males to withdraw from elementary/primary initial teacher education programmes (Edmonds et al., 2002) but there is no evidence that this is linked to the issue of competence. Evidence at point of graduation can be obtained from figures on the comparative levels of awards made to graduating male and female student teachers. Such courses include substantive components of classroom practice, which is evaluated through systematic observation. Figures from the case study country (Ireland) are presented in Table 1.1.

These data indicate that, in Ireland at least, there are no grounds for disparaging the level of achievements of entrants to teaching. A high proportion of these graduates achieved honours in their awards. The assessments on which these awards are based involve a combination of performance on practice in the classroom, on assignments and on examinations in the foundation and curricular areas

Table 1.1 Awards of initial teacher education graduates, B.Ed. and Higher Diploma in Education (HDE), 1997/1998–1999/2000; by gender, Irish universities and colleges of education

Award	B.Ed. Males %	B.Ed. Females %	B.Ed. Total[†] %	HDE Males %	HDE Females %	HDE Total %
1st Class Honours	2.3	3.0	2.9	6.1	9.7	8.7
2nd Class Honours[‡]	58.2	86.2	82.9	47.9	60.4	57.0
Pass	39.5	10.8	14.2	46.0	29.9	34.3
Total	100.0	100.0	100.0	100.0	100.0	100.0
N	129	956	1,085	707	1,907	2,614

Source: Figures from the Higher Education Authority (HEA)

[†] Results from the B.Ed. degree for one of the universities and its affiliate colleges are not included as exact comparisons are difficult. This institution awards a pass B.Ed. only after three years. A post-graduate year is required for an honours degree.

[‡] Only one university education department distinguishes between 2:1 and 2:2 so the figures are amalgamated for this department.

of education. Indeed, combined with the very competitive nature of entry to these courses, Irish teachers entering the profession appear to be at a high level of competence.

There are, however, important differences according to gender in the level of awards in initial teacher education. Similar to the overall pattern in the humanities as a whole at Bachelors degree level, and indeed to the pattern in all faculties in the university sector in Ireland (Drudy, 2004), women graduating from education courses are achieving honours in higher proportions than their male counterparts. On the basis of professional competence, therefore, increasing proportions of female entrants should not be a cause for concern. On the other hand, important issues in relation to the relative performance of males on education and other courses are raised by these figures. These are worthy of research, debate and analysis.

Professional status

There has been a great deal of debate concerning the issue of whether teaching is or is not a 'profession' (Drudy and Lynch, 1993: 90–1). Some sociologists (e.g. Johnson, 1972, 1977) have argued that 'professionalism' is a peculiar type of occupational control and that it is not an inherent expression of the nature of certain occupations. An occupation is called a profession when it exercises colle- giate control, i.e. when it is the primary authority defining the relationship between the giver and receiver of its services. Professional groups, Johnson claims, are those that exercise considerable control over the services they offer, hence the desire of emerging occupations to label themselves 'professional'. In Johnson's schema, teachers are not professionals because they do not exercise sufficient control over their services. On the other hand, Burke (1992: 216) suggests that when a sufficiently developed knowledge base exists to support, inspire and inform the practice of teaching – and he argues that it does – then one is dealing with a professional area and professional people. Burke also points out that professionals in bureaucratic employments are torn between maintaining their professionalism and striving for working conditions that benefit their status and responsibility (ibid., 194).

Lortie (1975: 10) describes the teacher's social position as being 'special but shadowed', and presents the following scenario of the 'status anomalies' that teaching bears:

> It is honoured and disdained, praised as 'dedicated service' and lampooned as 'easy work'. It is permeated with the rhetoric of professionalism yet features incomes below those earned by workers with considerably less education.

Part of the status problem with teaching in countries such as the United States and Britain (although less so in Ireland) arises from its eased entry, relative to professions in law, medicine and business. Formal certification at degree level is only relatively recent, teacher training is highly accessible, and admission policies for teaching have a non-elitist tradition (Lortie, 1975; Lacey, 1994).

Lacey argues that processes of 'anticipatory socialization' are involved in the choice of career, particularly for those entering the older, established professions. He states that:

> Prestigious training institutions are able to attract high-flying individuals from social elites who will go on to obtain prominent positions within their professions and therefore ensure the reputation and high standing of the training institution with the next generation of aspirants. Where competition for entry is fierce this hierarchy of institutions, usually backed by real advantages in career and income, can have a marked socialising effect. It is necessary for individuals to prepare themselves quite carefully to become the kind of person that the professional norms demand.
>
> (Lacey, 1994: 124)

Unlike the established professions, teaching does not recruit from any elite social group; rather it tends to be a means for upward social mobility, particularly for men (Lacey, 1994; Lortie, 1975).

Comparatively speaking, the induction system for teaching is relatively short and casual (Burke, 1996). Lortie states that most teachers are 'self-socialized' into the occupation and have definite ideas about their role before entering teaching. Self-socialisation tends to be based more on subjective experience (as pupil and later as teacher) than it is on initial training, induction or in-service training. This supports the common sense assumption that 'anybody can teach'; in addition it devalues the specific professional aspects of teaching: 'It is a potentially powerful influence which transcends generations, but the conditions of transfer do not favour informed criticism, attention to specifics, or explicit rules of assessment' (Lortie, 1975: 63).

Thus qualifications and induction procedures are areas which affect the status of teaching. Primary teaching may be further devalued by the fact that the professional training and academic development of most student teachers are combined into one preparatory programme, unlike other professions including secondary teaching. Burke (1992) suggests that the status of primary teaching in Ireland could be enhanced by separating these two aspects of preparation for teaching.

The status of teaching suffers also from its 'careerless' structure. As Lortie (1975: 84–102) argues, upward movement is the essence of career and there is little opportunity for this in teaching. The pay structure is 'front-loaded', and its rewards for long years of service are described as 'delayed gratification'. He argues that this 'gentle incline' suits women more than men; men look for other positions within the education system. Lortie's analysis of women's participation in paid employment may appear chauvinist from an early twenty-first-century perspective. Nonetheless, his comments on the implications of the reward system in teaching are still relevant:

It (the reward system of salary and promotion) subtly depreciates the status of classroom teaching; it is not enough to be 'merely' a teacher, for one must also be on the way to higher rank or, if a woman, married. This pattern of depreciation probably gives a certain fragility to relationships between younger and older teachers. Young men do not see older male teachers as models for emulation – their models are likely to be administrators.

(ibid.: 100)

According to Lortie (p. 6), teaching carries less prestige for men than it does for women: similar incomes have less 'value' for male teachers than they have for their female colleagues. In his analysis, a teaching salary makes an inadequate contribution to the male's principal economic role – as breadwinner. This, he argues, is confirmed by the higher proportion of males than females who find it necessary to take additional employment. It seems obvious to state that the economic roles of both men and women have changed somewhat in the past two decades. However, the idea of men as breadwinners (and women as homemakers) is one that persists and is sustained through domestic ideology. The issue is not whether a teaching salary is sufficient for a man, married or single. Rather, it is the perception of its adequacy that has the greatest influence on the status of teaching. As illustrated above, teachers and student teachers are sensitive to public beliefs about teachers' salaries.

Since the nineteenth century teachers have tended to be controlled by others: 'Those who taught school . . . were hired by local authorities for designated periods to perform stipulated duties for predetermined salaries' (ibid.: 2–3). Arguably, teaching still differs from other professions in these respects. Established doctors, solicitors and accountants are much more in control of their time, duties and income than are established teachers. Teaching also tends to be more bureaucratised than these professions. With the transition from rural to urban life 'the' teacher, a figure of respect and authority, is replaced by 'a' teacher, one of many who is answerable to his/her 'principal'. Assistant and principal teachers in turn are subordinate to administrators and academics and, as such, have a lack of control over professional practice (ibid., 10). An indirect form of control comes in the way of school organisation: teachers have always been physically separated from each other in practice, an organisational process which hinders professional interdependence and collegiality. Teachers have been slow to contest issues of control in education practice. The associative factor in teaching has come relatively recently and, according to Lortie, is closer in function to a blue-collar union than to professional organisations (ibid.: 17).

In Ireland the lack of a professional teaching council was identified as a concern as far back as the 1980s (Coolahan, 1981: 230). Burke (1996: 128) argues that: 'status is not the essence of professionalism but rather a corollary of it for professionality is concerned with competence, not prestige'. He suggests that the teaching body requires more self-regulation and more self-definition in order to identify itself as a profession (ibid.: 132). It must be said, however, that recent changes in Irish education have given more professional control to teachers. For example, teachers and union representatives now sit on curriculum review boards. As in parts of the United Kingdom, especially Scotland and Northern Ireland, the establishment of Teaching Councils has enhanced the professional status of teaching in a number of respects. In Ireland also, a national Teaching Council is under implementation, following the passing of the *Teaching Council Act*, 2001. When fully implemented under the terms of this Act, the role of the Teaching Council will include the establishment, publishing, review and maintenance of codes of professional conduct for teachers. Given the development of the educational knowledge base, the fact that teaching in the United Kingdom and in Ireland is now an all-graduate profession, the nature of teacher involvement in curriculum and policy development, the growth and importance of continuing in-career education for teachers, and the predicted involvement of teachers in the regulation of the profession and of the professional affairs of teachers through representation on Teaching Councils, it is reasonable to conclude that, in Ireland, and in the United Kingdom, at any rate, teaching is a profession in any sense of the term (Drudy, 2001). However, the international literature and the level of regulation of teachers in the United Kingdom and Ireland illustrate that, relative to the older established professions, teachers are still subject to much control, and this level of control may continue to undermine the professional status of teachers. The issue of control is closely related to gender and to the feminisation of schooling, and the hierarchical relation between teachers and administrators is to some extent gendered (Miller, 1992; Robinson and Huffman, 1982). The feminisation of teaching does not refer solely to gender imbalance; it describes also the processes by which male and female teachers have been made to conform to the pervasive constraint, of educational systems and environments.

Occupational status is often associated with the designation of an occupation as 'professional'. Teaching is not afforded the same professional prestige as many other occupations which require university degrees, and the principal factors which undervalue its prestige have been suggested above. Etzioni (1969) uses the term 'semi-professions' to describe those occupations which attract a high proportion of women, are subject to tight external control and involve a 'caring' role. From this point of view, teaching and nursing are regarded as having the same occupational status. Basten (1997) reports that, in the Soviet era of Eastern Europe, both the prestige and monetary rewards of medical doctors decreased as they became more feminised.

Teaching's long association with service has also influenced its social status. The idea of teaching as a vocation may have compensated for its ill-defined professional status. As Lortie has argued, teachers, as well as the general public have sustained the ideology that, in teaching, the theme of service is incompatible with that of material rewards. Both culturally and structurally then, teaching has tended to be rigorously controlled. There are indications which suggest that, in both societal and individual terms, the theme of service is not valued to the extent that it was previously.

Additional problems have emerged in recent years, notably, the public criticisms of teaching standards (Coolahan, 1981; Burke, 1996) and, of particular significance for men, the growing public suspicion of occupations which involve work with children (Penn, 1997; Johnston et al., 1998). This is not to put forward a pessimistic view. What needs to be recognised is that ideas and beliefs about teaching are undergoing some change. The historical patterns are being repeated to some extent, but at the same time societal views about teaching as well as socialisation into teaching are being renegotiated. These changes need to be recognised if young men and young women of quality are to be recruited into the profession.

The impact of the numerical dominance of women in teaching has stimulated some contributors to this debate, from the 1950s onwards, to suppose that disastrous consequences will follow for the profession (Acker, 1994: 77). Some have argued that there has been a reduction in the social prestige of the teaching profession due to the high number of women now employed in it (Basten, 1997: 56). Acker points out that four professions are commonly classified as 'semi-professions'. These are school teaching, social work, nursing and librarianship. All four are highly feminised (Acker, 1994: 77). These writers point to an assumption (mainly in Britain and a number of other European countries, and the US) that the increasing dominance of women in teaching has a negative effect on the professional status of the occupation, or that women teachers are to blame for the low status of the profession (ibid.: 80; Wylie, 2000: 1).

In fact, it is likely that the reasons for changes in the status of teaching as a profession are a great deal more complex. In Ireland, for example, teachers, and most especially primary teachers, have been drawn from rural areas (Kelly, 1970; Clancy, 1988, 1995b). Prior to the era of economic expansion from the 1960s onwards, a small number of professional occupations were visible in rural areas. These were the Church, medicine, agricultural adviser and teaching. However, economic, social, structural and labour market change has led to a much greater diversity of occupations. Some of the newer occupations, such as those in information technology or the media, may be perceived as very glamorous because of their relative novelty, or the amount of public attention they receive. Some professions receive significantly higher pay than teaching. The level of remuneration attaching to a profession relates to a variety of factors. These include the level of autonomy and control it has over its membership and conditions, and whether it can set its own remuneration rates or fees; the structure of the career path (Lortie, 1975); how comparatively scarce personnel with the requisite qualifications/expertise are; and the relative bargaining position of the professional group if employed by the state.

International comparisons of pay illustrate that there are considerable differences in salaries between countries. After 15 years experience teachers' salaries are generally above per capita GDP. In most countries teachers are well paid relative to the average earnings of wage and salary workers (OECD, 2003a: 369). However, the late 1990s saw a relative decline in teachers' salaries compared to per capita GDP in a number of countries, including Ireland, France, the Netherlands and Switzerland. A number of other countries (e.g. Germany, Italy, Japan, Mexico and New Zealand) registered an improvement (ibid.: 371). In fourteen of the nineteen OECD countries with relevant data, the salary of a teacher with 15 years' experience grew more slowly than GDP per capita between 1994 and 2001 (OECD, 2004: 2). Satisfaction, or lack of it, with levels of pay depend, of course, on relativities and comparators. In an all-graduate profession, teachers are more likely to compare themselves to other graduate professions than to per capita GDP. Teachers in secondary schools tend to earn less than executive officials with third level/tertiary qualifications, although they may earn more than some professionals in other caring occupations such as social work and pre-primary education (OECD, 2003a: 372).

From the point of view of the feminisation of teaching two observations must be made. First, research in many countries has suggested that the more feminised any occupation is, the more likely it is to be poorly paid (O'Connor, 1998: 198). Second, although teaching is highly feminised in most countries, in those where men are proportionately more represented at primary and lower secondary, pay is not necessarily better. Thus, as regards the levels of pay attaching to teaching, while the proportion of women may be a factor, other factors undoubtedly play a part. Indeed, the strength and relative bargaining power of the teacher unions themselves are a key factor. In Ireland the three teacher unions have long been recognised as a powerful collective bargaining force.

Public debate has also suggested that the status of teaching as a profession has declined. The reasons for changes in the status of teaching are complex, and it is difficult to be precise or definite about the effects of feminisation on this. If it is the case that numerical dominance of women in teaching, or any other profession, is associated with a decline in the status of that profession, this raises fundamental questions about the role and position of women in society. In particular, questions arise concerning the level of social and economic equality between men and women, and parity of esteem. These go well beyond consideration of an individual occupation such as teaching.

There are some issues in respect of which increasing levels of feminisation at point of entry to teaching may be considered problematic. The first is the issue of equality in the labour market. It is undesirable from this perspective that any occupation, be it engineering or primary teaching, is unduly dominated by one gender or the other. Labour market equality has become a central plank of European Union and national government policy relating to employment. International research has shown that women are under-represented in courses and careers in the physical sciences, in technology and in engineering (Drudy, 1996; 1998). It is generally agreed that in contemporary society this disadvantages women in the labour market. At entry to third level, the only courses which are as gender differentiated as engineering are primary/elementary teaching courses. If gender imbalance in the one is a matter of legitimate concern and policy intervention to foster equality, so too is it in the other.

A further problem is that of the hidden curriculum of schooling. The figures presented above indicate the proportionately low representation of women in positions of authority in schools. It has been argued that this has become part of the hidden curriculum of schooling – that 'women teach and men manage' (Lynch, 1994). If the low representation of women in authority is part of the hidden curriculum, so too is the low representation of men in the classroom, especially the primary/elementary classroom. It has been argued that the sexual division of labour among teachers contributes to the reproduction of the patriarchal and/or capitalist social order. It does this through providing models to students of male–female power relations and sex-differentiated responsibilities that reinforce the connection of 'femininity' with caring, serving, conforming and mothering (Acker, 1994: 87), while divorcing these concepts from 'masculinity'. What, then, are pupils learning about male–female power relationships if the teaching profession, and its management structures, are highly sex-differentiated?

The issues of labour market equality, the socialisation of young children, and the hidden curriculum of schooling present a basis for considering the levels of feminisation in teaching as problematic. The very universality of the under-representation of men in teaching at primary/elementary level is problematic in itself, in a historical, psychological and sociological sense. Notwithstanding debates on whether teaching is a 'profession' (by whatever definition), on rates of pay, or status, there is no doubt that in a society increasingly dependent on the knowledge industry, and one where citizenship and equality are so greatly affected by education, the role of the teacher is a crucial one. The teacher plays a pivotal role in the areas of both the formal and the hidden curriculum. Teaching has been, and will undoubtedly continue to be, an important professional career path for women, one in which they have distinguished themselves very well. It has also been an important career for men, one in which they too have made notable contributions. It is, thus, of very great relevance to examine the perceptions and attitudes towards teaching, most especially primary/elementary teaching, among school leavers and among students preparing for the profession. It is also highly relevant to provide an interpretive framework for the findings on men, women and teaching. Those are the issues with which the research in this volume is concerned.

Summary

This study of men, women and teaching draws upon international material and on research conducted in Ireland. In order to understand the relationship between gender and teaching, it is important to distinguish between 'sex' and 'gender'. The latter refers to culturally specific patterns of behaviour attaching to the sexes. International figures indicate a predominance of women in teaching, especially in primary/elementary schools, with variations by levels of economic development in different countries. International debates on the feminisation of teaching, and the corresponding phenomenon of low rates of male entry to the profession, have revolved around the areas of male role models, the relative competence of male and female teachers and the professional status of teaching. While it is difficult to be definitive about these matters, in part because of lack of substantive evidence, the areas of labour market equality and the hidden curriculum of schooling emerge as problematic.

Chapter 2

Gender and teaching

The data presented in Chapter 1 demonstrate that there is a considerable gender 'imbalance' in the teaching profession throughout the vast majority of the world. In most countries the imbalance is in favour of women, particularly in primary and lower secondary teaching. The exceptions to this are in the less economically developed regions of the world. This study addresses concerns in economically more developed countries about the low number of males who choose teaching as a career. In this chapter not only 'the feminisation of teaching' but also 'the construction of masculinity in schools' is examined. These issues are related to the central research question of the low proportion of men entering teaching. Data from a case study of entrance to teaching are used to illustrate the patterns.

Historical patterns

Tyack and Strober (1981) argue that, from its inception, institutional education has reflected an overall 'structuring of society', particularly in relation to distinctions of sex. In an historical analysis of gender and public education policy in the United States, they report that, in the early part of the nineteenth century, when education was not so tightly regulated, male teachers outnumbered female teachers:

> Until well into the twentieth century the people who hired teachers did not set high educational standards; they typically required that instructors be literate and reasonably well versed in the three Rs, of certified moral character, of native birth, and generally possessing middle-class appearance and habits.
> (Tyack and Strober, 1981: 134)

Similarly, Williams (1995: 23) writes that it was not uncommon for men to be teachers or nurses prior to the American civil war, but that this situation changed drastically when these occupations were institutionalised. Although other forms of employment were available to males, teaching was attractive to men as a short-term proposition. This was especially the case with those living in rural areas who combined the occupation with farming or who regarded it as a stepping stone to a more elevated position within the community (Tyack and Strober, 1981: 134–5). However, although recruits were sought from the middle-class sector of the population, the terms of remuneration for teachers were relatively poor, roughly on a par with that offered to casual labourers: 'They wanted to pay proletarian wages and still keep teaching a white-collar occupation' (ibid.: 135). Tyack and Strober look to factors other than the sex of teachers in their analysis, and they point to significant differences between developments in rural and urban areas. They argue that it was not accidental that school teaching first became feminised in the areas where industrial capitalism began its take-off into sustained growth (ibid.: 136).

However, when higher standards for rural schools were implemented, a similar process of 'feminisation' began in rural areas, although not at the same rate:

> In effect, the longer terms and increased standards for entry turned teaching into a 'para-profession'. . . . A little 'professionalization' of this sort drove men out of teaching, for it increased the opportunity costs without resulting in commensurate increases in pay.
>
> (ibid.: 140)

This economic factor alone does not account for the decline in the number of male teachers in the United States from this period. Ideological factors played their part. Many pioneers in women's education espoused a rationale for their replacement by trained female teachers:

> they claimed that women were by nature and God's design the ideal teachers of little children: nurturant, patient, able to understand young minds, and exemplary in their moral influence on the rising generation. . . . Recognizing how powerful the 'cult of true womanhood' was, they did not promote the idea that women should be teachers instead of being mothers. Rather, they argued that teaching prepared women to be better mothers and that it was but a step from the parental home to the schoolhouse and then back again to the conjugal home as wife and mother.
>
> (ibid.: 136)

It was ironic, according to Williams, that the increasing participation of women in institutionalised occupations was accompanied by the ideology of domesticity, 'that defined women solely in terms of their domestic function. This same ideology was employed to justify the lower financial rewards offered to female teachers, and also worked to exclude them from high-ranking positions' (Williams, 1995: 25, 31–9).

The patterns in gender distribution were not unrelated to those of hierarchy and control. Tyack and Strober identify 'a strong emerging sexual pattern of employment in city schools whereby women outnumbered men by about ten to one and taught in the lower grades, while men worked in the higher grades and as managers' (1981: 141). Moreover, they argue that alongside economic constraints, the patriarchal values of Victorian society and the strict moral codes set out for teachers made the occupation less attractive for men:

> Had mature men constituted a majority of the teaching profession, it is hard to imagine that school patrons would have insisted on such tight supervision of the morals and mores of teachers as they did in the case of young women.
>
> (ibid.: 145)

As indicated in Chapter 1, the 'feminisation of teaching' refers to the processes by which teaching became a mostly female occupation. Tyack and Strober (1981) identify a number of factors which contributed to this development in the United States, namely, the economic policy of education administrators, beliefs about the nature of women, and patriarchal control. They also show that these factors were less influential in rural areas than in industrialised, urban areas.

The contemporary international comparisons in Chapter 1 show that gender imbalance in the teaching profession is almost universal in developed countries, especially in primary/elementary teaching. Historically, the proportion of males in primary/elementary teaching has been higher in Ireland than in the United Kingdom or in the United States. Nevertheless, the paucity of male teachers, particularly at primary level, has been a concern for many years (Coolahan, 1981; Kelleghan et al., 1985). Indeed, one has to go back to 1874 to find an equal proportion of men and women in the profession in Ireland (Akenson, 1970: 354). However, in the latter part of the twentieth century the proportions of male primary teachers in the UK and Ireland were identical at 19 per cent, whereas the proportion of male primary/elementary teachers in the US was lower at 14 per cent (UNESCO, 2003).

In the nineteenth century and the first half of the twentieth century, teaching was, perhaps, a more attractive career for men in the US, the UK and Ireland and in many other countries. This no longer remains the case. The figures presented in Table 1, Appendix 1, show the decline in the proportion of males in primary teaching in Europe and America in the last part of the twentieth century. In Ireland there has been a steady decrease in the proportion of male entrants to colleges of education which in recent times has dropped to between ten and fifteen per cent (O'Connell, 1993: 146; Clancy, 1995a: 37). A similar trend was noted by Evans (1993: 226–9) in her study of teacher recruitment and retention patterns in Jamaica. Evans reported that, in the early years of independence, teacher training was the only form of professional education accessible to black Jamaicans, and as such was a highly valued occupation among males. Participation by males began to decline when entry to other previously exclusive occupations became accessible.

The changing profile of the teacher is reflected not only in the quantitative changes discussed above, but also in the changing perceptions of the teacher's role and status within the community (Quinn, 1982; INTO, 1995). Concerns about teacher status and professionalism are found in virtually every member state of the European Union (Adams and Tulasiewicz, 1995; Archer and Peck, 1990). The issue is the subject of a policy review and development by the ministries of education in 25 OECD countries (OECD, 2003b).

The term 'feminisation of teaching' has already been used with reference to the high proportion of females in the teaching profession, particularly in the primary sector. Eileen Byrne has argued that, historically:

> Woman's commitment to teaching is a tradition second only to her domestic role, throughout recorded history and in both East and West, and has acquired an aura of 'inborn gifts' and extended maternality that seems ineradicable. It is curiously noticeable that from the earliest days of state education, women have gravitated to and concentrated on younger children, on the infant and junior schools, the elementary and non-advanced sectors within the profession.
>
> (Byrne, 1978: 213)

The issues of the proportion of females and the age-levels of the pupils can be linked by suggesting that, the younger the pupils are, the stronger the perceived associations between teaching and nurturing will be. Some historical reasons why teaching attracted more women than men were noted earlier. Byrne states that, in addition to these factors, many women had no other opportunities for professional employment due to their own inadequate education and to discrimination against women in other professions. According to Byrne, the legacy of this 'tradition' is that many women still tread 'the unthinking path to the classroom' (ibid.: 214). She reports that, at the time of writing, the idea of teaching as an ideal career for women was perpetuated by the curriculum and by the career advice offered in secondary schools. Chief among the suggested reasons was what Byrne describes as the 'compatible with marriage' syndrome. However, given that a majority of women teachers were found to have chosen teaching at an early school age, she suggests that girls are socialised into teaching in much more subtle ways (ibid.: 216).

Gaskell (1992: 88–90) states that such predilections among girls result from a socialisation process which is perpetuated through 'domestic ideology', that is, the belief that women's careers ought to be compatible with homemaking responsibilities. She notes that, while the extent to which young women accept the values of domestic ideology is decreasing, many nonetheless continue to plan their lives around the inevitability of marriage and domestic responsibilities. This idea of domestic ideology could have implications for young men's attitudes to teaching. If it is generally assumed that teaching is compatible with the married life of women, would the corollary of this common sense belief be that it is less suitable for men, single or married?

Assumptions about women and teaching

Teaching is probably the best example of the ambiguities inherent in all paid work performed by women. Their qualifications for doing such work at all have usually rested on what they were thought to know and be able to do 'naturally'. This often meant no more than an extension of what they were in the habit of doing anyway.

(Miller, 1996: 2)

These beliefs undermine both the work of teachers and what women do 'naturally'. Furthermore, Miller reports that this association with women's 'nature' has led to attacks on a feminised teaching profession. Most recently, these criticisms arise from: concerns about the lack of male role models, a belief that there is a bias away from science and technology, a suspicion that education and assessment are becoming more 'moulded' to suit females, anxieties about the relative underachievement of boys in some areas, and the particular unemployment problem experienced by unqualified male school leavers (ibid., 4–5). Miller argues against such reactionary tendencies in which women, in particular, feminists, are held responsible for the alleged problems arising from a feminised teaching profession. This argument is supported by Mills and Lingard who reject the 'mythopoetic stance' of those who regard men and boys as being the new victims of pro-feminist education policies and practices (Mills and Lingard, 1997: 278).

Janet Miller (1986) reports on the attitudes of women teachers towards themselves as professionals. While most of the respondents in her study believed that they had abilities which were natural to women and important for teaching – 'mothering' and 'nurturing' – many of the same group were apologetic about these qualities in the context of teacher professionalism. Miller interprets this as a conflict of identity between, on the one hand, teachers' roles as 'nurturers' or 'carers' and, on the other hand, their professional roles as educators. Although this analysis by Miller is confined to women's perceptions of themselves as teachers, it can be inferred that there are implications here too for men as teachers. If the skills involved in teaching are believed to be the natural domain of women, then, by implication, men would be deemed to be less suitable as candidates for the teaching profession. Paradoxically, it is the assumption of 'natural' teaching abilities which undermines the professional status of women and, arguably, of all those involved in teaching. These themes are returned to in subsequent sections which address the experience of men in teaching and the status of teaching as an occupation.

Boys, men and schooling

Studies on and policy for gender equality have mainly been associated with the education and employment of girls and women. With regard to gender imbalances in primary teaching, as already indicated in Chapter 1, some of the debate has revolved around the issue of the education of males. Thus the position of boys and men in education must be examined. Hansot presents an historical view on the gendered organisation of schooling in the United States, and begins her analysis by commenting on the origins of coeducation. In the early stages of public education, and largely for economic reasons, boys and girls were schooled together. By the end of the nineteenth century, she reports that vocational education, differentiated by gender, became more widespread, especially for older children (Hansot, 1993: 14). Hansot's analysis illustrates how the institutional practice of coeducation did not necessarily translate into equal educational experiences for boys and girls. Criticisms of coeducation have come from a number of fronts:

> Whereas opponents of coeducation in the nineteenth century had claimed that high schools were too virile for girls, in the Progressive era critics claimed that they feminised the boys. In the 1970s, the new feminist reformers reversed the charge, arguing that public education made the girls too feminine and the boys too masculine.
>
> (ibid.: 18)

Male education is defined here as the 'boy problem'. Hansot argued that the 'boy problem' was real even though much of the rhetoric about it was exaggerated. However, its other face was the 'woman peril', that is to say, the fear that there were too many women teachers and that they were creating a feminised environment in the schools in which boys could not prosper (ibid.: 14).

Referring to educational commentary that girls learn to read earlier, obtain higher grades and co-operate more with their teachers, Hansot pointed to a shortcoming in this type of commentary. Such views do not consider factors other than the sex of students, such as social class and locality. In particular, social class is a major factor in school retention for both boys and girls. However, fewer working-class boys than girls remain in school, largely on account of their early entry into the labour market. Hansot describes the 'boy problem' with its real and imagined components as 'an amalgam of alleged feminization by too many women teachers, a working-class, anti-school male counterculture, male under-achievement, and the high male dropout rate' (ibid.). To an extent the extension of the period of compulsory schooling exacerbated rather than ameliorated the 'boy problem': 'Some boys, forced to remain in school well beyond what their patience or interest counselled, reacted by forming a male counterculture in which the school figured as a place for sissies and girls' (ibid.: 15).

Some recent reports on the comparative attainment levels of boys and girls has resulted in reappraisals of the 'boy problem' or the 'boys debate'. Bushweller (1994) regards these issues within the wider contexts of the problems experienced by many boys and young men in society. Using statistical evidence from a variety of sources he points out that young males are far more likely to engage in self-destructive behaviour (suicide, drug-addiction, crime) than are young females. He asks, if society supposedly favours males, why do they have so many problems? Bushweller argues that since such self-destructive behaviour is tipped so sharply towards one sex, there is a need to examine the effects of society on young males, and how schools respond to these problems. He alludes to the patterns in special education and learning disability programmes, in which, consistently, boys outnumber girls. These patterns of difference are observable not only in relation to specific learning disabilities, but also with regard to emotional difficulties.

With reference to the fact that girls now outperform boys in most areas of educational attainment, it has been argued that:

> A general improvement in education provision for girls, changes in job opportunities, the foregrounding and making problematic the problem of gender: these are amongst the explanations on offer for what can look like an astonishing reversal. However, they are almost certainly inadequate as explanations for the relatively poor showing of working-class boys in recent years compared with girls. A central theme of the new anxiety is also, of course, the feminisation of schooling: all the ways in which the increasing presence of women in teaching may have led to the sense of education itself as somehow an unmasculine business, inimical to a majority of working-class boys.
>
> (Miller, 1996: 135)

As indicated in Chapter 1, Miller observes the tendency among journalists, policy makers and other social commentators to connect the issues of boys' performance in schools with the feminisation of teaching. In some cases, the latter is used as a scapegoat for the former. However, any interpretation of the situation in purely causal terms can be rejected, given that the values and mechanisms of the wider society need to be included in any such analysis (Miller, 1996: 157–8). Elwood and Carlisle (2003: 104–5) suggest that there are multiple factors that contribute to differential performance in public examinations by boys and girls such as: teaching and learning in classrooms, school organisation and culture, teacher expectations, availability of subjects, differential entry patterns for examinations, and personal choices of students.

> Two phenomena are most widely discussed in relation to the emergence of the boys issue: evidence of changes in achievement patterns for girls and boys, and discussions of a social 'backlash' against feminism and feminist reforms.
>
> (Yates, 1997: 337)

Yates argues that interventions alone do not bring about any desired change because the construction of masculinities and femininites takes place in the very same environment where 'affirmative action' programmes are introduced. In particular, it is possible to be critical of those policies which tend to look on gender as some kind of disadvantage, as was the case with many interventions on behalf of girls in schools (ibid.: 344). Yates points out that, over the past twenty years, most empirical qualitative work on gender, pedagogy, subjectivity and schooling has studied girls rather than boys: 'Frameworks and theories might have been concerned with both, but the substantive "findings" and insights were not equally spread' (ibid.). Post-modern feminist research could be employed to understand more about the experience of boys in education, she argued, especially with regard to the gendered subjectivity of boys, an area which might reveal more variation than had been heretofore assumed. There has been a tendency in some research and policy debates on schools to treat masculinity 'as a more crudely sketched out discourse against which femininities were examined' (ibid: 345).

Education and the social construction of masculinity

Thus far, a number of apparently conflicting images of gender and education have emerged. What can be said at this point is that, far from being neutral arenas, schools are primary sites for the formation of gender identities and hence gender differences. At a factual level, distinctions can be made between single-sex schools and coeducational schools, and on the disparities in the career patterns of male and female teachers. At an interpretive level, the 'feminisation of teaching' or the 'boy problem' can be explored. Explicitly or implicitly, these ideas are formulated within a relational framework of gender. It has already been noted that there are some concerns internationally about the participation and experience of boys and men in education. Some of the ways in which masculinity might operate in schools are now outlined, as this issue is closely tied to the formation of gender identity and, consequently, to how males and females develop attitudes and dispositions to different careers, including teaching.

With regard to the formation of masculine identities, Williams (1995: 115–18) adapts psychoanalytic theory to feminist analysis. She employs the psychoanalytic 'definition' of masculinity, which, negatively, delineates it as anything that is not feminine. This is related to general patterns of social organisation in Western society in which boys and girls are reared (and for the most part, educated) by women. At about age three, boys begin to construct masculine identities. This is a problematic process, in that it involves a distancing from the original maternal identity, and also because men are largely absent at the stage when gender identities are being formed (through the traditional patterns of male employment, and also in cases of single parent families). In this way a masculine identity becomes associated with everything that is not feminine. Like Mac an Ghaill (1994), Williams considers that this type of theory helps to explain variation in the subjective experience of masculinity:

> The theory explicitly recognises that not all men will experience the same needs and desires to differentiate themselves from women. Group differences in the definition of masculinity are even likely. For example, those raised in families where men participate in child rearing will probably not define masculinity as the opposite of nurturing and emotional expressiveness.
>
> (Williams, 1995: 117)

In addition, this psychoanalytical view of gender identity recognises that the formation of masculinity often entails conflict and ambivalence. However, Williams points to the limitations of this theory. First of all it fails to explain 'why men are able to force their psychological concerns on others . . . why men's preoccupations with difference and subordination prevail in our culture nor how they come to be embedded in our social institutions'. She states that Connell's concept of 'hegemonic masculinity'[1] helps to explain the 'ascendance of specific configurations of masculinity and femininity in particular social contexts' (ibid.: 118).

Connell (1995) argues that rather than speaking of masculinity, there is a need to recognise that a number of masculinities may operate at any given time, and that these are related to one another and to femininities. In opposition to 'hegemonic masculinity' are gay and 'pro-feminist' masculinities. He distinguishes also the category of 'complicit' masculinities, which give a support base for the values of hegemonic masculinity. As Williams puts it: 'Masculinity . . . is a cultural ideal that many men support, but do not necessarily embody' (Williams, 1995: 119).

Skelton (1993) suggests that in educational institutions the *overt* and '*official*' masculinity is often progressive and liberal, whereas the *real* ideology is closer in identity to the 'complicit' form of masculinity. In his case study of male P.E. student teachers, he found that the ethos of the formal curriculum (child-centredness, equality, and co-operation) was generally accepted by the students and staff of the college. However, this rationale was undermined by the ethos of the dominant student subculture which was informed by the values of hegemonic masculinity (competitiveness, aggression, authority). Other expressions of student masculinity were rejected by this dominant group. Moreover, Skelton suggests that some members of the college staff valorised the attitudes and behaviour of this student subculture by their very complicity, a type of hidden curriculum, as it were.

Although there are numerous such reports of masculine counter-cultures in educational institutions, Skelton's account differs in two major respects. First, the subversion does not take the form of open confrontation – in fact, the students formally accepted the rationale and ethos of their college curriculum. Second, the case study takes place within a college of education. In this case the type of masculinity can be mapped into a number of relational frames. First, the very concept of masculinity is dialectically related to that of femininity. Second, hegemonic masculinity defines itself partially by rejecting other masculine identities (for example, pro-feminist or gay identities). Last of all, in this case, the values of hegemonic masculinity appear to be in direct opposition to the educational ethos of the college, though tacitly so. This reflects the historical pattern already suggested by Tyack and Strober where the social and moral control of a predominantly female teaching profession is linked to the strong masculine behaviour of many male teachers: 'Although less strictly held to moral account than women, men teachers were also restricted – by the female Victorian stereotypes at their job . . . men teachers sought to escape the stereotype by becoming breezy, virile "he-men"' (Tyack and Strober, 1981: 145).

Mac an Ghaill (1994) has argued that masculine perspectives are pervasively dominant in (British) secondary schools, yet paradoxically, that masculinity has tended to be absent from mainstream education research. Gender studies have focused on girls' schooling and femininity whereas masculinity is assumed to be unproblematic (Mac an Ghaill, 1994: 1). Mac an Ghaill set out to deconstruct the identities of sex and gender:

> male heterosexual identity is a highly fragile socially constructed phenomenon. The question that emerges here is: How does this fragile construction become represented as an apparently stable, unitary category with fixed meanings? It is suggested that schools alongside other institutions attempt to administer, regulate and reify unstable sex/gender categories. Most particularly, this administration, regulation and reification of sex/gender boundaries is institutionalized through the interrelated material, social and discursive practices of staffroom, classroom and playground microcultures.
>
> (ibid.: 9)

According to Mac an Ghaill, schools are sites for contradictions and negotiations in identities. By adapting the perspectives of feminist deconstructionist theory he contends that, far from representing the power and gender relations of society in some static sense, the expression of hegemonic masculinity in schools is subject to a whole range of factors and relations. Furthermore, gendered identities are not simply determined by social forces but also involve individual subjectivities (ibid.: 10).

In this brief account of the relationship between masculinity and education it can be seen that it is a problematic one. First of all, the relation between the two can be described as complex in that, although education systems have been subject to tight patriarchal control, there is a tendency for some masculine identities to be formed in varying degrees of opposition to that authority. Second, it can be seen that there may be conflict and struggle in the definitions of various masculinites, and a whole range of problems ensue from this divergence. There are obvious difficulties for those who do not identify with hegemonic or complicit masculinites but, as has been suggested, oppositional forms of masculinity can sometimes be manifestations of male students' alienation from schools and the labour market. The study of school leavers' and student teachers' perceptions of teaching reported in this volume provides an opportunity to explore the degree to which perceptions of teaching as a 'woman's profession' affect the attitudes and choices of young males.

Boys, girls and choice of teaching

The focus of this study of men and their relationship to the classroom was to deepen the understanding of the processes by which males and females choose, or do not choose, to enter teaching. The study selected a cohort of pupils in the autumn of their final year at school in order to establish their higher education course choices and career preferences.[2] It was felt that school leavers' course choices would have crystallised by their final year at school. Only pupils intending to pursue higher education were selected as it was felt that this would permit more valid comparisons to be made concerning choice of teaching in relation to other occupations. Pupils' perceptions of different careers were explored and variations by background variables examined. Schools were classified by the research team as being either 'rural' or 'urban'.[3] Some 37 per cent of pupils were in schools in a rural or small/medium town area, and 63 per cent were in schools in large urban areas. The total number of valid questionnaires obtained from school leavers was 1,049. Of these 418 were from males and 631 from females. The average age of respondents (in the first term of their sixth – i.e. final – year) was 17.7 years, with boys slightly younger than girls.

A cohort of second year student teachers in all five of the colleges of education in Ireland was selected for comparison. Each of the colleges was attached to a local university and all were located in urban centres, four in the east and one in the west of the country. The students were in the second year of a three year concurrent teacher education degree course. It was felt that second year student teachers would, by the time of the survey (the second semester), have had some teaching practice experience. Furthermore, any potential drop-outs would have been most likely to have occurred in first year (Lynch *et al.*, 1997). The research team was also aware that the colleges would have greater difficulties scheduling the survey among third year student teachers who would be preparing for final examinations and assessments of teaching practice.

Questionnaires were completed by 457 student teachers – 46 males and 411 females. This reflected the gender balance at intake in the five colleges in the previous year.[4] Thus, just 10 per cent of the college of education respondents were male. Some 88 per cent of the student teachers were under 23 years old at the time of the survey. Their mean age was 21 years. In Ireland, entrants to third level are deemed to be 'mature' if they are 23 years old at entry. The data showed that 11 per cent of students at the colleges of education were mature students on entering college the previous year. This rate was somewhat higher than that for third level entrants as a whole; the most recent figure available at the period previous to the survey stood at just over 5 per cent (Lynch, 1997). However, it was well below the international average for third level entrants towards the end of the 1990s (OECD, 1996: 127–30) and also significantly below that in Northern Ireland and Britain (29 per cent and 33 per cent respectively – Lynch, 1997). It should be noted that the higher than average (at least for Ireland) proportion of mature students among the college of education respondents did not include students on the postgraduate courses who pursue a primary teaching qualification after an initial degree. At the time of the survey, these courses were offered on a cyclical, rather than an annual, basis and were not included in the survey.

The school leaver choice process: gender and career preferences

Third level course choices

Intention to apply for third level courses in the university or institute of technology sectors, or to third level courses abroad, was a precondition for inclusion of the school leavers in the database. There was no difference between boys and girls on certainty about their choice of courses. Three fifths of all respondents said they were certain of their choice.

Choice of teaching

Teaching in the Republic of Ireland is an all-graduate profession at primary and post-primary levels.[5] As primary education is the most feminised sector of the teaching profession there was a particular emphasis in the research on ascertaining choice of primary teaching, and attitudes to it, among school leavers and college students. Furthermore, primary teaching courses are the principal teacher education courses available to school leavers through the higher education central applications system, apart from a small number of places available on second level specialist programmes for areas such as home economics, technology and physical education. Most second level teacher education places are only available at postgraduate level.

As expected, there was a major gender difference among those opting for primary teaching as their first choice, with only 2 males (0.6 per cent of the total number of males) as against 55 females (10.4 per cent of total females) so doing (in the analysis, percentages are calculated and significance tests conducted throughout with missing values excluded). This difference was statistically significant. The issue of whether primary teaching was included in students' planning for their second and third choices was examined and the results are presented in Table 2.1.

Primary teaching was a very highly favoured choice of college course among the female school leavers in the sample, but not among the boys. It should be

Table 2.1 Choice of primary teaching as a course choice (planned first, second and third degree preferences), by gender

Primary Teaching	Primary Teaching as Degree Choice		
	Males as % of all males	Females as % of all females	All choosing primary teaching as % of all pupils
Course Choice 1	0.6	10.4	6.4
Course Choice 2	2.1	6.9	5.0
Course Choice 3	4.2	7.6	6.2

noted that the proportion of boys increased on second and third choices, whereas the percentage of girls decreased. This suggests that boys look on primary teaching as a fallback position, while for girls it tends to be a first choice. It is interesting to note that the gender breakdown here was very similar to that of another highly feminised group of occupations – i.e. nursing/physiotherapy/other healthcare. Of the 140 who put one of these professions in their three top preferences, 14 per cent were male and 86 per cent female. As will be seen later in this chapter, the very gender composition of these professions appears to have an impact on choices, thus reproducing gender differences with each fresh cohort of entrants.

Choice of other courses

Over the last quarter century there have been great changes in the occupational structure in Ireland and elsewhere. These have been accompanied by an ever-increasing diversity of courses on offer to school leavers. A generation ago teaching was one of the most visible of the professions to young people entering higher education, alongside professions such as medicine and law. This was particularly the case for rural school leavers. This has changed dramatically. In the year of the survey, teaching courses had to compete with some 717 separate degree, diploma and certificate course entries for higher education entrants' attention and applications (Central Applications Office, 2001: 5). This, of course, applied as much to female as to male applicants. As illustrated above, almost six times as many females as males in the school leaver sample had put primary teaching among their first three choices. Figure 2.1 illustrates first preference course choices for all areas of study. Individual courses are grouped into 15 broad areas of study (Clancy, 1995a).

As well as in preferences for primary teaching, there were marked gender differences among respondents in preferences for other courses. The major discrepancies between the sexes were statistically significant. Males predominated in technology, computers and commerce, with girls in the majority in humanities, teaching, nursing, social science, and also in medicine/dentistry. Males had a slightly higher preference for science. In agriculture, art and design, and law the sexes were fairly evenly matched. Boys seemed to choose within a much smaller range of courses than did girls – 56 per cent of boys had chosen in the technology, computers and commerce areas. Girls' choices were more widely spread. On second and third choices similar patterns of choice emerge. The gender differences were also statistically significant but the contrasts were somewhat less marked in a number of areas.

Some Irish school leavers apply to UK colleges each year, especially in parts of the country where access to Northern Ireland is convenient. However, applying to a third level institution outside the State (almost invariably UCAS in Great Britain or Northern Ireland) was a minority pursuit among the sample here. One hundred and twenty-seven respondents intended applying – significantly more girls (21 per cent) than boys (13 per cent; $p<.001$).

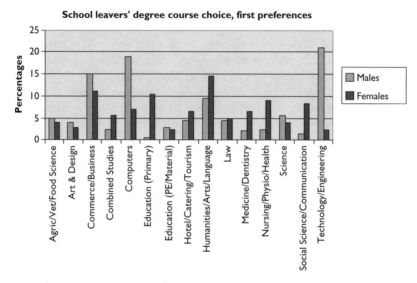

Figure 2.1 School leavers' degree course choice (Central Applications Office CAO) first preferences in fifteen course groupings, by gender

Career choice

The focus now turns to look at responses to the questions on career choice, as opposed to choice of third level course. For many students there was less certainty about career than course choice, given that one was more immediate than the other. Just 67 per cent of the respondents said they were 'certain' or 'reasonably certain' about their choice of career. There was little difference between the sexes on this point. However 93 per cent of those putting primary teaching as their first degree choice were 'certain' or 'reasonably certain'. Small numbers, however, mean that the Chi-square test of significance on the differences in degree of certainty between those choosing and those not choosing primary teaching could not be validly completed.

Some 97 pupils put primary teaching as a career among their top three choices. This was lower than the number who had indicated that they would include it among their first three degree choices (148). It formed 12 per cent of the total career choices, compared to 17 per cent of course choices. However, the percentages giving primary teaching as a *first* choice were similar for both course and career choices at 6.5 per cent and 6.3 per cent, respectively. Gender differences were, again, very pronounced in relation to primary education as a career choice. As regards other careers, some students had not thought beyond college and gave answers relating to courses rather than careers, which made coding difficult.[6] Table 2.2 shows the distribution of responses. The proportions giving primary education as a career choice are examined in more detail in Table 2.3.

The gender differences observed in the college choices recur in relation to career

Table 2.2 First career choice, by gender

Career area	First career choice	Male %	Female %	All %
1	Agriculture/veterinary/food science	4.1	2.5	3.2
2	Art and design	2.4	2.1	2.2
3	Commerce/business/account./banking/insurance/ marketing	17.6	12.6	14.7
4	Computers	14.4	5.6	9.2
5	Education – primary	0.6	10.3	6.3
6	Education – P.E./technology	0.9	1.6	1.3
7	Hotel/tourism/leisure/sport	6.2	11.1	9.1
8	Humanities/languages/music/journalism/drama	5.0	5.4	5.2
9	Law	2.4	4.1	3.4
10	Medicine	0.9	5.4	3.5
11	Nursing/physio/health/occup. ther./pharmacy	2.7	11.5	7.9
12	Science	2.7	2.5	2.5
13	Social science/social care/communications	3.5	13.8	9.6
14	Technology/engineer/construct/architect/pilot/ fireman	24.2	2.9	11.7
15	Secondary teaching	2.7	7.0	5.2
16	Trades/electrician/bricklayer/plumber	5.3	0.4	2.4
17	Police force/army	4.4	1.2	2.5
	Total	100.0	100.0	100.0 (n=824)

Chi-square=226.4; df=16; p<.000

Table 2.3 Primary teaching as a career choice, by gender

Primary teaching	Male* %	Female* %
Career Choice 1	3.8	96.2
Career Choice 2	11.8	88.2
Career Choice 3	25.0	75.0
Overall	11.3	88.7

*Note – percentages are within those choosing primary teaching.

choice. Males predominated in technology, computers, science and trades, and women formed the majority in education, medicine, nursing and social science. Males were clustered in three of the seventeen areas with more than half of them choosing careers in technology/engineering, commerce/business, or computing.

The divide between technical and caring professions to some extent coincided with the gender divide. An interesting feature is the fact that teaching was far from the only career lacking a profile with young people. For instance, both science and art/design received lower proportions of the pupils' first choices than either primary or second level teaching. The gender differences observed in many of the categories were statistically significant.

If the focus is on the three different types of teaching (i.e. rows 5, 6 and 15 in Table 2.2) there are marked gender differences in all three, with more females than males expressing a preference. However, small though the male numbers are, there were higher proportions of males choosing secondary and P.E./technology than primary teaching. When the picture was broadened to include all forms of teaching (i.e. secondary/high school or specialist – such as physical education, home economics or technology – as well as primary), approximately 13 per cent of respondents (the majority being girls) put one or other forms of teaching as their first career choice. However, the numbers choosing primary teaching were of particular interest in the study and Table 2.3 gives additional details on these.

The percentages of males choosing primary teaching as a career were similar to the percentage indicating that primary teaching would be one of their top three college preferences. The percentages for males were higher for choices 2 and 3. The overall proportion of males indicating primary teaching as a *career choice* was quite close to the figure for primary teacher college *entrants* in the previous three years (Drudy, 2004), which would suggest that the sample was reasonably representative. Gender differences were, again, very pronounced in relation to primary education as a career choice.

In addition to the questions on choice of course and of career, school leavers were specifically asked if they had ever thought about becoming a teacher. This question was aimed at finding out two things: (i) how many people had considered teaching, and what their reasons were for following through or putting aside their choice; and (ii) whether any candidates were opting for second level, as opposed to primary teaching. Two hundred and twelve second level respondents (20 per cent) indicated an interest in some form of teaching as one of their preferred college choices. Four times more girls' than boys' responses fell into this category. Two fifths of the total (42 per cent) indicated that they had considered teaching, while for the remainder it had never been an option. Proportionately, many more boys than girls fell into the latter category.

The proportion indicating a general preference for some kind of teaching was considerably greater than the proportions of those putting primary teaching as a first choice, somewhat more than those intending to put primary teaching in their top three CAO choices (20 per cent), and more than the number putting any form of teaching as a first *career* choice. A possible explanation is that for those considering an arts/humanities or science degree, secondary/high school teaching may be a vague possibility, whereas, for most people, primary teaching is a deliberate choice at the time of leaving school. In Ireland the most common form of teacher education for the lower and upper secondary/high school system is based on the consecutive model – i.e. a degree followed by a one-year, intensive, teacher education course.

The numbers putting any type of teaching as one of their first three choices were greater than numbers giving primary teaching as their first degree choice, therefore it is possible to pick out more statistically significant factors. Boys single sex schools were particularly remarkable in relation to choice of primary teaching.

Not a single pupil from this school type intended to put primary teaching as their first degree preference. Indeed, the single-sex boys' secondary schools produced the lowest percentage of all types of prospective teacher. This would suggest that the type of masculinist ethos found in many boys' schools (arguably one of hegemonic masculinity – see, for example, Lynch, 1989) is least hospitable to choice of teaching, especially primary teaching, as a career.

Student teachers' choice of teaching

Student teachers already in the colleges of education had chosen primary teaching as their course. However, it was not the first choice of all respondents. A total of 82.5 per cent of the respondents had put primary teaching as their first preference on their CAO form. These were mainly the school-leaver applicants, as although mature students go through the CAO somewhat different procedures are used. There were marked gender differences here. The proportion of males who had put primary teaching first was 69.8 per cent, while the female proportion was 83.8 per cent. The pattern of male and female CAO first preferences is shown in Figure 2.2.

This figure illustrates the greater propensity of male student teachers to have had other first preferences. These were spread between other Education courses – P.E./Materials/Technology and Nursing/Physiotherapy/other Healthcare

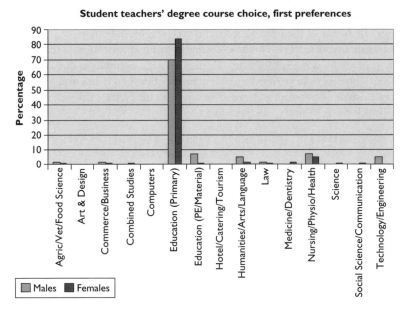

Figure 2.2 Student teachers' degree course choice (Central Applications Office) first preferences in fifteen course groupings by gender

(7 per cent of male preferences in each case). Arts/Humanities and Technology/ Engineering/Construction accounted for 5 per cent of males' first preferences in each group. Female alternative first preferences were proportionately more thinly spread. Nursing/Physiotherapy/Healthcare accounted for 5 per cent of female first preferences, with all other groupings proportionately lower. Some 14 per cent of the male first preferences not focused on primary teaching were for other caring professions (other education courses, Medicine/Dentistry, Nursing/other Healthcare, Social Science/Communications/Childcare). The corresponding figure for women was 9 per cent.

Altogether 84 per cent of male and 93 per cent of female student teacher first preferences were for courses leading to the caring professions (including primary teaching). This suggests a high orientation towards caring by this group, with an even greater orientation among females than males. In this sense it reflects the patterns observable among the school-leaver cohort.

Summary

The patterning of course and career choices by male and female school leavers, and the gender differences in the orientation towards the caring profession among student teachers, provides support for the argument that the relationship between masculinity and teaching (and other caring professions) is a problematic one. There is, however, also evidence that some masculine identities are formed in varying degrees of opposition to these overarching patterns. This is illustrated by the level of orientation of male student teachers in the study to the caring professions which, while lower than that of their female counterparts, was considerably greater than that of the male school leavers. This would suggest that men who choose teaching, especially primary teaching, differ from the general male population in a number of respects. Differences in perceptions and attitudes between males and females, and between males choosing and not choosing teaching, are explored in later chapters in this book.

Chapter 3

Perceptions of teaching as a career

Given the international figures on the representation of men and women in teaching, and the gendered nature of occupational choice, perceptions of teaching must be considered within the broader context of gender and the occupational structure. This chapter presents analyses of perceptions of teaching garnered from international research and from the views of school leavers and student teachers.

Occupational segregation or gendered occupations?

According to Siltanen (1994: 189), in late twentieth-century societies, employment continued to be characterised by a high degree of differentiation between women and men. The issue of whether occupations can be defined as 'gendered' purely by the number of men or women who are employed in them is raised by this observed differentiation. In Siltanen's analysis, the categories of 'men's jobs' or 'women's jobs' is rejected:

> Research conducted at the level of the workplace has shown that there is not a consistent relationship between the substance of job tasks and the gender composition of jobs: a particular job may be exclusively male in one workplace and exclusively female in another.
>
> (Siltanen, 1994: 190)

Thus, common sense views about appropriate jobs for men or women cannot be substantiated. 'There is a need to deconstruct gender categories in order to highlight the diversities in experience they mask' (ibid.: 189). Factors such as domestic responsibilities and career structures may be experienced differentially by different individuals and groups. Siltanen's research also suggests that, in occupations where the gender imbalance is seen to be significant, those 'who were in a minority position in relation to their gender . . . shared other social characteristics with those whose gender was the majority' (ibid.: 191). As illustrated in Chapter 2 of this volume, males who had already made the choice of teaching shared an orientation to the caring professions with their female counterparts (albeit to a somewhat lesser degree).

With regard to human behaviour, as argued earlier, gender refers to the culturally specific patterns of behaviour which may be attached to the sexes. It is, thus, culturally determined and highly variable. This applies to occupational choice and behaviour as much as to any other area.

Bourdieu and Passeron, in their path-breaking analysis of education, point out that the apparently most deliberate or most inspired 'choices' (of French female university graduates) may be viewed as taking into account, albeit unconsciously, the system of objective probabilities[1] which result in women's concentration in professions requiring a 'feminine' disposition, e.g. welfare work. The system of 'objective probabilities' may dispose them to accept and even unconsciously demand those types of work requiring a 'feminine' relation to the job (Bourdieu and Passeron, 1977). Studies of occupational choice among school leavers have provided evidence of the segregation of male and female choices, with a notable proportion falling into the categories of 'traditional' female and male occupations. Such structuring of choices by sex suggests that, in the matter of choice, school leavers also take into account (consciously or unconsciously) the probability of success attaching to each sex (Drudy, 1981: 160–1, 378).

The socialising influences of domestic ideology for both women and men with regard to entry to female-dominated professions have already been noted. It is possible that this too may play a role (either positively or negatively) in entry to teaching. Williams (1995: 50–64) in her interviews with male nurses, social workers, elementary teachers and librarians found a measure of conflict between the individual identities and 'gendered' occupational identities of her subjects. Thus, while there may be changing ideologies about gender and occupational choice, these may not necessarily be accompanied by changes in behaviour when choosing careers.

Wharton (1994) rejects any idea of a direct correspondence between the economic and the 'affective' consequences of gender segregation. For females working in male-dominated settings, feelings of well-being arise from the social status attached to male-dominated occupations more than from the economic rewards of working in such occupations (1994: 192). With regard to the 'psychological well-being' of men the field is quite complex and it may not always be helpful to make crude distinctions between 'male' and 'female' occupations. Wharton's study suggested that men in all-male work settings were significantly more satisfied than men in predominantly male settings, and men in mixed settings were clearly the least satisfied of all the groups (ibid.). Interestingly, men in 'all-female' occupations (i.e. where men were in a minority of less than 16 per cent) in general displayed higher levels of job satisfaction than those who found themselves in more substantial minorities (see also Williams, 1995). These figures and balances may be of significance in the case of primary teaching. Chapter 1 of this volume showed that the proportion of males in many countries is at, or below, 16 per cent. In countries where the proportion of males in primary teaching is a minority, but above 16 per cent, it could be expected that the satisfaction levels of many males already in the profession (who form a more substantial minority) would be lower than in those countries where the proportion of males in teaching has fallen even lower. 'Minority-majority relations deteriorate as the ratio between the two groups approaches parity' (Wharton, 1994: 186). Jacobs (1993) also found that men's interest in female-dominated fields is less usual than women's interest in male-dominated fields. These findings have a number of implications for the perceptions of careers which are segregated according to gender. The patterns may have some impact on male school leavers' perceptions and choices.

The development of career interests

As reported earlier, cross-cultural comparisons reveal a pattern of relatively low interest in teaching as a career option. Most of the material on this subject originates in the United States, where teacher recruitment and retention has been the concern of administrators and educators for some time.

Berry *et al.* (1989), Kelly (1989), Kemper and Mangieri (1987), Mack and Jackson (1993), Newby *et al.* (1995) Page and Page (1984) and Peterson (1992), all have reported on the low levels of interest among American high school seniors in teaching as a career. The findings of these surveys consistently report the following discouraging factors for entering teaching: poor salary, discipline problems with pupils, and difficult working conditions. Berry *et al.* (1989: 15) summed it up thus:

> Most of the students – irrespective of school location, race or gender-viewed teaching as a very low-paying job that is characterized by thankless, frustrating and routine tasks. These students generally viewed teachers as lower-level functionaries who must meet unreasonable demands placed on them by contentious students, administrators and parents.

Peterson (1992) also cited other career interests and 'no interest in teaching' as reasons why interest levels are so low. Han (1994) found that the factor of salary is more significant for males than for females. In all of the studies cited above girls as a group indicated more interest in teaching than did boys. Kemper and Mangieri's study looked at the differences between boys' and girls' attitudes in some detail. They found that, among the minority of pupils who indicated some interest in teaching as a career, males differed from females in a number of respects. First, a preference was shown by males for teaching higher grades (post-primary/high school). Second, males were less attracted to teaching low ability groups than were females. Males also differed from females in that they were less inclined to indicate life-long commitment to teaching as a career – most expected to change career after an initial period of teaching. If these patterns are universal, it could be argued that the crisis in recruiting male teachers is not just a matter of under-representation. These 'male' perceptions of teaching, even among those who elect to teach, tend to be negative ones, especially where primary/elementary level education is concerned.

Paradoxically, though, it would appear that a majority of high school students believe that teaching is an important profession (Newby *et al.*, 1995), and generally would regard teaching as a good occupation, especially for women (Page and Page 1984). There is some evidence from the United States to suggest that school career counsellors tend not to give positive support to those students who express an interest in teaching (Page and Page, 1984; Kelly 1989). Kelly's survey also examines how the age and gender of pupils can influence their attitude to teaching as a career. She found that very young pupils and school leavers were more favourably disposed towards teaching and teachers than were those who were in the adolescent phase of their development.

These 'stages' correspond with Ginzberg's formulation of three phases in the development of career interests: (a) the fantasy period (infants to age eleven); (b) the tentative period (early to mid-teens); (c) the realistic period (beginning at the age of seventeen) (Ginzberg *et al.* 1951). Kelly (1989: 13) suggested that, 'as students near the age when they have to make more serious decisions about their own careers, teaching regains some status and credibility as a career choice'. It is noteworthy that the most negative attitudes to teaching emerge at the adolescent phase, especially among males. This may be related to the processes of 'gender intensification', which were discussed above. Both Kelly (1989) and Wong (1994) argue that it may be necessary to examine the transition from elementary to high school as it would appear that negative attitudes about school and teaching are exacerbated in this period.

The perceived salary scale of primary schoolteachers has been found to be a greater disincentive for young males than for young females (INTO, 1991). However, there is evidence that among school leavers occupational status is interpreted both in terms of non-material benefits ('intellectually stimulating', 'respect in the local community') and material benefits (Johnston *et al.*, 1998: 40–2). In addition, male school leavers have been found to be sensitive to the societal interpretation of men working with children, and to consider this to be a major disincentive to choosing teaching (ibid.: 48).

In Britain, it has been found that a minority of male school leavers identify teaching as a possible career option – even though a majority feel that teaching would be a good career choice for both men and women. The most negative features of teaching identified by school leavers in this British survey were mis-behaving students, long hours, low pay and stress. Long holidays, working with children, and job satisfaction were cited as the main reasons for considering teaching as a career (TTA, 1998).

Arguably, teaching is somewhat special among the various occupations which require a university degree, in that it tends to be considered more often as a 'backup' option (Lortie, 1975: 50; O'Connell, 1993: 144). In Berry *et al.*'s interviews with academically talented high school students in the United States, the majority did not believe that teaching required any degree of technical prepa-ration, adeptness or proficiency – the respondents repeatedly stated that teachers 'are born not made' (1989: 22). This perception of teaching among some school students may reflect ambiguities about its status as a profession.

Another observable trend in the American, British and Irish studies is that, while the majority of school leavers consider teaching to be a 'good' and 'important' job, these perceptions are not translated into declared career interests. This suggests that the set of values applied to careers in their more general societal contexts is not necessarily the same as those applied to individual motivations and choices.

School leavers' and student teachers' perceptions of different careers

The choice of teaching as a career today takes place within a much wider spectrum of occupations than was the case in previous generations. Clearly, it would have been impossible to ask school leavers or student teachers to evaluate teaching as a career in relation to the entire range of occupational possibilities. However, in the surveys which formed the basis of the present study it was felt that it would be very useful to establish their perceptions of teaching in comparison to a selection of reasonably popular alternative professional occupations. Respondents were given a list of nine careers and asked to evaluate them in terms of job satisfaction, suitability to men and to women, financial reward, prestige and benefit to society. They were asked to give their top three rankings from the list of nine careers in relation to each of the above characteristics. In the context of the low uptake of primary teaching by young men, it was of particular importance to examine the gender differences in the students' perceptions. In order to compare the views of student teachers on a range of careers with those of the school leavers, and the gender differences in these views, they were asked to evaluate the following nine careers:

1. Primary teacher
2. Engineer
3. Lawyer
4. Computer programmer
5. Accountant
6. Social worker
7. Television producer
8. Doctor
9. Secondary teacher

Job satisfaction

Figure 3.1 presents the nine careers ranked by the school leavers and student teachers on the dimension of offering the 'most job satisfaction'.

The most frequently ranked career among school leavers with respect to job satisfaction was medical doctor, ranked highest by 37 per cent of all leavers. Social worker was also perceived by many as offering most job satisfaction. Primary teaching came in third on this dimension (15 per cent of responses). Interestingly,

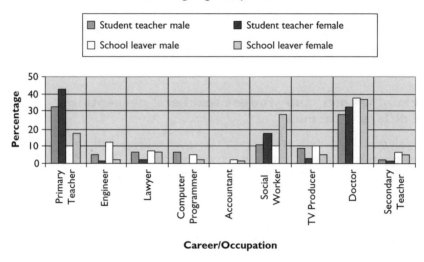

Figure 3.1 Job satisfaction rating of careers by school leavers and student teachers, by gender

Note: Student teachers consisted of all the males and a sample of the females.

secondary teaching was much less frequently chosen as offering most job satisfaction. It came seventh of the nine, chosen by 5 per cent of respondents. Accountancy was least frequently chosen on this dimension (by 1 per cent of respondents).

There were statistically significant gender differences in the perceptions (Chisquare =117; df=8; p<.000). Girls were more likely than boys to perceive a job in social work and primary teaching as offering most satisfaction. Boys were more likely than girls to perceive engineer, computer programmer, television producer and, to a lesser extent, secondary teacher in this light. A similar pattern was in evidence on second and third choices.

Those who intended to put primary teaching as their first degree choice (almost 7 per cent of the respondents) were more likely than others to see primary teaching as giving most job satisfaction – 51 per cent of this group, almost all girls. 'Doctor' and 'social worker' came next for this group (at 25 and 18 per cent respectively), with 'secondary teacher' a very rare choice for them at 2 per cent. It would appear that a strong perception of primary teaching as very satisfying does not necessarily spill over into second level teaching for this group. The 'newer' careers such as computer programmer or television producer did not figure prominently with regard to job satisfaction for those intending to put primary teaching first on their degree application. It would appear that those intending to put primary education first on their application form strongly perceive the 'caring' professions as offering most job satisfaction.

The responses of those who indicated that they had at least thought seriously about becoming a teacher (some 20 per cent of the total), showed they were more likely than others to see primary teaching as offering most job satisfaction (29 per cent as opposed to 11 per cent). Doctor, social worker and secondary teacher were disproportionately chosen in second, third and fourth positions by this group. Secondary teachers formed just 13 per cent of their top rankings. The differences in job satisfaction rankings between this group and others were statistically significant (Chi-square=2.52; df=8; p<.001). This again indicates a strong orientation to the caring professions among those giving serious consideration to any form of teaching.

Figure 3.1 shows that primary teaching was perceived as offering the highest job satisfaction by the majority of the student teachers (some 40 per cent), followed by medical doctor and social worker. Greater proportions of females than males identified these three careers, although they were the top three choices for both sexes. Although the proportions were small, more males than females suggested that engineer, lawyer, computer programmer or television producer would offer higher satisfaction. Just over two thirds (68 per cent) of the students put primary teaching among the top two, and 92 per cent put it among the top three for having highest levels of job satisfaction. Secondary teaching received the lowest proportioned ranking of all of the occupations listed for higher job satisfaction (apart from accountancy, which received none). However, in the cumulative ranking of the top three choices for higher level of satisfaction, secondary teaching came fourth (at 30 per cent), after primary (90 per cent), doctor (77 per cent) and social worker (57 per cent). Again the ranking of careers offering highest job satisfaction shows a strong orientation towards the caring professions by these student teachers.

If the careers receiving the top ranking for job satisfaction by third and second level students are compared, there are some notable differences – as would be expected. The most marked of these relates to perceptions of primary teaching. The proportion of second level pupils perceiving primary teaching as offering most job satisfaction was third highest at 15 per cent, compared to 40 per cent of student teachers. However, in the case of both samples, males gave top ranking to primary teaching proportionately less often. Second level male pupils rated doctor highest, followed by engineer. Third level males rated primary teacher highest, followed by doctor.

Careers most suited to men and to women

Figure 3.2 illustrates the perceptions of the school leavers and student teachers on the career they felt most suited to men, from the selection of nine careers offered to them.

There is evidence of rather stereotypical views on the part of a high proportion of both the school leavers and the student teachers. Just over 60 per cent of respondents identified engineering as the career most suited to men. There was

Career most suited to men

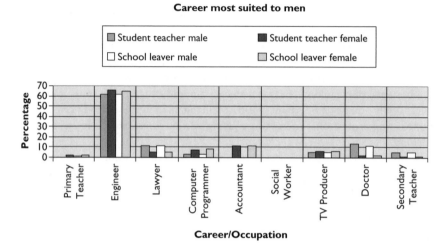

Figure 3.2 Career perceived as most suited to men by school leavers and by student teachers, by gender

Note: Student teachers consisted of all the males and a sample of the females.

little difference between boys and girls in this regard. No other career came even close to this figure. There were some gender differences with regard to the other occupations. An interesting feature was that 9 per cent of female school leavers, but hardly any of the male school leavers, refused to choose – some stating that the question was sexist. The distributions on the figure above refer to those who did indicate a view on the selected occupations and do not include the 9 per cent. Male school leavers and student teachers were more likely to view lawyer, doctor and secondary teacher as most suited to men. Females were more likely to see computer programmer and accountant as most suited to men.

Although they were doing a course leading to primary teaching *no* male student teacher thought it most suited to men, of the nine careers listed, and just one man made it his second choice. Less than 2 per cent of the sample thought that second level teaching was the career most suited to men, while cumulatively just 8 per cent of the sample put it in their top three choices. The data suggest that in choosing primary teaching, males make choices that run contrary to their own conceptions of gender identity.

Figure 3.3 illustrates the perceptions of the school leavers and student teachers on the career they felt most suited to women, from the selection of nine careers offered to them.

Again there is evidence of some rather stereotyped views among the school leavers and student teachers. A majority (57 per cent of school leavers and 61 per cent of student teachers) saw primary teaching as most suited to women. A further 27 per cent of school leavers and 32 per cent of student teachers saw social worker

Career most suited to women

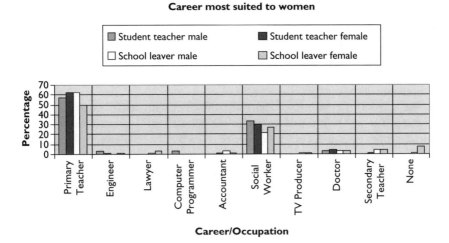

Figure 3.3 Career perceived as most suited to women by school leavers and by student
teachers, by gender

Note: Student teachers consisted of all the males and a sample of the females.

in this light. This indicates a strong connection in the perceptions of the respondents between femininity and the caring professions. There is no evidence of a
connection between masculinity and caring.

Some gender differences were evident. Boys were more inclined than girls to
see primary teaching as most suited to women (66 per cent compared to 50 per
cent). This gives an indication that girls may be somewhat less stereotyped in their
perceptions than boys. It is reinforced by the differences among those that gave
'none' or refused to give an answer on this item. Some 8 per cent of females,
compared to just 1 per cent of males, gave no answer in this category (again, this
group was not included in the above distribution).

Among the student teachers, although second level teaching was seen as most
suited to women by just one female, it did receive more second and third choices.
Cumulatively primary teaching as the most suitable career for women fell into the
first, second or third choice of 93 per cent of the student teachers, while social
worker was mentioned by 88 per cent, secondary teacher by 61 per cent and
engineer by 5 per cent. In contrast to their male colleagues, females who had made
a choice of primary teaching had made a selection that was in tune with their
general perceptions of careers.

In addition to the data on the perceptions of the teaching profession presented
above, its suitability to men and to women, and in comparison to a range of other
careers the study did some additional exploration of the respondents' perceptions
of teaching's suitability to men and to women. This time respondents were offered
the options of suitability to men and to women and to 'both equally'.

Somewhat in contrast to the responses to the earlier question illustrated in the two figures above, when offered an option of 'suited to both equally', over half of the school leavers selected this option. Nevertheless, a substantial proportion (46 per cent) still selected the 'best suited to women' option for primary teaching. There were significant sex differences here – boys were a great deal more likely to choose 'best suited to women', while girls were much more likely to select 'suited to both equally'.

The pattern of responses is markedly different with regard to second level teaching. The vast majority of school leavers (79 per cent) evaluated this as equally suited to both men and women. Six per cent saw it as best suited to women. Here too there were significant gender differences in the responses. More than seven times the proportion of boys to girls thought secondary teaching would be best suited to men, whereas considerably more girls thought secondary teaching was suited to men and women equally. Overall, it is clear that there is greater gender stereotyping of primary teaching than of second level teaching, with boys much more likely to have stereotyped views than girls.

As regards the student teachers' perceptions of the suitability of males and females to primary teaching, they were much less inclined to view primary teaching as better suited to females (23 per cent as opposed to 46 per cent of school leavers) and were more inclined to see it as suited to both genders equally (76 per cent as opposed to 53 per cent of school leavers). Again, there were gender differences among the student teachers with more men than women seeing it as better suited to females (35 per cent compared to 20 per cent). Just under two thirds (64 per cent) of the student teachers indicated that they had experience of male teachers during their primary schooling, with a significantly higher proportion of males (91 per cent) than females (55 per cent) giving this response. In response to a question on how they viewed a good male teacher almost two thirds (65 per cent) of the women, compared to just 42 per cent of the men, selected 'doing the same job as a good female teacher'. Males' preferred response (58 per cent) was 'bringing a different and valuable style to this job'. This response was selected by proportionately far fewer women (32 per cent). Only women selected the option 'having more difficulty carrying out the role' – 4 per cent of them. Thus, women's perceptions of their male colleagues would appear to be more predicated upon a concept of the female teacher as the 'norm' in primary teaching, than were the males' perceptions of themselves.

As with the school leavers, student teachers were more inclined to view secondary teaching as suited to both genders equally (84 per cent). A much higher proportion of male student teachers viewed secondary teaching as better suited to men than did female student teachers (35 per cent compared to 5 per cent).

Perceptions of women and men as 'best teachers'

As teaching is the only profession which children have a great deal of time to observe, and to which they are exposed at length through childhood and adolescence, they are in a position to evaluate it. Some of the respondents may have had limited exposure to teachers of the opposite sex if their education had been in the single-sex system; nevertheless, most pupils (even those in single-sex schools) would have had an opportunity to observe male and female teachers and to have formed a view on their relative competence.

Just over half of the school leavers (53 per cent) felt that, in their experience, women made better primary teachers. A third of the pupils felt that both men and women were equally capable as primary teachers, with a minority (6 per cent) perceiving men as better. Some 8 per cent had no opinion. There were significant sex differences in pupils' perceptions – girls were significantly more likely to evaluate women as better, or to go for 'both equally', although the proportion perceiving men as better was very low. Boys were over four times as likely as girls to have this perception. There were pronounced differences with regard to pupils' perceptions of second level teachers. Over 60 per cent of the pupils felt that men and women were equally capable as second level teachers, while 21 per cent felt men were better. Just 12 per cent of the respondents felt women were better at second level, with the remainder (7 per cent) having no opinion. Again, there were significant gender differences in pupils' perceptions. Boys were five times as likely as girls to feel that men made better second level teachers, and less than half were as likely to perceive women as better teachers at this level.

When the totals with 'no opinion' on the relative capability of male and female teachers are removed (7.5 and 7.1 per cent of respondents respectively in relation to primary and second levels), then it is possible to compare respondents' perceptions of whether men and women are 'best suited to' or 'make better' teachers. This recalculation and comparison gives rise to some interesting features. More of the respondents felt women made better teachers at primary and second level (57 and 12 per cent respectively) than felt that women were 'best suited' to primary (46 per cent) or to second level (6 per cent). Although relatively low, the proportion of respondents who thought that men made better teachers at primary (6 per cent) was fourteen times greater than that who felt men 'best suited' to primary (0.4 per cent). The proportion that felt men were better at second level (22 per cent) was also greater than that which perceived men as 'best suited' to second level (15 per cent). The position with regard to the 'both equally' option is that while 53 per cent of the respondents felt that men and women were equally suited to primary, and 79 per cent to second level, just 37 per cent and 65 per cent felt that they were equally capable at primary and second level respectively. This comparison suggests that pupils are capable of making two types of judgements on teaching. One of these assessments, in relation to gender 'suitability' to different types of teaching, involves a somewhat culturally stereotyped view of what is appropriate to male and to female roles. The other involves judgements, based on their own experiences, which see women in general as more competent at primary level, but at second level having more variety in their views.

Respondents were asked to indicate their reasons for designating 'men', 'women' or 'both equally' as the best teachers, in their experience. Taking the reasons given within the 'women best' spectrum, the greatest proportion (18 per cent overall) said that women were more patient, motherly, caring as primary teachers, and another 15 per cent said women were better with young children. As one pupil put it: 'Females are less scary than males when you are little.' Five per cent of school leavers gave the reason that children reacted better to a mother figure and 2 per cent thought women were better at controlling children. One young man wrote: 'Women have better patience and most are nicer than men.' Other responses could be summarised by the student who wrote, 'men have little patience compared with women'. Two per cent thought that women teachers communicated better.

Within the 'men better' spectrum the most commonly given reason was that men were stricter/had more control/got more respect (given by 5 per cent of the total). As one male student put it: 'Man is bigger, shouts louder and can make the laziest of students do their work.' This tallies with research which shows that men in jobs such as teaching and nursing tend to be given the more difficult cases (Allan, 1993). However, most of the rationale and the comments seemed to refer to secondary rather than primary teaching. One student wrote: 'All my female teachers are useless and can't control a class. Men are better able to handle teens, keep them interested.'

The idea that men were better at second level was suggested by a number of respondents – this again was usually linked to the question of control. An alternative viewpoint was given by a girl who said, 'sometimes male teachers have difficulty controlling a class of 30 girls'. There was also a small minority who felt same sex teachers were better in single-sex schools. A girl whose brother had a male primary teacher reported that: 'he looks up to him so much he is considering being a primary teacher himself'. The variety of responses is illustrated by another girl who wrote, 'men are also loving and caring, but can't show it' linking this to fear of child abuse allegations. Another wrote: 'Primary teaching includes a lot of affection – men may find this taxing on their personalities.' However, abuse allegations did not surface often as a reason that men were better or worse as teachers. As is illustrated in Chapter 5 of this volume, fear of false abuse allegations did not emerge as an important factor in male school leavers' decisions not to enter teaching.

Within the 'both equally' spectrum, the most frequently offered reason was that both were equal – no sex difference in teaching potential (11 per cent of the total). The second reason was that both could be good and bad (7 per cent of total), followed by 'depends on the individual' (6 per cent of total). Other reasons were 'depends on teaching skills'; 'at primary both equal'; 'at secondary both are equal'. Several students gave balanced comments contrasting each sex's skills: 'Women are better with younger children, more connecting and understanding . . . men understand criticism and are able to take jokes with teenagers.' One girl wrote that she had been 'taught about equality – this colours attitudes'. In the 'own experience' category 3 per cent said they had never had a male teacher, and 3 per cent said their answer was based on their own particular experience.

As to the perceptions of student teachers on which sex make better primary teachers in their experience, student teachers were much more inclined to suggest 'both equally' (58 per cent) than were school leavers (34 per cent). This difference was not as great with regard to the gender of second level teachers – 65 per cent of student teachers, compared to 61 per cent of school leavers said 'both equally'. However, male student teachers were much more inclined than their female colleagues to suggest that men made better second level teachers (35 per cent of men, compared to 7 per cent of women students). Reasons given for their responses fell into categories broadly corresponding with their views: gender egalitarian ones accounted for over two thirds. The two most frequently offered were that competence depended on the individual (17 per cent) or that there were no sex differences (16 per cent).

In sum, on the issues of which gender was most suited to, and better at, primary teaching student teachers were rather less stereotyped in their views than school leavers. Their views of male/female suitability and competence in second level teaching were more comparable to those of the school leavers. This would suggest that exposure to the professional demands of primary teaching and greater knowledge about it served to reduce the stereotyping.

Financial reward, prestige, benefit to society

Debates on teaching and the research literature already reviewed show that, from time to time, concerns have been expressed about the levels of prestige and pay attaching to teaching, although there would appear to be a general assumption that teaching is perceived to be of clear benefit to society. In Ireland there has been much debate in the media at the turn of the twenty-first century about the levels of pay and prestige attached to teaching, triggered by industrial action by teachers. Nevertheless, public opinion surveys have suggested that the public is generally satisfied with the education system and that a considerable proportion feels that teachers are entitled to more pay (*Education and Living, Irish Times,* 25 April 2000). This section explores the perceptions of the school leavers and student teachers in relation to these three aspects of teaching as compared to other careers. Figure 3.4 presents their views on which of the nine professions gives the greatest financial return.

Perceptions of the careers offering greatest financial returns are almost evenly split between doctor and lawyer. The 'caring' professions (other than medical doctor) – primary and secondary teaching, and social work – practically vanish from the bar chart. There are no significant gender differences in the distribution, nor were there any significant differences between those choosing primary teaching, or who had considered teaching as a career, and those choosing other careers. Teaching is not perceived as carrying great financial rewards. Thus, those who choose it do so for other reasons.

Figure 3.5 shows the results relating to the level of prestige, which the careers carry in the community, according to the respondents.

Career giving greatest financial return

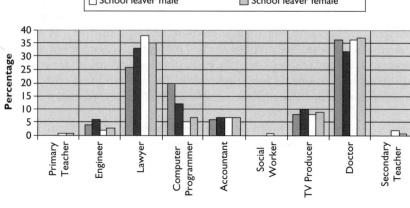

Figure 3.4   Career perceived by school leavers and student teachers as offering the highest rate of financial return, by gender

Note: Student teachers consisted of all the males and a sample of the females.

Career with most prestige

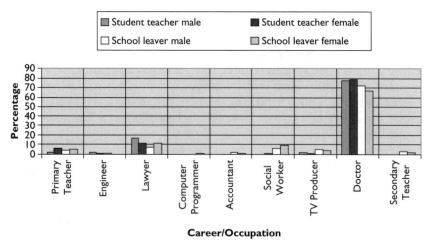

Figure 3.5   Career perceived by school leavers and student teachers as carrying the most prestige in the community, by gender

Note: Student teachers consisted of all the males and a sample of the females.

For both males and females, medical doctors emerge as having the highest prestige (perhaps influenced by the very high academic points level required at entry). Lawyers, social workers and primary teachers (females rank the latter slightly higher) follow (far behind) doctors. Interestingly, engineers, computer programmers and accountants, but also secondary teachers were chosen very infrequently as having the highest prestige. Student teachers, in the vast majority (78 per cent), identified medical doctors as having the highest prestige in the community. The proportion giving this their highest ranking was even greater than that of school leavers (70 per cent). There was little gender difference in this regard. Just 5 per cent of student teachers (of whom most were women) felt that primary teaching offered highest prestige, while no student teacher ranked computer programmer, accountant or secondary teacher highest. Again there are some similarities here with the school leaver distribution. Primary teaching was ranked highest for prestige by 6 per cent of pupils, but second level teaching by just 1 per cent. In sum, the caring professions listed here (albeit mainly medicine) were assessed as carrying the most prestige by 86 per cent of respondents.

While primary teaching was assessed by only 6 per cent of school leavers as having the highest prestige, there was a tendency for those who intended to put it first on the CAO form to rate it more highly. Some 14 per cent of these assessed it as having the highest prestige, compared to 5 per cent of those choosing other courses. None of those choosing primary teaching assessed secondary teaching as having the highest prestige. Indeed, just 1 per cent of the entire cohort did so. This is in contrast with a number of international studies where it has been found that, among school leavers and college students, secondary teaching was regarded as having higher occupational status than primary teaching, and that this perceived higher status was linked to the gender of those involved (Brabeck and Weisberger, 1989; Johnston *et al.*; 1998). Figure 3.6 presents the highest-ranking careers perceived as of most benefit to society.

Medical doctor was again given the highest ranking by the largest proportion of school leavers (55 per cent) in relation to benefit to society. This was followed by social worker at 24 per cent and primary teacher at 13 per cent. The figure for secondary teacher, while low at 4 per cent, was actually in fourth position. The other careers accounted for very low proportions on this characteristic. Accountancy, in particular, was ranked very poorly, with just one person (0.1 per cent) of the entire cohort perceiving it as being of greatest benefit to society. Overall, the caring professions were ranked highest on this dimension, by 96 per cent of the respondents. There were some gender differences. More males perceived the career of medical doctor as being of most benefit to society, while more females perceived social worker and primary teacher in this way.

Unsurprisingly, intending primary teachers were more likely to see their chosen career as the one of most social benefit – 25 per cent of them perceived it thus, as against 13 per cent of those choosing other courses. The broader group who had given some consideration to teaching also ranked primary teaching somewhat higher. No such difference was to be seen in relation to secondary teaching.

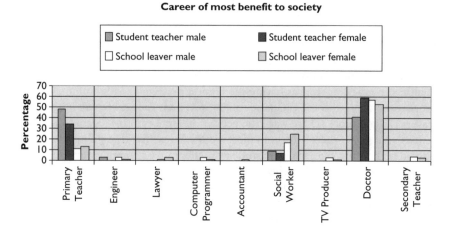

Career of most benefit to society

Figure 3.6 Career perceived by school leavers and student teachers as of most benefit to society, by gender

Note: Student teachers consisted of all the males and a sample of the females.

The lack of high ranking of secondary teaching on all of the variables was notable. Among these school leavers secondary teaching would seem to be held in a good deal lower regard than primary teaching. Another factor worthy of note was the level of unanimity and conservatism among the school leavers' perceptions – for example, engineering for boys, perceptions of high levels of pay, prestige, and social benefit attaching to the older professions, especially medicine and law. However, primary teaching appears to be a respected profession even among those not choosing it. Second and third choices were more wide-ranging.

As regards the perceptions of the student teachers, they ranked the careers of medical doctor (54 per cent) and primary teacher (37 per cent) as of most benefit to society. There were some gender differences. Proportionately more women ranked doctor highest, while proportionately more men ranked primary teacher highest. By contrast nobody ranked second level teacher, accountant or television producer highest.

There were some differences between the school leaver and student teacher patterning on this dimension. While school leavers had given their highest ranking to medical doctor, social worker had come second, and primary teaching third. However, second level teaching was given a low ranking by school leavers also.

Student teachers' rankings of careers within the top three of most benefit to society made some difference to the pattern. A total of 97 per cent of college students put primary teaching in their top three rankings, followed by medical doctor (88 per cent), social worker (53.2 per cent) and secondary teacher (45 per cent). Accountancy was least frequently in the top three rankings (0.5 per cent).

The student teacher cohort thus predominantly viewed the caring professions as of most benefit to society.

Perceptions of the level of enjoyment of different careers

Job satisfaction, money and prestige are only part of the career equation. For young people today enjoyment is very important. So how do they perceive the enjoyment index of different careers? Respondents were asked to assess the nine careers on the basis of how enjoyable they perceived them to be. They were asked to choose between four categories – *all the time/mostly/sometimes/never*. The responses were divided into those who assessed the careers as 'all the time' or 'mostly' enjoyable, versus those who did not. Figure 3.7 presents the proportions that perceived the careers as 'always/mostly' enjoyable, by gender.

Careers almost/mostly enjoyable

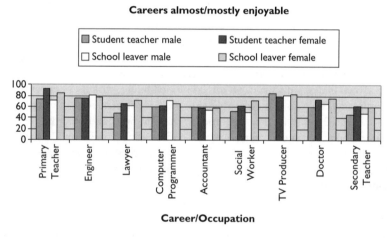

Figure 3.7 Career perceived by school leavers and student teachers as always/mostly enjoyable, by gender

Note: Student teachers consisted of all the males and a sample of the females.

Figure 3.7 illustrates that TV producer was perceived as always/mostly enjoyable by the highest proportion of school leavers (82 per cent), closely followed by primary teacher and engineer (both by 79 per cent). Secondary teaching attracted the lowest enjoyment rating of all, just behind accountant. Marked gender differences were in evidence:

- The two jobs rated **most** enjoyable by **male school leavers** were engineer and TV producer.
- The two jobs rated **least** enjoyable by **male school leavers** were secondary teacher and social worker, with males giving secondary teaching particularly low enjoyment ratings.

- The two jobs rated **most** enjoyable by **female school leavers** were primary teacher and TV producer.
- The two jobs rated **least** enjoyable by **female school leavers** were accountant and secondary teacher.

Girls had more positive perceptions than boys about how enjoyable primary teaching might be – 25 per cent as against 13 per cent of boys thought that primary teachers would enjoy their job all the time. Just 15 per cent of girls, as against 29 per cent of boys, indicated that primary teaching would be 'sometimes' or 'never' enjoyable. The two jobs which got a higher positive response from males as opposed to females were computer programmer and engineer. Primary teaching as a profession was considered more enjoyable by school leavers who aspired to it. Those students were also more likely than others to perceive secondary teaching as enjoyable, although their rating for this was a good deal lower than for primary teaching.

When the combined perceptions of both secondary and primary teaching were averaged and compared with the combined average enjoyment ratings for all nine jobs, half of the school leavers (50 per cent) gave teaching a 'less enjoyable' rating than that of the nine careers' combined average scores. There was a significant difference between males and females on this combined figure, with more males than females rating teaching as less enjoyable (58 and 45 per cent respectively; Chi-square=15.74. df=2, p<.000). The responses to this question confirmed the gender differential on perceptions of careers, observable throughout this survey. Boys were less likely to rate teaching, or indeed other caring occupations, as enjoyable.

Among student teachers primary teaching was perceived to be always or mostly enjoyable by the greatest proportion of respondents (88 per cent). There was, however, a marked gender difference here. A much lower proportion of males than females perceived primary teaching to be always or mostly enjoyable. There were similar gender differences in the perception of the enjoyability of primary teaching among school leavers, but in that instance the gap between males and females was smaller. The greater gender difference between males and females actually training to be primary teachers may well indicate dissatisfaction with the career, or a level of uncertainty about it. Second level teaching (as was the case with school leavers) was perceived as having the lowest rate of enjoyment, together with accountancy. Again males perceived second level teaching as enjoyable much less frequently than did females.

Indeed males tended to rate most of the careers less favourably than did females, with the exceptions of television producer and accountant. Nevertheless, the broad gender differences among student teachers were:

- The two jobs rated **most** enjoyable by **male student teachers** were television producer and engineer.
- The two jobs rated **least** enjoyable by **male student teachers** were lawyer and secondary teacher.

- The two jobs rated **most** enjoyable by **female student teachers** were primary teacher and television producer.
- The two jobs rated **least** enjoyable by **female student teachers** were secondary teacher and accountant.

In comparison to the school leavers the student teachers, as might be expected, were more positively disposed towards teaching. When the combined perceptions of both secondary and primary teaching were averaged and compared with the combined average enjoyment ratings for all nine jobs, just one fifth (21 per cent) gave teaching a 'less enjoyable' rating than that of the nine careers' combined average scores, compared to half of the school leavers. This more positive orientation to teaching was accounted for primarily by females and by a more positive orientation to primary teaching rather than to secondary teaching.

In sum, student teachers ranked primary teaching, followed by medical doctor, as offering the greatest job satisfaction. Similar to the school leavers, they were rather stereotyped in their perceptions of which careers were most suitable for men and for women – engineering for men, primary teaching and social work for women. Doctors, lawyers and computer programmers were perceived as having highest levels of pay, while primary and second level teaching were not mentioned at all. Doctors were viewed as having the highest prestige, although primary teaching was placed in the top three rankings by more than half the student teachers, and by just over one fifth of the school leavers. Doctors and primary teachers were viewed by students as being of most social benefit. Primary teaching was included in the top three rankings by almost all third level students and by almost half of the second level respondents. Primary teaching, but not secondary teaching, was perceived by high majorities of both school leavers and student teachers as being always/mostly enjoyable.

Not surprisingly, primary student teachers were very positive (if somewhat stereotyped) in their perceptions of primary teaching as a career – apart from the pay dimension. Second level teaching was far less positively ranked. It was perceived least often of all the careers, apart from accountancy, as offering the most job satisfaction. Students also perceived second level teaching as having lower prestige, and being of less social benefit than primary teaching.

Perception of selected aspects of primary teaching

Earlier in this chapter, data were presented on school leavers' perceptions of primary teaching as a career in comparison to a number of other careers. School leavers' perceptions of a number of characteristics pertaining specifically to primary teaching are now explored. The responses are related to gender and choice of primary teaching.

On the basis of criteria identified from previous research, respondents were offered a list of fifteen different characteristics associated with primary teaching.

They were asked to identify those which they felt would be attractive about primary teaching as a career, and those which would be off-putting.

School leavers perceived the most attractive aspects of primary/elementary teaching to revolve around extrinsic factors: the short day and good holidays, and job security. There were no significant differences either by gender or by intended choice of a primary teaching course with respect to these two factors. On 'making a difference in young people's lives', the third most attractive feature (perceived to be so by 94 per cent of all respondents), there was a significant gender difference. This was the second most attractive feature for girls at 98 per cent, but the third for boys at 88 per cent. This reflects the greater altruistic/other directed orientation of girls, observed earlier. There was also a significant gender difference, a fourth most attractive feature – a respected position in the community – was perceived as attractive by a higher proportion of girls. The remaining three features which were perceived as attractive by a high proportion of respondents were the levels of personal fulfilment in the work, job availability and being on one's own in control of the classroom. Two of these, namely personal fulfilment and autonomy, were significantly more attractive to girls, and to those intending to put primary teaching as a first course choice, while job availability was significantly perceived more often as attractive by those intending to put primary teaching as their first degree choice.

The least attractive aspects of primary/elementary teaching were after-school planning and correcting (89 per cent of all respondents), having responsibility for managing and disciplining up to 30 pupils (78 per cent) and upholding the schools' religious ethos by preparing children for church events (76 per cent). Girls were somewhat less likely than boys to perceive planning and correcting as unattractive even though three quarters of those intending to put primary teaching first on their degree application forms saw planning and correcting as unattractive. This was a considerably lower proportion than those putting other courses first. Likewise those planning to go into primary teaching found the prospect of classroom management and discipline less off-putting than others (62 per cent, compared to 79 per cent). Girls were somewhat less likely than boys to find maintaining church ethos unattractive – 73 per cent compared to 80 per cent of boys. Nevertheless, planning, correcting and classroom management are integral aspects of the teaching role in all contexts. Given the denominational nature of the primary sector in Ireland, the expectation that teachers will maintain the religious ethos is likely to remain part of teaching for the foreseeable future.

Five characteristics fell into the middle range with respect to their perceived attractiveness. Three related to opportunities for promotion, salary and maintaining good relationships with parents (deemed attractive by 56 per cent, 53 per cent and 50 per cent respectively). Opportunities for promotion were significantly more attractive to those intending to go into primary teaching, while girls were significantly more likely to see maintaining good relationships with parents as attractive. Two further characteristics relating to children's needs were perceived as unattractive by a high proportion of the respondents: having to adjust the curriculum for children with special needs (55 per cent) and being involved in catering for young children's needs (50 per cent). However, there was a significant gender difference on both of these items. Fifty-four per cent of girls (compared to 31 per cent of boys) indicated that they perceived adjusting the curriculum for special needs as an attractive feature. Some 54 per cent of girls (as opposed to 34 per cent of boys) found the idea of involvement with the day-to-day needs of children attractive also. Those intending to do a primary teaching course also were significantly more likely to find dealing with children's daily needs more attractive. These results support findings presented in Chapter 4 which indicate a more marked orientation towards children by girls in general, and by those (mainly girls) intending to put primary teaching as their first university choice.

In comparison, Table 3.1 illustrates that the aspects of primary/elementary teaching identified by the student teachers as most attractive were extrinsic factors – the short day and good holidays; job security and availability; a respected position in the community. School leavers had also seen most of these factors as the most attractive. Two other factors were also seen as very attractive by the student teachers: making a difference to people's lives and personal fulfilment. The first of these is an 'altruistic' factor, the second an intrinsic one. The other factors were also viewed by a majority as attractive: being on one's own in control of the classroom (by 80 per cent) and involvement with children's needs (61 per cent). The aspects of primary teaching identified by student teachers as most off-putting were after-school planning and correcting; having responsibility for managing and disciplining up to 30 pupils; and upholding the school's religious ethos by preparing children for church events. These three were also identified by school leavers as most off-putting. However, student teachers found two of these three even more off-putting than did the school leavers. The overall proportions finding after-school planning and correcting unattractive were 95 per cent of student teachers, compared to 89 per cent of school leavers. Managing and disciplining pupils were identified as unattractive by 89 per cent of student teachers and 78 per cent of school leavers. It would seem that experience of these two integral aspects of the primary teacher's job rendered them even less attractive, as the student teachers would already have had exposure to these aspects during teaching practice. Salary levels, promotion prospects, dealing with parents and with special needs were also generally viewed as unattractive aspects of primary teaching (by 67 per cent, 66 per cent, 67 per cent and 55 per cent respectively). In the case of only one of the fifteen aspects of primary teaching was there a gender difference. Females were significantly more inclined than males to view involvement with children's day-to-day needs as attractive.

In sum, as well as the short day and job security, where there were no differences between the sexes among either school leavers or student teachers, females were more attracted by the hands-on features of the job, than were males. These features included being involved with children's day-to-day needs, having control of the classroom, and adjusting the curriculum for children with special needs. Females were also significantly more attracted by the relational and altruistic aspects –

Table 3.1 School leavers' (SLs) and student teachers' (STs) perceptions of aspects of primary teaching which would be attractive for them, by gender and by school leavers' choice of degree course

Aspects of primary teaching which would be attractive	Male SLs %	Female SLs %	SLs Primary teaching 1st choice %	SLs Other course 1st choice %	Male STs %	Female STs %	Differences: statistical significance (based on Chi-square value)
Salary Level	54.7	51.3	60.7	50.8	28.3	35.0	Sex = NS Priml =NS STs sex:=NS
Respected position	89.6	94.4	96.5	92.1	86.4	92.3	Sex: p<.003 Priml =NS STs sex:=NS
Short day/good holidays	99.0	99.7	98.2	99.8	97.8	100.0	Sex = NS Priml =NS STs sex:=NS
Job security	95.7	96.1	100	95.6	100.0	99.3	Sex = NS Priml =NS STs sex:=NS
Job availability	77.5	75.3	87.5	75.7	93.5	93.9	Sex = NS Priml: p<.026 STs sex:=NS
Making a difference in young people's lives	87.8	97.9	98.2	93.9	95.7	98.7	Sex: p<.000 Priml =NS STs sex:=NS
Personal fulfilment	82.0	90.3	94.7	86.4	89.1	95.3	Sex: p<.000 Priml: p<.045 STs sex:=NS

Opportunities for promotion	55.7	55.6	69.6	51.8	31.8	34.0
						Sex: NS Priml: p<.007 STs sex:=NS
On one's own, in control	61.1	67.7	76.4	63.5	95.6	81.1
						Sex: p<.018 Priml: p<.035 STs sex:=NS
Responsibility for management/discipline	21.9	22.6	38.2	21.4	13.6	20.0
						Sex: p<.NS Priml: p<.005 STs sex:=NS
Involvement with children's daily needs	33.7	53.8	66.1	43.3	47.7	65.3
						Sex: p<.000 Priml: p<.001 STs sex: P=.028
Maintain good relationships with parents	44.1	54.1	57.1	47.4	26.7	34.9
						Sex: p<.001 Priml =NS STs sex:=NS
After school planning/correcting	9.0	12.4	26.3	9.7	4.4	5.4
						Sex: p<.05 Priml: p<.001 STs sex:=NS
Upholding school's religious ethos	20.4	26.8	32.1	22.2	15.9	26.1
						Sex: p<.012 Priml =NS STs sex:=NS
Adopting curriculum for special needs	31.1	54.4	54.5	44.8	41.9	46.2
						Sex: p<.000 Priml =NS STs sex:=NS

Note: Student teachers consisted of all the males and a sample of the females; NS = Non-significant; Priml = Primary teaching as 1st Choice on school leavers' degree application.

personal fulfilment, making a difference to others, and fostering good relations with parents. Females also found maintaining the religious ethos of the school less off-putting than males. The fact that only about a quarter of respondents found the maintenance of the religious ethos of the school attractive raises issues concerning the frequently stated view of the churches (now protected in law through the *Equal Status Act, 2000* – see Government of Ireland, 2000c) that the appointment of teachers of the relevant denomination is a mechanism for the preservation of church ethos in schools in a mainly denominational school system.

Perceptions of the nature and status of teaching and of gender issues

In order to expand the understanding of perceptions of a range of different aspects of teaching, particularly primary teaching, school leavers' and student teachers' reactions to twenty-one additional statements were sought. These related to further dimensions of teaching, to women's and to men's roles and teaching, and to issues of gender equality in teaching. As was the case with other elements of the questionnaire, these statements were derived from the previous research, and from the pilot studies. Respondents were asked to indicate their feelings towards each of the twenty-one statements along a five point scale from strongly agree (score = 1) to strongly disagree (score = 5). Thus, the lower the score on each scaled item, the more positive the perceptions of respondents to it. Mean scores on perceptions of each of the twenty-one scaled items were related to the student's gender, to whether or not they intended to put primary teaching as their first university choice, and to whether or not they had indicated any kind of preference for primary or second level teaching. Their responses are included under five separate headings:

1. perceptions of the nature of teaching;
2. perceptions of the status of teaching;
3. perceptions of women in teaching;
4. perceptions of men in teaching;
5. perceptions of gender equality in teaching.

The responses of respondents to the series of statements on primary teaching are set out in Appendix 1, Table 2. The responses are analysed by gender of respondent and, in the case of school leavers, by whether the respondent intended to put primary teaching as their first degree choice, and by whether the respondent had indicated that he or she intended to put any kind of teaching as a preference on their application form. 'Any Type of Teaching' refers to those who answered 'Yes' to a question on whether they had ever considered any type of teaching. (It thus includes those who intended to put primary teaching as their first choice as well as those intending to apply for other teacher education courses.)

When interpreting the table it should be noted that *the lower the mean score in each cell, the stronger the level of agreement* with the relevant statement. *The higher* *the mean score, the stronger the level of disagreement.* The test used to compute the significance of the difference between the means is the 't' test. Where the difference is statistically significant this is indicated in the cells in the following way: * p <.01 – p <.05; **p <.000 – p <.001 (see Appendix 1, Table 2).

There were significant variations between groups in their perceptions of the five dimensions of teaching explored: the nature of teaching, its status, women in teaching, men in teaching and gender equality in primary teaching. Let us turn now to consider this variation within the groups – i.e. the ideas to which each group was most well disposed and those with which they most disagreed.

From the mean scores it is evident that, among school leavers, boys were less inclined than girls to have strong feelings about any of the issues explored. Their mean scores fell within a narrow range and, although they differed significantly from girls on many individual scale items, the values were not at either extreme.

Of the twenty-one scaled items, boys were in greatest agreement with the following three: that being a good primary teacher depends on personality rating, not gender (mean = 2.01); that male teachers are better at controlling older pupils (mean = 2.08); and that teachers perform a moral service to society (mean = 2.19). They were in the least agreement with the three statements: that boys need male teachers as role models (mean = 2.85); that children have more respect for male teachers (mean = 2.83); and that there is a lot of interest and variety in primary teaching (mean = 2.73).

It would appear from the narrow range of their scoring then that boys were less engaged with the issues relating to primary teaching than were girls. While the statement that they gave their highest level of agreement to was a gender egalitarian one, they were also a great deal more likely to agree with a statement on male control than were girls, but were least likely to agree that boys need male teachers as role models. They also had a low level of agreement that primary teaching was a job with a lot of interest and variety.

In contrast, among the school leavers, girls' mean scores ranged more widely. They were more likely to have strong levels of agreement and disagreement with the statements, indicating that the issues were of greater interest and salience for them.

As with the boys, the statement with which girls most strongly agreed was that being a good primary teacher depends on personality and training, not gender (mean = 1.38). However, their level of agreement with this statement was significantly greater than that of the boys. The statement which attracted the second highest level of agreement from girls was that it is important to see men in caring roles (mean = 2.00). Their third highest level of agreement was that primary teachers are able to influence children for the good (mean = 2.04).

Girls disagreed strongly with the following three statements: that children have more respect for male teachers (mean = 3.75); that male teachers are better at organising sporting and other activities (mean = 3.64); and that men are more suited to secondary teaching (mean = 3.62). In short, girls appeared to find the issues under examination to be of greater salience, and to have significantly greater orientation towards equality and caring.

The school leavers intending to give first preference to primary teaching were, of course, of particular interest in the context of the present study. As might be expected, the range evident in their scoring on the twenty-one scaled items was greater than that of any other group, ranging from strong agreement to strong disagreement. This would indicate that the issues under consideration were of more interest to them than to other groups.

The statement with which intending primary teachers were most in agreement was that being a good primary teacher depends on personality and training, not gender (mean = 1.16). Their second highest level of agreement was with the statement that there is a lot of interest and variety in primary teaching (mean = 1.68). In this they differed significantly from the other pupils and, as such, indicated a very positive, intrinsic focus on primary teaching. Their third greatest level of agreement was with the idea that teachers perform a service of moral value to society (mean = 1.74).

As might be expected, because those intending to enter primary teaching were mainly girls, there was some overlap with the patterning for girls' responses as a whole in the study. Although the three statements with which intending primary teachers most disagreed were the same as those chosen by girls as a whole, there were differences in the intensity with which they disagreed. Levels of disagreement were expressed (higher than by any other group) with the ideas that male teachers get more respect (mean = 3.89); that males are better at organising sports/other activities (mean = 3.88); and that males are more suited to secondary teaching (mean = 3.72).

As regards school leavers who expressed a preference for any form of teaching, again, as might be expected, the patterns were very similar overall to those who intended to give primary teaching their first preference (who are a sub-set of this wider group). Although the range of scores was not as great as that of intending primary teachers, there were variations which indicated high levels of agreement and disagreements with the notions expressed among the scaled items. This wider group differed from those who put primary teaching as their first preference in one noteworthy respect. They appeared to be less focused on the intrinsic aspects of teaching. Unlike intending primary teachers whose second highest agreement was with the assertion that there is a lot of interest and variety in primary teaching, the wider group had their second highest agreement with 'primary teachers influence children for the good' (mean = 1.83), and their third highest agreement with the notion that teachers perform a service of moral value (mean = 1.85). Their three highest levels of disagreement were with the same issues as those of intending primary teachers, but with the somewhat lower mean scores of 3.68, 3.54 and 3.43 respectively.

From the student teachers' responses to the twenty-one items on perceptions of teaching it can be seen that there was greater agreement with the gender egalitarian statements and on those relating to the nature and status of teaching, than there was with those which related to stereotypical roles and perceptions of men and women in teaching. Where stereotypical responses were espoused this was significantly more likely among men than among women. However, both men and women student teachers expressed high levels of agreement with the suggestion that it is important for children to see men in caring roles.

When compared to the perceptions of teaching among the school leavers, there was greater agreement among student teachers that primary teaching is a demanding and exhausting job but also that there is a lot of interest and variety in it. Scores on these two items had been proved to differ significantly between school leavers choosing primary teaching and others. There was greater agreement among student teachers of both genders than among school leavers that teachers perform a service of moral value to society, and that they are able to influence children for the good. These two items had also given rise to significant differences among the school leaver respondents selecting primary teaching and those selecting other courses. On the whole, student teachers had rather less stereotyped views in relation to women in teaching, as measured by their average scores. Male student teachers were less inclined than male school leavers to endorse stereotyped views on men in teaching. As regards the two statements presenting egalitarian views on gender equality in education, levels of agreement among student teachers were higher than among school pupils as a whole. However, among school leavers these too had been significantly related to choice of teaching, with greater agreement among those selecting primary teaching than among others.

Summary

International research on perceptions of teaching suggested that men's interest in female-dominated fields is, in general, less usual than women's interest in male-dominated fields. Although there are perceptible patterns, practices and ideologies in various careers, the structural configurations of gender differences vary from job to job, as do individual, subjective experiences of masculinity or femininity. The perception of particular occupations as female-dominated, and the associated perceptions (both negative and positive) of the minority of men who work in them, may have implications for school leavers' perceptions and decision-making. Previous studies on men in teaching suggest that there are conflicts and contradictions in their role.

School leavers' and student teachers' perceptions of primary and second level teaching in the study reported in this volume were established, with statistically significant gender differences evident in perceptions of teaching and other careers listed. The lack of high ranking of second level teaching on all of the variables was notable. For both the school leavers and student teachers secondary/high school teaching would seem to be held in a good deal lower regard than primary/elementary teaching. Another factor worthy of note was the level of unanimity and conservatism among the school leavers' perceptions – for example, engineering for boys, perceptions of high level of pay, prestige and social benefit attaching to the older professions, especially medicine and law. However, primary teaching appears to be a respected profession even among those not choosing it. The extrinsic features of teaching were the most attractive to the vast majority of both the school leavers and student teachers – the short day, long holidays and job security. There were significant gender differences with regard to other aspects perceived as attractive. These reflected the greater altruistic/other directed orientation of girls. The aspects of primary teaching perceived as most off-putting were intrinsic ones – after-school planning and correcting, classroom management and discipline, and upholding the religious ethos of the schools. Significant gender differences were found here too – females found these aspects less off-putting than males, as did school leavers intending to put primary teaching as a choice. Females were more oriented to the needs of children. The attitudes of the school leavers and student teachers to five dimensions of teaching were explored: the nature of teaching, its status, women in teaching, men in teaching and gender equality in primary teaching. It would appear from the findings that males were less engaged with the issues relating to primary teaching than were females. They were less inclined to have strong feelings about any of the issues explored. Females appeared to find the issues under examination of much greater salience, and to have a significantly greater orientation towards gender equality and caring.

Chapter 4

Social background and choice of teaching

This chapter considers the interaction of class and gender across a variety of occupations, with particular emphasis on teaching. It also examines the influence of social background on the choice of teaching versus other occupations. The trends and possible explanations for entry patterns into teaching as a career are presented.

Teaching and the class structure

In spite of the cultural differences between the US and other countries such as Ireland, Britain and elsewhere in Europe, the analysis of Allan (1993: 113–7) in his commentary on the paucity of male elementary teachers in the United States is relevant to concerns explored in this study. Allan sums up the problems of the male classroom teacher thus:

> In spite of the initial advantages offered by affirmative action, welcoming male principals, and widespread public perception of the need for more male role models in the socialization of children, men who choose elementary teaching experience stressful disadvantages, posed by conflict and contradiction focused on their maleness. In fact, each advantage is itself potentially a disadvantage or source of uneasiness.
>
> (1993: 126)

Allan presents a scenario where men in primary teaching find themselves in a 'no-win' situation. If hired simply because they are men, 'this raises suspicions among their female colleagues about their suitability as teachers' (ibid.). He also notes that there may be hostility from (male) school principals who may regard the maleness of others as a threat to their own authority. On the other hand, forming an alliance with either the male principal or female colleagues can be misinterpreted as, respectively, preferential treatment or effeminacy – both of these potential problems arise from the location of males in a female-identified job. Like Christine Williams, Allan contends that the same conditions that appear to be advantageous also carry with them disadvantages. 'Erring' on the masculine side of their identity raises doubts about male teachers' suitability and competence, whereas an emphasis on nurturing and sensitivity leads to suspicions and charges of effeminacy. Allan concludes that male elementary teachers suffer because they upset the gendered ordering of the social institutions in which they work.

Rose and Birkelund (1991) note that the labour markets of most Western countries are highly segregated by gender. They make a distinction between horizontal and vertical segregation and both of these patterns are reflected in the occupation of teaching. Rose and Birkelund adapt Goldthorpe's class model, one which is based on the work and market situations of men (Goldthorpe 1980), to their own study on the inter-relationships between class, occupational segregation and gender. In this seven-tier model a distinction is made between the Service Class and the Junior Service Class, with teaching falling into the latter category. In their analysis of census data from the United Kingdom, they conclude that socio-economic categories are related to occupations that are segregated by gender. In general, men and women who are employed in male occupations enjoy a significantly higher average annual income than those employed in female occupations. Their survey finds that there are fewer female occupations in Class I but that in Class II there are:

> relatively large and almost equal numbers of male and female occupations (in which) the income differences are both large and statistically significant. . . . In this case there is at least *prima facie* evidence that it could be occupational segregation which might explain the market situation differences between men and women.
>
> (Rose and Birkelund, 1991: 16)

In addition they report that the differences in credentials between male- and female-dominated occupations are either not significant, or, where there are comparable numbers, tend to favour the female occupations (ibid.: 14–15). Placing such statistics within a gender-relational frame, Miller (1996: 157) reports that, in Britain during the early 1990s, there was a general political contempt for higher education. The view taken was that education was more feminine than masculine, and was generally 'out of touch with the tough demands of a modern technological world'.

Rose and Birkelund gathered data on satisfaction in work situations and found significant differences in Class II in favour of male occupations (ibid.: 16). The differences were in the areas of autonomy, decision-making and supervision. Rose and Birkelund conclude that in classes where women's employment is concentrated 'there are not only significant differences in the market and work situations of men and women but also similar differences between male and female occupations' (ibid.: 17).

Delamont (1980: 73–7) has suggested that there is an interaction between sex and social class origin, and that this accounts for the different experiences of male and female teachers. In Britain, she has argued, the social class origin typical of male teachers is 'lower-middle class', and the conventional stereotypical view of gender which many male teachers have stems from their own childhood. Women who go into teaching are characterised as being 'middle-class' and as having limited career targets. However, as has been seen already, class is just one of a number of social and cultural categories of factors which may operate in the segregation of occupations or in the 'gendered subjectivity' of employed persons. There are cultural variations in patterns of entry to teaching in different countries. For example, there has traditionally been a lower proportion from manual working-class backgrounds at entry to primary teaching in Ireland than has been the case in England, because of the high proportion from rural and farming backgrounds (Kelly, 1970; Drudy and Lynch, 1993; Clancy, 1988 and 1995a).

Benton DeCorse and Vogtle (1977) speculate that there may be contradictions in how men feel about the conditions of teaching. For example, men may be attracted by the earning power of teaching, but this is devalued by the traditional perception of women teachers providing a 'second income' for households (ibid.: 42). They reported that male teachers' reasons for entering teaching are not fundamentally different from those of their female colleagues, but they suggest that, among male teachers, there is a greater conflict between individual career decisions and perceived societal concepts of 'appropriate' male occupations. For example, many of their subjects did not receive the support of their fathers at the initial stage of their career choice (ibid: 41). However, they reported that there have been some changing patterns in the career paths of men in the 1990s, and these have tended towards greater flexibility and intrinsic motivation. This is particularly the case with men who enter teaching as their second career: 'Generally, for these participants, intrinsic reward and personal satisfaction have replaced earlier perceptions of financial security' (ibid.: 41).

Freidus (1990; 1992) found many similarities in the negative experiences of both male and female second-career teachers (financial, social image, staff relations). However, the men in her study had additional problems and pressures:

> Men who come into elementary classrooms are expected to succeed. In our society, elementary school teaching continues to be viewed as women's work. As such it is not considered by most to be particularly challenging in an intellectual sense or taxing in a physical sense. Hence, the logic goes, it should be easy for men who have been able to garner success working in the arduous and competitive fields of business and the professions to excel in the classroom.
> (Freidus, 1992: 21)

The reality, according to Freidus, is quite different: the world of the classroom is one that requires constant decision-making, a wide range of content knowledge, and the capacity to meet the emotional, cognitive and physical needs of large groups of children on an ongoing basis. Most of the men in her study apparently could not fathom the complexities that would be involved in a teaching career, whereas her female subjects had more realistic expectations. Both male and female second-career teachers felt emotionally vulnerable, sometimes 'out of control', and dependent on experienced colleagues. These feelings, she argues, are not compatible with the traditional vision of what men should feel, and as such, they present to male teachers a number of personal and professional challenges. Thus, there is a conflict between the prior gender socialisation of men and the roles that are required as teachers.

From a theoretical perspective the concept of class concerns relationships to property and the ability to command income, wealth and other resources. However, in empirical research the vast majority of researchers from all theoretical backgrounds use occupation as an indicator of income, wealth and resources when trying to establish social class. Previous work has suggested that, with regard to the majority of children who are selected in sample surveys in the educational system, classifications of parental occupation based on the census classification of occupations can be used as an indicator of class position, but to a limited extent (Drudy, 1991). There are difficulties in relying on occupational categories, which are exacerbated in the case of studies of school or college students, as their knowledge of their parents' occupations is sometimes inadequate. On other occasions students may have fears (irrespective of how groundless these may be) of revealing parental occupations as sources of income.

When the focus of attention is on the cultural and attitudinal area, such as educational and career decision-making, other approaches have been used (Drudy, 1995: 295–323). For example, in a study of second level student performance Breen (1986) used the qualifications of mothers and fathers as an indicator of 'cultural capital', i.e. the cultural goods transmitted by different families (Drudy and Lynch, 1993: 155). Using educational qualifications implied that parents' education could be used as a referent for the skills, attitudes and abilities of pupils that 'derive from their home environment' (Breen, 1986: 89). The next section examines the influence of parental social class and a number of other selected background factors on career choice and, in particular, on choice of teaching.

The influence of selected factors on choices

Parental social class background

In the light of the debates highlighted above, two measures to indicate parental social class background were used in this survey – parental occupations and parental educational levels achieved. Some of the difficulties encountered when classifying occupations in other research emerged in this study also. For example, the information supplied by students about parents' occupations did not always correlate with educational levels. Some parents appeared to have jobs which were not compatible with their educational levels – unless a lot of informal night study had been undertaken. In other cases the information given on occupation was insufficient to make a totally accurate classification according to central statistical office guidelines. For example, few sons and daughters of civil servants oblige researchers by giving their parent's grade. In most cases where there was ambiguity, it was decided to make an estimate of class position if it was possible, but these estimates would contain a higher degree of error than would be the case if fuller information were available.

Parents' occupations were coded according to the social class categories of the 1996 Census Classification of Occupations. This classification system is seven-fold, with occupations ranked from Social Class I through to Social Class 7. Where a mother's occupation was given as housewife/homemaker or social equivalent this was coded accordingly. Where housewife and another occupation were given the other occupation was coded. In the case of full-time housewives, the number of respondents giving mother's former occupation was too small to be useful. 'Unemployed' was coded accordingly. There were also some students who omitted to include data on parental occupation – some 45 omitted anything on fathers' occupations, while 109 omitted any details on mothers' occupations. These have been eliminated from the tables below.

The seven-point Central Statistics Office (CSO) social class scale was recoded into three categories for the purposes of analysis. These were:

- Social Class 1 and 2: Higher and Lower Professional, Employees and Managers
- Social Class 3 and 4: Intermediate Non-Manual/Skilled workers
- Social Class 5 and 6: Semi- and Unskilled Workers

The remaining categories were coded as 'other/housewife/unemployed/ deceased'. However, only classifiable occupations are used in Table 4.1.

According to the school leavers, some 49 per cent of their fathers had jobs which fell into Social Classes 1 or 2 – the professional, employer and manage-rial categories. The largest group of mothers (42 per cent) fell into the 'other' category, mainly housewives, although this group is not included in Table 4.1. Approximately 57 per cent of school leavers' mothers were working outside the home, many in part-time employment. This is higher than might have been expected for this age group of women, and most likely reflects the improved economic situation at the end of the 1990s. Of those who were in classifiable occupations, they were fairly evenly divided between the professional, managerial and employer social classes and the intermediate and skilled social classes.

According to the student teachers, approximately 83 per cent of their fathers worked full-time and 3.9 per cent part-time. A further 13.5 per cent were retired or deceased. A total of 28.9 per cent of mothers worked full-time in the home. Of the remaining 61.1 per cent, almost two thirds (63.8 per cent) worked full-time, 26.8 per cent part-time and the remainder (9 per cent) were retired or deceased. The proportion of mothers of the college students who worked outside the home was thus somewhat higher than that for the school leavers. For both groups, the occupations (including farming, appropriately assigned by acreage) were classified into the six social class categories.

Table 4.1 Social class of respondents' parents

Social class category	School leavers' fathers %	Student teachers' fathers %	School leavers' mothers %	Student teachers' mothers %
Social Class 1 and 2 (Professional etc.)	49.1	57.9	42.1	59.3
Social Class 3 and 4 (Intermediate Non-Manual and Skilled)	43.5	32.8	45.1	25.7
Social Class 5 and 6 (Semi- and Unskilled Workers)	7.4	9.3	12.8	15.0
Total	100.0	100.0	100.0	100.0
N	819	192	539	113

Notes:
i.   Low responses to questions on parental occupations are normal in surveys; those for whom no definitive information was provided were excluded from analysis.
ii. Farmers were distributed throughout the social classes according to acreage. Overall, some 15 per cent of the fathers in the survey were farmers.
iii. The occupational classification appendices in Clancy's reports on access to higher education (1988 and 1995a) were very helpful and a very useful additional resource when an occupation proved elusive.

Responses from the sample of student teachers indicated that 36.5 per cent of their fathers, and 11.2 per cent of their mothers, were farmers. Of those who were from farm families, 59.7 per cent were from farms of 100 acres or over – that is, for the most part, from the more viable, higher income, farming sector. The proportion of fathers who were farmers was disproportionately large, considering the present proportion of farmers in the male labour force – 14.9 per cent in 1997 (Central Statistics Office 2005). In this survey the proportion of student teachers from farm backgrounds was surprisingly substantial, in the light of the decline in agricultural employment in Ireland.

When occupations were divided into social class categories (allocating farmers to the appropriate social class based on acreage), it is clear that the two professional categories (Social Class 1 and 2) predominated in student teachers' backgrounds. The finding that student teachers in the primary colleges of education come mainly from farm and middle-class backgrounds confirms and replicates earlier findings (Kelly, 1970; Greaney *et al.*, 1987). The proportions to be found in the two professional/managerial categories (1 and 2) are even greater than indicated by higher education applicants in the second level schools, illustrating the greater level of social selection at entry to third level. Forty-two per cent of the student teacher respondents were in receipt of a grant.[1] Student teachers were asked also to indicate if they worked during term time (apart from teaching practice) – 36 per cent stated that they did. The jobs were mainly bar, restaurant and shop work, child-minding and other miscellaneous jobs in the services sector. A high proportion (41 per cent) of those in part-time employment worked for 6–10 hours per week, while 13 per cent worked for sixteen hours or more.

As suggested earlier, the level of parental education can also be used as an indicator of social class position. Table 4.2 examines the level of education achieved by parents of the school leavers and student teachers in our survey. Respondents were asked to indicate the highest educational levels achieved by parents. These were grouped into three categories:

1. Finished formal education at or before the end of Junior Cycle (age 15/16)
2. Finished formal education at end of Senior Cycle (age 17/18)
3. Finished formal education at Third Level (degree/diploma)

It would appear from the information on parental education given by school leavers that the average educational attainment of mothers was greater than for fathers. The numbers declaring that parents had reached third level education is higher than would be expected for the general population in their middle years. However, what must be borne in mind here is that the school leaver group is itself more highly selected than their general age-cohort, as the survey focused on those intending to apply for a third level place through the higher education application system. It is therefore to be expected that parental educational levels would be higher than average.

The information provided by student teachers indicated a higher average level of educational achievement among mothers than among fathers. Student teachers' mothers were more likely to have a third level qualification than the mothers of the school leaver cohort, although the educational attainment of fathers was notably lower in the case of the student teachers. This may well be associated with the preponderance of rural and farming backgrounds represented among the student teachers. There has long been a tradition of rural females staying on longer at

Table 4.2 Highest educational level achieved by respondents' parents

Highest level achieved	School leavers' fathers %	Student teachers' fathers %	School leavers' mothers %	Student teachers' mothers %
At or before end of Junior Cycle	43.4	52.1	35.7	31.4
At end of Senior Cycle	24.6	19.8	31.3	27.8
Third Level Diploma/Degree	32.0	28.1	33.0	40.8
Total	100.0	100.0	100.0	100.0
N	990	192	1,001	194

school than their male counterparts (Morren, 1970). Some 58 per cent of fathers fell into Social Classes 1 and 2 (Table 4.1), and many of these would have been farmers. It is likely that the very close connection between education and social class that is normally observable in more urban populations does not pertain to such a high degree among the families represented here. It is interesting to compare the proportion of fathers of student teachers who had left school before or at the end of the junior cycle (52 per cent) with the fathers among the school sample who fell into this category (43 per cent). A much higher proportion of urban families were represented in the second level sample (see sampling procedures outlined in Appendix 2) and thus the fathers in the second level sample are likely to be more typical than the fathers of student teachers.

Academic achievement

Entry to post-primary teacher education programmes in the Republic of Ireland is highly competitive. Analysis of figures provided by the Central Applications Office showed that in 2003, for example, there were over 10,000 applicants for just under 1,000 places in the primary colleges of education, of which 16.1 per cent were from males (although males formed just under 10 per cent of those who received offers). Data from the Higher Diploma in Education Application Centre, which processes applications for the 800 places on the Higher Diploma in Education in the four NUI universities, illustrated that in 2003 there were 3,034 applicants, of whom 27.1 per cent were males, with males forming 27.2 of those who accepted offers. In the context of the Irish situation of very competitive entry to teaching in Ireland, it was evident that academic achievement would play an important role in the process of entry to teaching. The main measure of school leaver academic achievement in this study was based on the results in the Junior Certificate Examination, as reported by the respondents themselves.[2] The Junior Certificate Examination is the first public examination taken by Irish students and marks the end of the junior cycle of second level education at age 15–16. Although pupils normally take between 8–10 subjects at Junior Certificate level, the Grade Point Average in this study was based upon their reported performance in the three core subjects – English, Irish and Mathematics as these three subjects are taken by almost all pupils. In the calculation of Grade Point Averages an adaptation of the method used to obtain single scores by the National Council on Curriculum and Assessment (NCCA) in its study of the 1992 Junior Certificate Examination (Martin and Hickey, 1993: 7) was adopted. A combined grade point average for the three subject areas was computed (see Table 4.3 in the notes for details).[3]

International research had pointed up important gender differentials in educational achievement transnationally. Therefore, it was clear that gender would be an important intervening variable. Before examining the relationship of the social class of the school leavers and student teachers, the relationship of gender to academic achievement is first presented. The relationship between gender and academic performance for school leavers is presented in Table 4.3.

Table 4.3 Distribution of Junior Certificate Grade Point Average for English, Irish and Mathematics, by gender

Grade Point Average	Males %	Females %	All %
0–6	3.7	4.1	3.9
6.1–8	15.4	8.2	11.1
8.1–9.4	42.2	38.5	40.0
9.5–10.9	28.5	33.1	31.3
11+	10.2	16.1	13.7
Total	100.0	100.0	100.0
			(n = 1,020)

Chi-square=20.02, df=4, p<.000

The distribution of GPAs for the school leavers is skewed towards the upper bands, most likely because the sampling procedure involved selecting only those who intended to be third level applicants later in the year. In this context, it may be somewhat surprising to find 15 per cent whose GPA in these three subjects falls below 8, which is equivalent to a Grade B on an Ordinary Level paper, or a Grade E on a Higher Level paper.

There were significant differences between boys and girls on grade point average scores in the junior cycle. The overall GPA for the student sample was 9.34, with girls having a GPA of 9.48 and boys a GPA of 9.14. When means were compared this difference was found to be statistically significant. So too were the differences in scores between boys and girls throughout the categories of the GPA distribution as presented in Table 4.3, which illustrates the gender differences in Junior Certificate performance which were evident from mean grade point averages. While slightly more girls scored in the bottom band, they were much more likely than boys to have scores in the top two bands. These gender differences were statistically significant. The higher levels of academic performance of the girls here mirror similar gender differences among the school population as a whole in performance in public examinations in Ireland (Martin and Hickey, 1993; Drudy, 1995) and internationally (OECD, 2003a).

Another important measure of academic performance (and of academic potential) is the number of higher level subjects taken by students at Senior Cycle. School leavers had been asked to indicate the number of higher level subjects they intended to take at Leaving Certificate. Almost 87 per cent of the sample planned to sit four or more higher level papers at Leaving Certificate. In the light of their Junior Certificate grade point averages, these plans may have been somewhat optimistic for some of the respondents. It is likely that changes would have been made subsequent to the survey in the light of the Leaving Certificate 'mock' examinations in the Spring. However, the number of honours papers gives some indication of students' academic level. The average number of higher level papers was 5.23, with girls average 5.39 and boys average 4.99. The differences between boys and girls were statistically significant.

Junior Certificate GPAs and the numbers planning to sit higher level papers at the Leaving Certificate examination show that, on average, girls were achieving better academic results and had greater academic potential at Leaving Certificate than boys, although in some cases students are restricted by school policy on when decisions about higher level papers are taken. From the point of view of primary teaching, which requires relatively high examination grades (i.e. Leaving Certificate 'points'), the pool of suitably qualified boys was smaller than the equivalent pool of girls. It may be important that, as will be seen elsewhere in this book, boys were slightly more likely than girls to mention 'high points and Honours Irish' as reasons for not choosing primary teaching.

One obligatory requirement for entrance to primary teaching in Ireland is that candidates must have a minimum of a grade C in higher level Irish in their Leaving Certificate Examination. Irish is the first official language (although English is the mother tongue of the majority of the population). It is a compulsory subject at primary school and all primary teachers are expected to teach it, except in exceptional circumstances. There were significant differences between boys and girls as to the level at which they intended to take the subject at their Leaving Certificate Examination. Less than half of the total sample (44 per cent) planned to take Leaving Certificate Irish at higher level. This was a good deal higher than the proportion of those taking Irish at higher level nationally in the Leaving Certificate Examination for the survey year cohort (31 per cent – Department of Education and Science, 2000: 99–107). This reflected the fact that the sample was confined to those who intended to apply for a university or other third level place and thus could not be expected to reflect the patterns of other groupings among the wider Senior Cycle population. There were statistically significant gender differences, as half the female respondents planned to take Irish at higher level, as against just over a third of the male respondents. This again reflects national patterns (bearing in mind the selected sample) where nationally a much higher proportion of females than of males took higher level Irish (ibid.).

At Junior Certificate, some 54 per cent of male respondents, compared to 63 per cent of female respondents, had taken higher level Irish. This difference was significant also (Chi-square = 9.78; p<.002). The drop in uptake of higher level Irish from Junior to Leaving Certificate was steeper for boys than for girls. Low uptake of higher level Irish at Leaving Certificate reduces the pool of suitably qualified primary teaching applicants, but of male applicants in particular.

Many studies have demonstrated that a strong relationship exists between social class and academic attainment (Breen, 1986; Hannan et al.; 1996; Clancy, 1996; Smyth, 1999). It was felt that this might well be a factor influencing school leaver academic achievement. As 43 per cent of the mothers were not in paid employment outside the home, father's occupation was used as the indicator of social class.

School leavers' social class background, as indicated by social class of father's occupation, is significantly related to grade point average in the three core subjects at Junior Certificate. This relationship is evident even though this group does not represent the whole age cohort, or even the entire Senior Cycle population in the sample schools. Only those who expressly intended to apply for a third level place are included in the sample. Nevertheless, even within this group some influence of social class background on academic performance is apparent. The most marked differences in GPAs are between those from Social Classes 1 and 2 (the professional, management and employers group) and the others. Pupils from these two social classes are a great deal more likely to have had GPAs in the two highest bands, and a great deal less likely to have had scores in the two lowest bands. There were some interesting variations in the two other categories. Pupils with fathers in Social Classes 5 and 6 were less often (than any other group) in the lowest band, and proportionately more frequently in the top band than pupils from Social Classes 3 and 4, although less often than Social Classes 1 and 2.

Social class and educational background and school leavers' choice of teaching

The relationship between school leavers' social class background, parental education and decision-making about teaching is now examined. Table 3 (Appendix 1) presents these relationships in relation to (a) respondents' intentions to have primary/elementary teaching as their first choice on their degree application form and (b) whether they had ever considered teaching at primary or second level as a career choice. While, as shown in Table 4.4, social class background had an impact on respondents' academic performance, Table 3 (Appendix 1) illustrates that it had little overall impact on preference for teaching, or for selection of primary/elementary teaching at third level. There was a slight tendency for pupils whose mothers fell into Social Classes 1 and 2, and for pupils whose fathers fell into Social Classes 5 and 6 to favour choice of primary teaching. The latter finding is combined, with some apparent contradiction, with the most notable feature of the table: i.e. that no student whose mother fell into Social Classes 5 or 6 expressed a preference for primary teaching. Some caution must be applied when interpreting

Table 4.4 Junior Certificate Grade Point Average in English, Irish and Mathematics, by father's social class

Grade Point Average	Social classes 1 and 2 %	Social classes 3 and 4 %	Social classes 5 and 6 %	All %
0–6	2.8	4.3	1.7	3.3
6.1–8	8.6	13.7	20.3	11.6
8.1–9.4	30.3	47.8	45.8	39.1
– 10.9	39.3	27.9	18.6	32.9
11 +	19.0	6.3	13.6	13.1
Total	100.0	100.0	100.0	100.0
N	399	351	59	809

Chi-square = 60.30; df = 8; p<.000

this. First, the numbers are inevitably small; and second, only mothers working outside the home are included. When children of housewives as a group are examined, 8 per cent chose primary teaching. However, it is possible that the pupils whose mothers were in the semi- and unskilled groups were among the lowest income groups, and may therefore not have been targeting a 'high points' course. Overall, it must be said that the data presented in Table 4.4 and Table 3 (Appendix 1) suggest that social class and parental education had little direct influence on choice of primary teaching, although it may have had an indirect effect, as social class was related to academic performance.

The data suggest an inter-relationship between gender, academic achievement and preference for primary teaching. Among the sixth year pupils in this survey, the measures of academic attainment used indicate significantly higher academic performances among girls than among boys. Higher level Irish – a compulsory requirement for primary teaching – was more often taken by girls at this level than boys, and this difference was statistically significant. These trends mirror those found in other studies at national level (Drudy and Lynch, 1993). Those planning to put primary teaching as their first degree choice had higher levels of academic performance and were almost all girls. From the point of view of entry to primary/ elementary teaching, which requires relatively high points, the pool of suitably qualified boys is smaller than the equivalent pool of girls. Among the respondents in the sample, the proportion of boys prioritising primary teaching was very small indeed, indicating that primary teaching was a very tentative choice for them.

Academic achievement of student teachers

As already indicated, students apply for higher education places through the Central Applications Office. The procedure is competitive and places are allocated on the basis of points calculated from the Leaving Certificate results in six subject areas of the curriculum. Typically, students sit for seven subjects and the best six are used for the calculation of third level entry points. The maximum number of points attainable is 600. The points level for entry to the Colleges of Education is comparatively high. In 1999, for example, it varied between 385 and 460, depending on the college and whether the course was through the medium of Irish or English. In the two largest colleges, from which 79 per cent of respondents come, the final cut-off points for offers varied between 445 and 460. In 1997, the year of entry of the student teachers in this research, the figures for the two larger colleges varied between 425 and 470. In fact, many students enter the college with points levels well above the minimum requirements. This is indicated by the average number of points held by respondents. The mean point score of the 457 respondents in this study was 481 points. However, many had scores well above this average, as is illustrated below.

The majority of student teachers had points falling in the band retaining the mean, median and modal values (445–499). Only 13 per cent of the respondents fell below this range. Higher proportions of males than females were in the lowest

Table 4.5 Distribution of college entry points categories, by gender

Points category	Male %	Female %	All %
410 and under	15.2	7.1	7.9
411–444	2.2	5.6	5.3
445–499	58.7	57.7	57.8
500–529	17.4	18.7	18.6
530+	6.5	10.9	10.4
Total	100.0	100.0	100.0
N	46	411	457

Chi-square not applicable

category. However, 29 per cent of the respondents had points in the two highest categories: 19 per cent had between 500–529 points, and a further 10 per cent had over 530 points. There was a somewhat higher proportion of females with these higher scores. In this latter grouping, a substantial proportion would have been eligible for any course in the higher education system, including most of the so-called 'high-prestige' courses.

As might be expected, the majority of student teachers had high grades (B or better) in higher level Irish. However, men were significantly more likely to have had lower levels of achievement in Irish at Leaving Certificate than women. Yet male student teachers were less likely (46 per cent) than females (51 per cent) to express the opinion that they found any of the requirements for entry to college difficult. Although they were slightly more likely to have lower points, just 24 per cent of men, compared to 33 per cent of women, said they had found the high points for entry to be a difficulty. Some 17 per cent of men, compared to 15 per cent of women found the higher level Irish requirement difficult. Student primary teachers were therefore good academic performers, with females having higher average scores than males.

Influence of teachers in the family

The analysis indicates that the social class background of the respondents had relatively little influence on their choice of primary teaching, as compared to other higher education courses. However, the research also set out to examine whether the special insights arising from having a teacher in the family would have an influence on the choice of teaching as a career. Just over 10 per cent (108) of the school leaver sample had a mother who was currently or formerly a teacher at first or second level. Some 5 per cent (51) had a father who was a current or former teacher. A larger group, 35.9 per cent (377) had a relative within the wider family (including parents) – i.e. mother, father, sibling, uncle, or aunt, who was, or had been, a teacher.

The data suggest that respondents who had teachers within the family circle were significantly more likely than others to have given some consideration to teaching as a career, and were significantly more likely to intend to put primary teaching as their first preference on their degree application form. Indeed, of the 57 people who expressed a definite intention to put primary teaching first, over half (53 per cent) had a relative who was, or had been, a teacher. This would suggest that exposure to teaching within the family gave a very positive orientation to students towards the profession, in spite of whatever complaints they might also have heard about teaching and its conditions.

The influence of having family members who were teachers was also explored with the student teachers. Among the sample of student teachers in the colleges of education, 24.5 per cent had mothers and 13.3 per cent had fathers who were teachers. Some 60 per cent of the mothers who were teachers were (or had formerly been) primary teachers, while three quarters of the fathers were (or had formerly been) second level teachers. Altogether a total of 61.7 per cent of respondents in the colleges had a close relative who was a teacher (compared to 53 per cent of the second level students who intended to put primary teaching first on their higher education application forms). Clearly, having a parent, sibling, or close relative in the profession favourably predisposes these young people towards the profession. Given the high points levels required for entry to primary teaching there may be a form of 'double effect' at work here. First, teachers as an occupational grouping fall within Social Classes 1 and 2, whose members were more likely to have achieved higher levels of academic performance in public examinations and were thus more likely to be candidates for a third level course in the first place. Second, exposure to teaching at home may have provided a positive orientation to the profession.

Reaction of 'significant others' to the decision to become a teacher

Preliminary discussions with key informants, and previous research suggested that a number of important people in young peoples' lives – 'significant others' – could play an important part in their decision-making. Specifically, the issue was how a decision to become a primary/elementary teacher would be/was perceived by the school leavers'/student teachers' family and friends. School leavers were asked if they felt their father, mother, teacher, guidance counsellor and friends would react positively if they announced they were going to become a primary teacher. Student teachers were asked to indicate how the same significant others in their lives reacted when they told them of their decision to become a primary teacher.

School leavers perceived that the most positive support for a decision to go into primary teaching would come from their mothers, and that the most negative reactions would be from friends. Teachers and guidance counsellors were perceived by respondents as potentially much less positive towards primary teaching than were parents.

Table 4.6 School leavers' perceptions of responses of significant others to the choice of primary teaching as a career

Reaction	Father			Mother			Teacher			Guidance counsellor			Friend		
	Boy %	Girl %	All %	Boy %	Girl %	All %	Boy %	Girl %	All %	Boy %	Girl %	All %	Boy %	Girl %	All %
Positive	39.3	60.4	52.0	51.6	66.7	60.8	37.7	46.7	43.1	35.0	42.0	39.3	17.9	49.9	37.3
'Would not mind'	33.7	28.7	30.7	33.8	23.1	27.3	28.9	32.8	31.2	29.0	30.0	29.6	35.1	35.3	35.2
Not sure/Negative	27.0	10.9	17.3	14.6	10.2	11.9	33.4	20.5	25.7	36.0	28.0	31.1	47.0	14.8	27.5
Total	100	100	100	100	100	100	100	100	100	100	100	100	100	100	100
N	404	606	1010	405	616	1021	405	607	1012	400	611	1011	396	603	999

Table 4.7 Student teachers' perceptions of responses of significant others to the choice of primary teaching as a career

Reaction	Father			Mother			Teacher			Guidance counsellor			Friend		
	Male %	Female %	All %	Male %	Female %	All %	Male %	Female %	All %	Male %	Female %	All %	Male %	Female %	All %
Positive	50.0	79.1	76.2	68.2	91.1	85.7	58.5	75.0	71.3	44.1	61.8	58.2	25.6	73.3	62.4
'Would not mind'	40.5	17.4	22.6	22.7	4.8	9.0	29.3	19.3	21.5	32.4	20.6	23.0	39.5	19.2	23.8
Not sure/Negative	9.5	3.5	4.8	9.1	4.1	5.3	12.2	5.7	7.2	23.5	17.6	18.8	34.9	7.5	13.8
Total	100	100	100	100	100	100	100	100	100	100	100	100	100	100	100
N	42	144	186	44	145	189	41	140	181	34	131	165	43	146	189

Note: Student teachers consisted of all the males and a sample of the females.

There were statistically significant gender differences as boys perceived propor-tionately much lower levels of support from each category than did girls. In relation to negative reactions, the perceived negative responses of friends showed the most marked gender differences of all, with more than three times the proportion of boys than girls envisaging such a response.

The perceptions of teachers' and guidance counsellors' reactions could, perhaps, be explained by a possible policy of 'non-directiveness'. Most guidance counsellors said during interviews that they would not point a student in any particular direction, but would endeavour to discover the young person's own inclination. Perceived negative reactions could, of course, possibly be explained by a negative attitude towards primary teaching among secondary teachers generally. It was not possible to assess this in this research and should prove a fruitful avenue for further research. However, there was a belief among some teachers that a high achiever – particularly a boy – should 'do better' for himself. This was a sub-text to several of the interviews with guidance counsellors where 'waste of talent' and 'possible unsuitability through lower boredom threshold' were mentioned (see Chapter 5). One school leaver wrote: 'They'd think I was wasting my time and talents and they'd think I didn't have the right qualities – patience.'

A young man going into primary teaching clearly expects reaction to be generally less than wholeheartedly positive, and may therefore hide his decision until the last moment. Indeed, during the course of the interviews, a guidance counsellor from one of the rural schools which had a steady, if small, number of male entrants to primary teaching over the years, gave examples of just such patterns. Boys, undoubtedly, perceived that there would be relatively less support for them from significant others for a decision to go into primary teaching. A young woman, on the other hand, was likely to perceive herself as having the support of almost everyone.

Student teachers perceived others' reactions to their career choice as being, in general, more positive than did school leavers. This was to be anticipated as they had already made this choice. In each of the categories the proportions reporting favourable reactions to a primary teaching career decision were higher than among the school leavers, while the proportions who were unsure or reported negative reactions were much lower. Although more positive, the variations of the responses showed similarities with the patterning of the school leavers' perceptions of others' reactions. In both cases mothers were viewed as having the most positive reactions (followed by fathers) while student teachers reported guidance counsellors and friends as least positive.

In both school leaver and student teacher samples there were significant gender differences in relation to the perceived reactions of most of the significant others. Male student teachers reported much lower levels of positive reactions in all categories than did female students. The differences were large in all instances but most especially in the case of friends and of fathers. The criterion for Chi-square significance testing (i.e. no cell has less than 5 expected values) was met in the case of respondents' perceptions of just two groups mentioned – guidance counsellors and friends. The gender differences in perceived friends' responses were highly significant at the p<.001 level. However, if the responses of male school leavers and student teachers are compared there are some interesting differences between them. For example, male student teachers proportionately more frequently indicated that fathers and teachers were positive to a choice of primary teaching. Nevertheless, the overall gender differences in the perceived responses of others to a decision by student teachers to take up primary teaching as a career confirmed the finding among school leavers that young men get less positive reinforcement and support for this career choice than do women. In this context it is likely that many young men would find it difficult to make such a 'non-traditional' choice.

Place of origin and choice of teaching

The figures on the representation of men and women in teaching presented in Chapter 1 illustrated that, while the predominance of women is evident in most countries, globally there are regional variations in the proportion of men in teaching. Indeed, examination of the proportions of women in teaching in the different regions worldwide suggests that the levels of feminisation could reasonably be taken as indicators of economic development. Previous research on entrants to primary teaching in Ireland had indicated considerable disparities among students with regard to the geographical areas of origin. Entrants from the capital (Dublin), these studies indicated, were under-represented, accounting for half the numbers one would expect based on population statistics, while western seaboard regions and some southern counties were strongly over-represented (Greaney *et al.*, 1987; Clancy 1995a).

As pointed out in Appendix 2, to generate the school leaver sample, a form of cluster sampling was used in the selection of schools in which a county was randomly selected from each of the four provinces, followed by random selection of schools within each county. The Dublin metropolitan area (city and county) was treated as a separate region, as it contains approximately half of all schools in the country. In terms of counties/provinces, Mayo/Connacht, Offaly/Leinster and Donegal/Ulster had the highest proportion of prospective teachers (just under 30 per cent in each case) compared with Dublin/Leinster (the most urbanised areas) and Cork/Munster (16 and 17 per cent respectively).

The sixteen schools surveyed were in either urban areas (Dublin and Cork cities) or rural areas/small towns. When schools were divided into either 'rural' or 'urban' in this manner, the rural schools had 26 per cent of the potential teachers against 17 per cent for their urban counterparts. These differences in counties/provinces and rural/urban areas were statistically significant (p<. 000 in both cases).

With regard to the student teachers, respondents were asked to indicate their home county and also to indicate the population size of the area in which their family home was located, from a range of options ranging from rural area to large conurbation. The data showed that student teachers in the colleges of education were disproportionately drawn from Munster (southern part of the country) and

Table 4.8 Place of origin, classified according to size of area and compared to the population distribution (1996 Census)

Place of origin	Student teachers			Distribution of total population*
	Male %	Female %	All %	
Large Urban Areas (50,000 + population)	15.2	10.7	11.2	32.8
Medium Sized Towns (1,500–49,999 population)	28.2	39.7	38.5	59.9
Towns/Villages under 1,500 and Rural Areas	56.6	49.6	50.3	7.3
Total	100.0	100.0	100.0	100.0
N	46	411	457	3,626,087

*Source: Central Statistics Office, 1997: 20

Connacht (the west of the country). This was particularly the case for the small number of male students in the colleges. Leinster, in the east (the most urbanised and industrialised province) was under-represented in the student population – particularly among males.

While the regional disparities were marked, and were not unexpected in the light of previous research, the study wished to establish whether propensity to enter teaching was greater in rural rather than in urban areas. Obviously, even in regions from which entrants to primary teaching have traditionally been drawn, such as Munster and Connacht, there are urban as well as rural areas. Table 4.8 shows the distribution of student teachers' family home locations, compared with distributions for the population as a whole (all ages).

Over half of the student teachers surveyed were from small towns of less than 1,500 population and rural areas. This compared to a national population distribution in such areas of just over 7 per cent. The greatly disproportionate numbers from rural areas were counterbalanced by the under-representation of student teachers from large urban areas – just over a tenth of student teachers, compared to almost a third of the general population, were from cities of over 50,000 population. There were some variations by gender in the distributions. More males than females were from rural areas, but also from large urban centres. A greater proportion of the female student teachers came from medium-sized towns. Nevertheless, rural backgrounds predominated for both male and female students. This confirms earlier findings and the findings from the second level survey. More strikingly, it sets out the heavy preponderance of students from rural backgrounds entering the primary teaching profession and, in particular, the much greater likelihood of men from rural areas than from urban areas to be attracted into teaching.

Summary

International research on social class and teaching emphasises the way in which teaching is positioned within horizontally segregated labour markets. Conflicts and contradictions have been found in teachers' roles. There are country-specific and cultural differences in the social origins of teachers. In the study on which this volume is based, and with regard to the influence of social class background on academic achievement, the research showed that pupils from the professional, employer and managerial social classes were a great deal more likely than others to have had grade point averages in the highest achievement band, and were less likely to have scored in the two lowest bands. The student teachers in the colleges of education had been high academic performers. Indeed, a substantial minority had higher education entry points levels which would have qualified them for entry to most courses in the university system, including the so-called 'high prestige' courses. The differences between males and females on points levels were not large, although male performance was somewhat lower. While social class background had an impact on academic performance, it had little overall impact on preference for teaching among the school leavers, or for selection of primary teaching at third level. However, when the question of the influence of having *teachers* within the family circle was specifically examined, it was found that school leavers who had teachers as family members were significantly more likely than others to have given some consideration to teaching as a career. They were also significantly more likely to have declared an intention to put primary teaching as their first preference on their university/college application forms. It would appear that exposure to teaching within the family gives a very positive orientation to students towards the profession, in spite of whatever complaints they might also hear about teaching and its conditions. Among student teachers this was even more evident – over 60 per cent of them had a near relative who was a teacher. Given the high points levels required for entry to primary teaching, there may be a form of 'double effect' at work here. First, teachers as an occupational grouping fall within Social Classes 1 and 2 (the professional, employer and managerial grouping) which are more likely to achieve higher levels of academic performance in public examinations. They are thus more likely to be candidates for a third level course in the first place. Second, exposure to teaching at home provides a positive orientation to the profession.

As regards place of origin of the student teachers the more rural regions of Ireland were over-represented. Fully half of the student teachers were from rural areas, with less than a third of the proportion that would have been expected from large urban areas, given the population distribution in the country as a whole. An even greater proportion of the male students were from rural areas. There was a disproportionate representation of students from middle-class and farming backgrounds.

The influence of 'significant others' in the students' decision-making in relation to primary teaching was explored. Students were asked how they felt that others would react if they chose primary teaching as a career. In general students felt that parents would be more positive than any other group (including teachers and guidance counsellors), and that mothers would be more positive than fathers would. Girls felt much more often than boys that others in their lives would be positive about primary teaching as a choice for them. Although just over a tenth of the students felt there would be a negative reaction from their peer group to such a choice, boys were a great deal more likely (over seven times as likely) to feel this as were girls. Young men, undoubtedly, perceived there would be relatively less support for them from significant others for a decision to go into primary teaching. A young woman, on the other hand, was likely to perceive herself as having the support of almost everyone.

Chapter 5

Careers: advice, choice and orientations to work

This chapter considers the orientations and interests that students bring to their choice of career. It assesses the impact of their orientations on choice of teaching. It examines gender differences in these orientations to work and relates these to choice of teaching. Their perceptions of the influence of the careers advice they received are also explored.

Men, women and orientations to work

The socialisation of males and females, and the formation of gender identities, have been demonstrated to be important factors in the way that men and women orient themselves to teaching. Earlier, the term 'domestic ideology' was used to describe the processes by which men and women are believed to have different responsibilities in relation to work. The idea of 'marriage compatibility' in relation to women's work has been suggested by a number of authors as playing a different role for males and females in occupational choice. Such research does not suggest that all girls passively accept such an ideology. For many, the choice of a 'marriage-compatible' career might arise from a pragmatic assessment of their actual situation. On the other hand, boys are less likely to consider careers that are compatible with home responsibilities but are more likely to view their future careers in the role of 'breadwinner' – this in spite of the increased participation of women in the labour force. Hannan *et al.* (1983: 75) reported on the different expectations of boys and girls in relation to their careers. Of particular relevance to this research project was their finding that part-time work was considered to be compatible with the perceived responsibilities of married women. It should go without saying that primary teaching is not a part-time job, but as will be discussed later, the perception of primary teaching as being 'part-time' and therefore compatible with marriage is one that is linked to the status of teaching as a profession. On the basis of such findings there has been an argument that boys will put a greater emphasis on factors relating to income and promotion prospects, while girls will be less likely to give great importance to these considerations.

With regard to the differences, by the end of the 1980s there were criticisms of traditional views which explained gender-typed careers in terms of the 'natural' personality traits of girls and boys (e.g. Agnew *et al.*, 1989: 2). A more plausible explanation suggested was that gender-typed career decisions are heavily influenced by the presentation of typically 'masculine' and 'feminine' careers. As an example, female students might find that science has a predominantly male learning culture where teachers are, for the most part, male, where models of instruction are oriented towards traditional masculine interests (e.g. boys' books and toys), and where the physical layout of the science laboratory reflects a 'masculine' environment (ibid.). Similarly, one could speculate that some young men do not consider teaching as a career option because of what they perceive to be an overwhelmingly feminine learning environment in colleges of education and in schools.

Lightbody *et al.* (1997) suggest that, in general, males may be more 'gender typed' in the selection of professions than are females. This form of stereotyping is most evident in perceptions of careers in the technological sector. This study was critical of government and educational initiatives that are concerned with the low levels of participation by females (and males) in science and technology. Lightbody *et al.* argue that, in an education climate which favours science and technology, girls who have superior examination results but do not opt for 'male' subjects and careers are regarded as being 'misguided'. This, they argued, is to undervalue the choices that many young women (and presumably, some young men) make. They reported on research that suggested that 'females place more importance than males on people-related values, enjoyment of their work and self-efficacy, and have higher levels of emotional expressiveness'. Women tend to avoid careers in science and technology because these professions do not meet the criteria of 'people contact' or 'service to society' (ibid.: 35). In other words, they are not misguided but are aware of what they are looking for in their lives. This thesis challenges some of the implicit assumptions made about women's (and men's) career-related values.

With regard to orientations to work, one of the best known approaches in social psychology was that developed by Super (Super, 1968). This approach subdivided attitudes, or orientations, to work under three headings: intrinsic, extrinsic and concomitant. This subdivision was originally developed in order to help explain patterns of choice across a wide range of occupations. Studies of teaching and of choice of teaching as a profession have identified another dimension – that of caring, altruism or orientation to others or to children (Lortie, 1975; Hubermann, 1991; Johnson *et al.*, 1998). These issues are explored in the surveys of school leavers and student teachers reported in this chapter.

Another, though not unrelated theme, is the sex-stereotyped model of career interests. A survey of academically talented high school students by Oppler *et al.* (1992) demonstrated that gender differences in occupational interests are consistent with this model. In their sample, boys rated quantitative, scientific, and vocational occupations higher than females, whereas girls rated teaching and the arts higher than boys. Similarly, Berry *et al.* (1989) found that a disproportionate number of females intended to enter 'service' occupations. However, in both of these studies, and for males and females alike, the preferred occupations of advanced post-primary pupils were in the areas of business, law, architecture, medicine/health, and science/engineering – but not in teaching. Thus, existing research shows that while there are some differences which are consistent with a stereotyped model of gendered occupations, there are also observable similarities in the patterns of career choice among academically talented boys and girls.

It can be concluded then that a number of factors operate in relation to the career decisions that school leavers make. First, the socialisation processes that occur both inside and outside the school environment must be taken into account. However, because these processes may be experienced differentially by individuals, it must also be recognised that the subjective experience of school leavers in relation to gender, stage of development, educational attainment and socio-economic background may vary. Less obvious, perhaps, are influences such as presentation and image of careers, and the prevailing ideologies which support these.

Career guidance and career choice

One of the research objectives was to establish the role of career guidance in career choice, with particular reference to teaching – especially primary teaching. Eighty-seven per cent of school leavers reported having received career advice from the guidance counsellor in their school. About 63 per cent found it useful – slightly more males than females. School leavers were given a list of other people who might have given them career advice and were asked to indicate who was most influential.

While guidance counsellors were considered 'most influential' by a substantial percentage of respondents, parents were considered the most influential source of career advice (by 22 per cent of the school leavers). Some school leavers were more likely to be influenced by their parent of the same sex – 18 per cent of girls put 'mother' first, against 9 per cent of boys; while 16 per cent of boys put father first, as against 6 per cent of girls. Evidently, the advice of the same sex parent was influential for many students.

'Guidance counsellor' was placed first by 21 per cent of boys, and 15 per cent of girls. The differences were significant at the $p<.000$ level. When 'other' was chosen it was quite often 'employer', which may reflect the prevalence of part-time work. There was a significant minority who put self alone. One respondent added 'I do not let others influence me in life-altering decisions.'

As regards the part played by guidance counsellors in career choice, it is clear that they play an important, but not a predominant role. The most influential people in relation to advice on careers, according to the students themselves, are parents.

When it came to student teachers, the majority of the 457 respondents had made the choice of primary teaching while still at school (90 per cent). Girls were a good deal more likely to have decided on primary teaching while still at primary school, or in the junior cycle of second level, than were boys (56 per cent and

14 per cent respectively). A higher proportion of boys, 54 per cent, reported that they had decided while aged 15–18 (thus mainly at senior cycle/senior high school), than did girls – 36 per cent. It might thus be hypothesised that career guidance teachers would have been more influential for male students, as career guidance is infrequently available to younger pupils in Irish schools.

Some 37 per cent of female student teachers reported that they had not been influenced by career advice; for males the figure was 30 per cent. Parents (combining the categories of 'parents', 'mother' and 'father') had by far the greatest influence on students. Male respondents were more likely (57 per cent) to give both parents as the greatest influence than were females (40 per cent). On the other hand, females were much more likely to pick 'mother' (20 per cent, compared to males at 7 per cent) or 'other relative' (17 per cent compared to 0 males). 'Teacher' as a category was offered as most influential adviser by 13 per cent of the total sample, with more males (27 per cent) than females (9 per cent) choosing it. 'Guidance counsellor' was chosen by less than 4 per cent of the students, with no gender differences on this item. It would appear that, in retrospect, student teachers evaluated guidance counsellors as having had very little influence on their decision-making. However, more than a quarter of males found the more general category of 'teacher' to have been influential.

Values, orientations and choice of teaching

What exactly motivates people in choosing a career is open to much discussion. Over the years a considerable literature has been developed on the subject with a range of competing theories on occupational choice (Drudy, 1981). As pointed out earlier, one of the best known approaches in social psychology was that developed by Super (1968). This approach subdivided attitudes, or orientations to work, under three headings: intrinsic, extrinsic and concomitant. 'Intrinsic' covered issues such as job satisfaction, fulfilment and creativity; 'extrinsic' covered issues such as pay, prestige and job conditions; and 'concomitant' issues such as job surroundings, or relationship with co-workers and supervisors. Studies of teaching had indicated the need for a measurement of orientation to others or caring – an 'altruistic' scale.

During the pilot phase of the study, a scale was developed to assess the career-related attitudes of the school leavers and the student teachers. The second level pilot study suggested that the notion of a distinctive 'concomitant' orientation, or set of attitudes to work, was not relevant to these school leavers.[1] Three sets of career-related attitudes, or orientations, were identified – intrinsic, extrinsic and altruistic. These were measured by means of a fifteen item scale.

Reliability tests were carried out on the scales. The altruistic scale held together best with an alpha score[2] of 0.78 – i.e. if a respondent thought 'making a difference to others' was very important, s/he was likely to think the same about 'helping children', 'caring for others', 'contributing to the community' or 'combining work and family'. The reliability value was next highest for the extrinsic scale at 0.67 –

i.e. if a respondent thought being 'well paid' was very important, s/he was likely to think the same about having 'high prestige and status', 'plenty of time off', etc. With an alpha score of 0.55, the reliability level of the intrinsic scale was lower than for the other two, but still acceptable. In other words, those who thought job satisfaction very important were likely to think the same of learning new things, fulfilment and creativity.

Among the student teachers the values on the Alpha (Cronbach) reliability tests used on each of the scales were higher than those for the second level students, indicating a greater level of internal consistency on the scales. The reliability coefficients were: intrinsic attitude scale – Alpha = 0.65; extrinsic attitude scale – Alpha = 0.71; altruistic attitude scale – Alpha = 0.76. As was the case with the school leaver scales the altruistic scale held together best, with the lowest level of internal consistency on the intrinsic scale. Nevertheless, all reached acceptable levels of reliability. School leavers and student teachers were asked to indicate the factors that they felt were important when choosing a career.

School leavers attached greatest importance to intrinsic values when choosing a career. This is followed by extrinsic values. The school leavers attached least importance to altruistic values. There were significant gender differences on each of the scales in the case of school leavers. Females attached greater importance to intrinsic items than did males. Males, on the other hand, placed greater value on extrinsic items than did females. As regards the altruistic scale, the scores indicated that females attached significantly greater importance to these items than did males (although with females, as with males, altruistic values were deemed to be of less importance than either intrinsic or extrinsic ones). When the school leaver

Table 5.1 Mean values of all school leavers and student teachers on intrinsic, extrinsic and altruistic scales, by gender

Scale	Mean value		Scale	Mean value	
---	Male school leavers	Female school leavers	---	Male student teachers	Female student teachers
Intrinsic t=4.15; df=753; p<.000 (SLs);	1.54	1.39	Intrinsic t = 2.13; df = 194; p<.034	1.65	1.47
Extrinsic t=-4.61; df=901; p<.000	1.93	2.14	Extrinsic t = -.275; df = 194; p<.784	2.57	2.60
Altruistic t=11.17; df=828; p<.000	2.90	2.24	Altruistic t = 3.93; df = 194; p<.000	2.17	1.73

Note: 't' – values relate to gender differences on each of the three different scales. The lower the mean value score, the greater the importance attached to the scaled items (student teacher sample included all male respondents and a sample of female respondents).

data were tested to assess the relationship between values and choice of primary teaching, there were significant differences on each of the scales between those who intended to put primary teaching as their first degree choice (and were, therefore, likely to be the most committed to primary teaching) and others. Those prioritising primary teaching attached most importance to intrinsic values, significantly more, indeed, than did those who intended to place some other course as their first choice. Those choosing primary teaching were also significantly more likely than other students to have attached high importance to altruistic values. On the other hand, students choosing primary teaching were significantly less likely to have attached importance to extrinsic items.

The pattern of higher priority given to intrinsic and altruistic values by school leavers choosing primary teaching was confirmed by the findings among student teachers. Student teachers were also more oriented to intrinsic values than to any other career related values. In comparison to the school leavers' average scores on the scales, student teachers were more strongly oriented to altruistic values than were second level pupils. In comparison to the school leavers' average scores on the scales, both male and female student teachers were more strongly oriented to altruistic values than were second level pupils. This was particularly marked in the case of females. The student teachers were less oriented towards intrinsic values, but particularly towards extrinsic values, than were school leavers. This stronger orientation towards caring among the student teachers confirms the linkages between caring and primary teaching already observed in this study. When the difference between the means of school leaver males and student teacher males on the altruistic scales was tested for statistical significance it proved to be highly significant ($p<.000$). The differences between male school leavers and male student teachers were not significant on their intrinsic scores, but significant for extrinsic scores ($p<.02$). This suggests that males studying to be primary teachers are most markedly different from other males in relation to their attitudes to caring.

Both school leavers and student teachers were asked to rate which factor was most important to them when choosing their career. 'Job satisfaction' – an intrinsic factor – was rated highest by over 60 per cent of both sexes, and by those choosing and not choosing primary teaching. This would suggest that most students are making their career choice on the basis of a value. Indeed, in interviews, guidance counsellors reported putting an emphasis on this. 'Good pay' came second as the most important factor. The majority of respondents choosing this were male.

When the 'most important' factors listed by respondents were grouped according to whether they were 'intrinsic', 'extrinsic' or 'altruistic', the differences between the sexes were significant. Females were somewhat more likely than males to give an intrinsic item as the most important factor, and a great deal more likely to give an altruistic item as most important, when making a career choice. Males, on the other hand, more often listed an extrinsic factor. The chance to be creative and inventive in one's work was the only intrinsic factor rated more highly by boys than by girls. It is difficult to be sure of the implications of this greater male emphasis on creativity. Overall, the findings among school leavers suggested that while intrinsic factors were usually most important for both girls and boys in choice of career, ancillary reasons (i.e. second or third most important) are different for each sex, with girls tending to rate altruistic factors higher and boys rating extrinsic ones.

Among the student teachers, as was the case with the second level pupils, the majority (just over 60 per cent) rated intrinsic factors highest. The positioning of the other two types of attitude were reversed. For the student teachers altruistic factors were listed second most frequently (by 28 per cent), with a higher proportion of females prioritising them. Extrinsic factors came third, at 6.3 per cent, but with proportionately more boys favouring them.

The chief contrast between student teachers and school leavers was between the proportions choosing extrinsic and altruistic factors as most important at second and third level. Both males and females at both levels gave proportionately more top rankings to intrinsic factors, and proportionately less to extrinsic values. This was particularly noticeable among males. However, some 22 per cent of the male student teachers ranked altruistic factors as most important, compared to just 7 per cent of the second level males. By contrast, 33 per cent of the second level males gave top ranking to extrinsic factors, compared to just 13 per cent of male student teachers. Thus, males going into primary teaching are much less oriented towards factors such as pay and prestige, and much more oriented towards caring and towards others than are males in general.

Summary

A number of factors operate in relation to the career decisions that school leavers make. Socialisation processes that occur both inside and outside the school environment must be taken into account, although these may be experienced differentially by individuals according to gender and other characteristics. In this study, guidance counsellors played an important, but not a predominant role in career choice, as perceived by school leavers and student teachers. The advice of guidance counsellors was more important in the case of males. The most influential people in relation to advice on careers, according to the students themselves, are parents. The attitudes or orientations of students towards work were assessed using a measure of the things highly valued by them when they were thinking about a career. Three different types of attitude/orientation to work were identified – 'intrinsic' (high value on job satisfaction, fulfilment, creativity); 'extrinsic' (high value on pay, prestige, job conditions); 'altruistic' (high value attached to caring, 'making a difference', or to helping children). Overall, intrinsic values were most highly valued, followed by extrinsic, and finally by altruistic values.

There were significant gender differences. Girls attached greater importance to intrinsic and altruistic values; boys to extrinsic. The findings suggest that, while intrinsic factors are usually most important for both girls and boys in choice of career, ancillary reasons were different for each sex, with girls rating altruistic factors higher and boys tending to value extrinsic ones. People choosing primary teaching (and they were mainly girls) attached most importance to intrinsic values and were also significantly more likely than other respondents to have attached high importance to altruistic values. They attached less importance than others to extrinsic values.

As with school leavers, the career-related attitudes of the student teachers were explored. In comparison to the school leavers' average scores on the scales, both male and female students were more strongly oriented to altruistic values than were second level pupils. This was particularly marked in the case of the female student teachers. The students were less oriented towards intrinsic values, and particularly towards extrinsic values, than were school leavers. This stronger orientation towards caring among the student teachers confirmed the linkages between caring and primary teaching already observed in this study. The data also suggested that males studying to be primary teachers were most markedly different from other males in relation to their attitudes to caring. Indeed, males going into primary teaching were much less oriented towards factors like pay and prestige, and much more oriented towards caring and altruistic factors than were males in general.

Chapter 6

Why so few men?

This chapter outlines the findings in a number of countries on people's reasons for becoming teachers. It considers the influence of school cultures on the experience of teaching and on choice of teaching. It explores the reasons offered by the school leavers and student teachers in this study for choosing teaching. It gives their views on the reasons for the declining numbers of men in teaching and their suggestions on what should be done.

Previous research on reasons for choosing teaching as a career

Lortie's study of the teaching profession in the United States (1975) is, arguably, a sociological classic. He identified five 'attractors' to teaching, which he describes in terms of themes. These are: the interpersonal theme, the service theme, the continuation theme, material benefits, and the theme of time compatibility.

The interpersonal theme, or 'working with people', is not exclusive to teaching. This gregarious aspect is found also in the highest professions, and so, it adds prestige to the occupation. Lortie (1975: 27) found, though, that among the teachers he interviewed, very few placed importance on the creative interpersonal skills that might be involved in teaching – for most respondents, the 'skills' of interpersonal relations were considered to be more important than 'creativity' in interpersonal encounters. The service theme is one that has long been associated with teaching, and comes from such nineteenth-century notions as a 'mission in society' and 'moral worth', ideas that are grounded in both sacred and secular beliefs. This attractor proved slightly more significant for women than for men, and also more for primary teachers than secondary teachers. Lortie argued that the concept of 'service' is more likely to appeal to people who approve of the prevailing education system than to those who are critical of it (ibid.: 28–9). The continuation theme referred to the process whereby schoolchildren are so attached to their learning environment that they wish to continue as teachers. As with the service theme, the continuation theme appears to have a conservative bias. Lortie found that the theme of material benefits was underplayed by teachers – for two reasons. First of all there is the public perception of teaching as being badly paid, and second, since values such as 'dedication' and 'service' are emphasised, teachers feel uncomfortable about considering the attractions of money, power and prestige. Teachers in Lortie's study were also sensitive to the theme of time compatibility, which refers both to the length of teachers' working days and to the duration of teachers' vacations. Summing up the attractions of teaching, Lortie (ibid.: 32–3) states that:

> Teaching is special in at least two respects: few occupations can offer similar opportunities for protracted contact with normal [sic] children, and few can provide such compatible work schedules. The definition of teaching as service (the aura of its mission) sets it apart from many other ways to earn a living. Although muted, material benefits play their part in drawing persons into the occupation.

These, he argues, are the values, which one would expect to find among new entrants to teaching.

Lortie argued that the effects of material benefits are experienced differently by males and females. He used the concept 'alternatives foregone', a term from economics, to describe the 'opportunity cost' of becoming a teacher: this is based on an assumption that those who become teachers have the opportunity to enter other, higher-paying occupations. According to Lortie, entering teaching is subjectively more costly for males than for females (ibid.: 33). Both the status and the pay of women's work have been progressively improving in the past few decades. Nonetheless, it is arguable that the difference in 'cost' obtains, especially if the different attitudes of male and female school leavers to teachers' salaries are considered. The results of this condition are twofold. First, in straightforward economic terms, teaching is more attractive to women than to men, and therefore, women will continue to constitute the great majority in teaching. Added to this is the problem of male identification with the job. Lortie argued that the sense of material loss experienced by many male teachers has 'a depressing effect on the recruitment of younger men':

> We can reason that male teachers will have greater material motives for regretting their fates and are thus less likely to project high enthusiasm for their work. . . . To the extent that a subjective sense of deprivation makes male teachers less acceptable as models, there is a systematic tendency for the occupation to attract more women than men. The differential distribution by sex of material rewards of money and prestige therefore probably has effects beyond its role in the original calculus of choice.
>
> (Lortie, 1975: 34)

Lortie's conceptual model of attraction and facilitation into teaching was adapted in a number of subsequent studies. A study of pre-service teachers by Morales (1994) indicated that the majority chose to teach due to their service orientation and that the material benefits theme did not feature in the student teachers' responses. Like Lortie, she interpreted this pattern as being part of teacher socialisation: teaching is publicly perceived to be low-paying, and in any case the theme of material benefits does not converge with that of service to society. Research by Evans (1993) and by Hutchinson and Johnson (1993–4) mirrors Lortie's work more closely, with the interpersonal, service and continuation themes being rated more highly than those of material benefits and time compatibility.

Other American-based studies indicate that patterns of attraction to teaching have been changing slowly. Marso and Pigge's survey of education majors (1994) shows that, in addition to the traditional reasons, one in five respondents enter teaching with a desire to change society – such a pattern seems to go against what Lortie describes as the 'conservative outlook' of aspiring teachers. Su (1997) notes that although 'altruistic' reasons still predominate, the desire to transform society is cited by many students, notably by those from ethnic minority backgrounds. Peters Behrens (1997) also reports on the changing perspectives of teaching candidates, and presents the five core values which are most salient among her (all female) group. These are: socio-political empowerment (teachers as agent of change), spiritual empowerment (teaching as a vocation, upholding publicly stated values), intellectual empowerment (excitement about the learning process and about knowledge) and child-centred pedagogy (teaching described within an interpersonal context). Although this work does not present sufficient quantitative evidence, it nonetheless serves to suggest that values related to teaching are not as homogenous as they once might have been. In the past few decades the idea of teaching as a service to society was surpassed by the interpersonal theme of child-centred pedagogy (Evans, 1993), but the supremacy of such values does not appear to be infinite. Just as Lortie does, Serow (1993) argues that the motivational statements of those entering teaching ought not to be taken at face value. Altruism, he states, refers to the psychic needs of individuals as much as it does to the welfare of others (ibid.: 197). Moreover, student teachers are subject to specific social-isation processes, and their responses will be influenced by the dominant education ideology, in which knowledge-oriented strategies are less valued than child-centred ones (ibid.: 202). On a more practical level, Su (1997) reports on the lack of future teachers' commitment to teaching as a lifelong career. This compares badly with the commitment of student teacher groups in earlier surveys. The above quoted studies indicate that while there is a certain consistency in the career-related values and motives of student teachers, these values and motives are also subject to change. Lortie's theory of teacher socialisation was based on the conditions of his time; arguably, new configurations of career values among student teachers can also be interpreted in this way.

Studies of motivations for teaching have found that both men and women attribute the highest degree of importance to a liking for working with children (Kelleghan et al., 1985: 56). For women, the second and third most important motives have been identified as, respectively, academic interest, and hours and conditions; in the case of men, the order of importance of these was reversed. The next most important motivations for the females were time compatibility and salary, and again, these motives were reversed in order by the male group (ibid.). Interestingly, Kelleghan *et al.* found that both women and promoted teachers tended to be more positive in regard to intrinsic motivations than did males and non-promoted teachers. The group that was least inclined to cite intrinsic motivations was that of non-promoted males (ibid.). These patterns would appear to be consistent with those reported in research in other countries.

Green and Weaver (1992: 237) analysed a range of studies on the motivations of entrants to teacher colleges. They found that the differences between intending primary and secondary teacher groups were paralleled by the differences observed between female and male students – even where there was an even distribution of men and women in these groups. The male/secondary theme was mainly subject-centred, whereas for the female/primary groups the theme was predominantly child-centred. A similar pattern was observed by Marso and Pigge (1994).

Reid and Caudwell (1997) investigated the motivations for entering secondary teaching in Britain. The reasons put forward by their respondents were generally consistent with the frameworks of both Lortie and Huberman. Many of the motives were other-directed ones, the principal theme being interpersonal (working with children). However, when the other motives were analysed, it appeared that the choice of secondary teaching over primary was closely related to the students' academic interests (Reid and Caudwell, 1997: 54). The working conditions of secondary teaching were also considered to be more attractive – wanting to teach more than one class and a preference for the abilities and responsiveness of secondary school pupils. The main reasons put forward for not selecting primary school teaching were: not wanting to work with the age group, not wanting to generalise, and feeling that they would be frustrated with the job. Other frequently cited reasons were: a waste of one's academic knowledge, inability to teach at primary level, insufficiently creative and, a perception that primary teachers acted too much like a nurse (ibid.: 56). It should be noted that most of these negative reasons arose from personal concerns rather than concerns about the nature of primary teaching as a job. By omission, it would appear that these students preparing for second level teaching regarded primary teaching as a job lacking in specialisation, academic or otherwise.

Brookhart and Loadman (1996) present a profile of a group of American males who enter elementary teacher preparation. The concerns of their study were not only with the quantity of male candidates but also with the quality of those entering education programmes. Their research indicated the following tendencies among male student teachers: they were less academically oriented than female candidates; had fewer academic subjects from high school; were less likely to have chosen teaching because they enjoyed school; reported more prior experiences with children than did males who entered secondary teaching programmes; decided to enter teaching later in life than did female students; reported lower expectations of the usefulness of teacher preparation for developing the knowledge and skill necessary for teaching (Brookhard and Loadman, 1996: 208).

Thus there may be a distinct male student teacher profile, one that is somewhat different in background from that of the female student, and substantially different in terms of their perceptions about teaching. Brookhart and Loadman also found that, based on their declared intentions, male students and newly qualified teachers are less likely to remain in teaching for life, and are more likely to move into education administration than are their female counterparts. The fact that these decisions are made at such an early age seems to suggest that young men (and young women) are socialised into sex-type career roles prior to entering colleges of education.

This is not to imply that all males are passively involved in a single socialisation process. After all, the decision for males to become teachers would appear to go against the dominant socialising influences, which were discussed in earlier sections. However, the perceptions of male student teachers might actually support popular assumptions, which are made with regard to the 'nature' of primary school teaching. For example, Johnston *et al.* (1998: 17) found that primary teaching is ranked as being 'least suited to males' and 'most suited to females' by a majority of their male and female respondents alike, as did the respondents in this study (see Chapter 3). They further report that males tend to agree with the view that teaching very young children is an extension of motherhood, and that it is therefore less appropriate for males to teach this age group.

It has been suggested that, broadly speaking, male and females do not differ in their initial motivations for choosing teaching as a career. However, as Morales (1994) found, this convergence of viewpoints is not evident in the perceptions males and females have about their roles as teachers. The divergence of male/ female views might arise, in part, from the differential trends in the academic and socio-economic backgrounds of male and female candidates. However, these cannot be interpreted in simple causal terms. Such differences are inextricably linked to overt and covert socialising influences.

The influence of school cultures

Measor and Sykes (1992) distinguish the informal culture of a school from its formal culture. Examples of the former would include processes of gender social-isation, adolescent culture and pupil–teacher interactions. The formal curriculum identifies those areas of the curriculum that are regarded as having an objective existence such as timetables, syllabi and rules. Lynch (1989) made a similar distinction between the formal curriculum and the hidden curriculum. However, the idea of a hidden curriculum refers to the ethos of institutions and systems as well as to the cultures of participating groups. Moreover, in this view, the formal curriculum to some extent *is* the hidden curriculum. Drudy and Lynch (1993: 182–5) argue that implicit socialisation is effected through the operation and selection of subjects, texts and syllabi. They go on to suggest that between boys and girls schools the differences in the hidden curriculum may be more significant than the observable differences within the formal curriculum. Research conducted by Lynch (1989) has pointed out that the aesthetic, moral-religious and socio-personal development of pupils receive higher priorities in girls' schools than in boys' schools. Furthermore, girls' schools place greater emphasis on developing qualities such as caring for others, sincerity, gentleness, 'refinement' and self-control than their male counterparts (ibid.). This research also illustrates that there tends to be a stronger ethos of achievement in girls' schools than in boys' schools.

Hannan *et al.* (1996) show that the 'mixed' arrangement of the coeducational school does not lessen the extent to which boys' and girls' experiences of the hidden or informal curriculum tend to be differentiated.[1] Thus, while the socialising power of single-sex institutions has long been recognised, the evidence with regard to coeducational schools suggests that the processes of socialisation involved here work in more subtle ways. Schools reflect the ethos and culture of the wider society. The fact that distinctions between a 'masculine' and a 'feminine' educational ethos can survive in the context of coeducation is significant because it shows the extent to which these socialising influences transcend organisational structures.

Both Riddell (1992) and Acker (1994) argue for interventionist strategies to combat both formal and informal manifestations of sex differentiation in education. The interaction of teachers and pupils proved crucial in this respect. Riddell's case study research in British schools revealed that the majority of her subjects believed that the sex-stereotyped attitudes and behaviours of their pupils were completely due to external socialising forces, with only a minority of those interviewed acknowledging the additional presence of intra-school socialising forces. This issue of teacher ideologies is discussed also by Acker, utilising R.J. Alexander's definition of educational ideologies, namely, 'the networks of beliefs, values, assumptions about children, learning, teaching, knowledge and the curriculum'.[2] Teachers' ideologies appear to be in favour of gender equality and against negative sex-stereotyping, but there are many aspects of teachers' ideologies which, unconsciously, go against these ideals (Acker, 1994: 98–100). One of these is the ideology of child-centred learning which, for some practitioners, becomes a set of attitudes that focuses exclusively on the individual learner and does not take into account their interaction as members of social groups like gender, race or class. The second ideology that underpins many teachers' assumptions and beliefs is that of environmental determinism. With this type of view it would be implicitly assumed that differences in the education and career aspirations of boys and girls are determined by biological sex differences, or by prior external social-ising forces. Janet Miller (1993: 46) argues that a concept of neutrality is embedded into what is described variously as the 'formal' or 'official' curriculum:

> the fact that we often construct ourselves and our relationships to others and to bodies of knowledge through a prevailing system, say, of gender, often is erased by supposedly 'neutral', 'objective', 'unitary', and 'essential' views of what constitutes our experiences and relationships as males and females to one another as well as to school knowledge, to what is commonly termed 'the curriculum'.

Of course, the pupils themselves are also agents in the socialising processes that may influence their individual behaviour and decisions. Eccles and Bryan (1994) suggest that there is a process of gender intensification during the adolescent stage of identity development. However, they do not interpret this in terms of environmental determinism alone and argue that the identity development of each individual takes place within a specific social milieu, and as such it is negotiated, rather than formed. Socialising influences have been found to be more pronounced during adolescent stages of development. Mills and Mills (1996), in an empirical study of American middle schools, examined students' beliefs with regard to male and female stereotypes. Comparing this cohort with similar studies from ten years earlier, they found that there was no significant 'improvement' (i.e. reductions in stereotyping) in the student group's beliefs about appropriate female and male roles. However, their findings indicate that their teachers believed that there had been significant positive changes in their pupils' attitudes. This represents an example of how unchallenged teacher ideologies can lead to misinterpretations of pupils' experiences and perceptions.

Morgan and Lynch (1995: 536) argue that: 'Differences in types of courses undertaken by women and men relate directly to the central issue of stereotyping in subject choice.' Studies of the provision, allocation and choice of subjects in second level schools in Britain, with particular reference to the experience of girls, report that gender-based differences in subject take-up increase as pupils progress through the education system (Measor and Sikes, 1992: 72–7). While this appears to be consistent with the theory of adolescent gender intensification, it is argued that an additional, though not unrelated, factor is involved. This is the different form of curricular structures for primary, and for the junior and senior cycles of post-primary education, which move progressively from a compulsory core curriculum to one that involves more individual choice (ibid.). Morgan and Lynch (1995) report that this pattern is reflected in the Irish education system, commenting that there is still a level of variation between categories of schools and between individual schools in terms of subject provision and allocation. Very often, differences in the range of subjects offered to boys and girls appear to be related to assumptions of appropriate male and female interests – typically, in girls' schools there is a tendency to emphasise arts/humanities whereas in boys schools the emphasis will be on science/technology.

Curricular choice is just one part of the structural socialisation that takes place in any school. As Acker (1989) suggests, it is much easier to remove the material causes of difference than to challenge the ideologies that sustain beliefs about such difference. For example, while girls are moving into 'boys' subjects', there has been no equivalent increase in the take-up of 'girls' subjects' by boys (Drudy and Lynch, 1993; Morgan and Lynch, 1995). Burnstyn (1993: 107–25) states that the widespread use of computers has introduced a new level of gendered segregation in education and in employment. In educational settings, the use of information technology tends to be dominated by males and is appropriated by masculine subcultures. Burnstyn contends that the association of technology with masculine interests has a detrimental influence on girls' and women's engagement with computer-based learning.

The research on gender and the influence of school cultures provides some indication as to why males may be less focused on the classroom and less likely to orient themselves to teaching. These are: higher retention rates for girls at second level/high school; higher aggregate levels of attainment for girls than for boys; a greater participation by girls in arts and humanities subjects; traditional sex-role socialisation through school ethos and the hidden curriculum. Nevertheless, gender analysis recognises that the operation of difference is, to a large extent, mediated by wider socialising factors and by ideological constraints. The relative advantage that girls might have with regard to the entry requirements to university courses does not, in itself, explain why so few boys consider teaching as a career option. Recent patterns of similarity in subject choice may also be a cause for concern, insofar as, increasingly, arts and humanities subjects appear to be valued less by boys and girls alike (see, for example, Drudy and Lynch 1993), and the decline in their status at school may reflect a wider societal reappraisal of educational aspirations.

School leavers' and student teachers' reasons for choosing or avoiding teaching

School leavers who were considering teaching as one of their higher education choices were asked to indicate (from a menu of ten possible reasons, derived from previous research and the pilot study) why they were doing so. In the case of student teachers, they were asked why they had chosen teaching. If school leavers had indicated that they were not considering any form of teaching, they were asked to indicate their reasons from a separate list of ten – again derived from the pilot study and previous research. In all cases respondents were asked to rank their top three reasons for choosing or not choosing to become a teacher.[3]

There were some marked gender differences on the top ranked reason for selecting some form of teaching, as one of the school leavers' preferred college choices. The most popular reason for choosing teaching was '*satisfaction of showing children how to do things*'. This was ranked first by almost one third of those choosing teaching, but was the most frequently top ranked reason by girls (37 per cent) with just 14 per cent of boys indicating that this was their reason. Girls were also more likely to choose '*liking children*' as a reason (14 per cent of girls, 6 per cent of boys).

The greatest gender difference was on the item '*job conditions*'. This was the most popular reason boys put for choosing teaching (41 per cent of male respondents) followed, far behind, by '*satisfaction of showing children how to do things*' and '*teaching is a worthwhile calling*'. The high percentage of boys who chose '*job conditions*' as a reason suggests that boys opting for teaching were choosing it for very different reasons than girls, mainly for extrinsic reasons.

Table 6.1 Top ranked reasons given by school leavers (SLs) and student teachers (STs) for choosing primary teaching, by gender

Reasons for choosing primary teaching	Male SLs %	Female SLs %	All SLs %	Male STs %	Female STs %	All STs %
I get satisfaction out of showing children how to do things	14.3	36.5	31.8	22.2	27.0	26.4
I have experience working with children	4.1	6.2	5.7	8.9	2.2	2.9
I enjoyed school myself	8.2	3.4	4.4	6.7	4.9	5.0
I was attracted by the job conditions	40.9	8.4	15.4	20.1	6.1	7.5
I've always liked children/ young people	6.1	14.0	12.3	6.7	26.8	24.8
I feel teaching is a worthwhile calling	14.3	12.4	12.8	22.2	16.3	16.9
I identified with/was influenced by one or more good teachers	6.1	10.1	9.3	4.4	5.6	5.5
I see opportunities for promotion	0.0	0.0	0.0	0.0	0.2	0.2
There's a tradition of teaching in my family	2.0	0.0	0.4	4.4	1.7	2.0
I see it as a way of helping disadvantaged children	2.0	3.4	3.1	2.2	4.6	4.4
Other	2.0	5.6	4.8	2.2	4.6	4.4
Total	100.0	100.0	100.0	100.0	100.0	100.0
N	49	178	227	45	411	456

Among the second ranked reason of those choosing teaching, 'teaching is a worthwhile calling' was the most common, overall, and for males. More girls chose 'satisfaction of showing children how to do things'. The same pattern held good for the third ranked reason, with more girls choosing 'experience working with children' this time. Some respondents gave personal reasons. On the whole girls appeared to be more oriented towards children than boys, although one girl wrote, very positively, under 'other': 'I see it as a job which has a variety [sic] and has room for you to be your own boss . . . You have some personal input and can be quite creative.'

The top ranked reason given most frequently by student teachers for their choice of teaching was that they 'get satisfaction out of showing children how to do things'.

This was followed by another child-focused reason – '*I've always liked children/ young people*' and, third, by the perception that '*teaching is a worthwhile calling*'. There were some gender differences. Female top ranked reasons were equally split between the two child-focused reasons, with '*worthwhile calling*' in third place. The top ranked reasons given by males split evenly between '*showing children how to do things*' and '*worthwhile calling*'. However, males ranked '*job conditions*' in third place, giving it top priority more than three times more frequently (proportionately) than did females. The pattern was repeated when first and second rankings were combined.

On this variable there was a similarity with the school leaver patterning. Among school leavers who expressed a preference for teaching, '*job conditions*' was ranked much more highly by males than by females. Males who had actually gone into teacher education gave higher priority to '*showing children how to do things*' and '*worthwhile calling*' than did male school leavers who had expressed a preference for teaching. These data provide further evidence that boys are more inclined than girls to make choices, even of primary teaching, for extrinsic reasons. The responses of the male student teachers, therefore, differed from those of the male school leavers who had expressed a preference for teaching in five noteworthy aspects – as reasons for choosing teaching male student teachers gave top ranking in larger proportions to having gained satisfaction from showing children how to do things, having had experience with children, considering teaching a worthwhile calling and having a tradition of teaching in the family. Male student teachers attached less importance to the job conditions of teaching than did the boys who were considering teaching at the end of their schooling but, nevertheless, males in both groups attached higher importance to this than did females.

Although just a small proportion (3 per cent) of student teachers had given '*I had experience of working with children*' as their main reason for choosing primary teaching, it was clear from the responses that the vast majority of the student teachers had actually had some experience of working with children before entering college. Some 81 per cent indicated that they had done so. There was a marked gender difference – a total of 84 per cent of the women students, compared to 57 per cent of the men students, had such previous experience. The majority of the females (40 per cent) gave babysitting as their experience, the majority of the boys (40 per cent) gave youth club work. This again suggests a stronger orientation towards younger children by females than by males.

Student teachers were also asked to indicate why they had chosen primary teaching rather than second level teaching. The most frequently cited reason (given by 29 per cent of the sample) was that they '*liked young children*' or liked helping/ working with them. However, proportionately more women (34 per cent) than men (13 per cent) offered this reason. A quarter (25 per cent) suggested that young children were easier to manage or gave rise to fewer discipline problems. A higher proportion of men (30 per cent) than women (23 per cent) gave this reason. A further 7 per cent of the sample said they 'liked forming young minds'. The remaining responses included 'more job satisfaction and fulfilment with young children' (7 per cent), 'primary learning is life skills rather than exam orientated' (4 per cent) and 'no guarantee of getting the H.Dip.' (4 per cent).

In order to gauge their views on whether primary teaching was a 'job for life' or a phase in a career, student teachers were asked if they could see themselves in primary teaching in twenty years' time. Approximately two thirds (65 per cent) said that they could. A somewhat higher proportion of females than males (67 per cent compared to 61 per cent) saw themselves still in primary teaching. The main reason offered for envisaging themselves still in primary teaching in the future was 'enjoyment' of the job (given by 39 per cent of those with a long-term commitment). The main reason for envisaging a career change given by those who gave a negative response to the question was that they would 'like a break' or would like to have a change and development in their career (given by 62 per cent of those who intended to change).

In sum, student teachers offered child-focused reasons most frequently for the choice of primary teaching, although these were offered proportionately more frequently by women. Many more women had had experience of working with children before college. A liking for young children was the most frequently cited reason for choosing primary rather than second level teaching – again more frequently cited by women students. Two thirds of the sample could see themselves in primary teaching in twenty years' time, with somewhat more women than men expressing this kind of commitment. Enjoyment of the job was the most frequently given reason for staying while wanting a break was the most frequently envisaged reason for moving on.

School leavers who had not chosen teaching were also given a menu of reasons. These are set out in the following table.

Table 6.2 School leavers' top ranked reasons for not choosing teaching, by gender

Reasons for not choosing teaching	Male %	Female %	All %
Wouldn't get necessary points	17.6	23.3	20.7
Don't have Honours Irish	14.4	18.5	16.6
Don't have the right personality	11.6	8.2	9.8
Don't have enough patience with children/young people	11.6	9.2	10.3
Feel managing children is stressful	6.6	5.9	6.2
Feel job is frustrating	8.9	5.9	7.2
Don't like school myself	9.1	3.2	5.9
Would be doing same job for 40 years	8.9	14.0	11.7
Feel there's a risk of false child abuse allegations	0.3	0.0	0.1
Would like more opportunities for advancement	5.5	6.6	6.1
Other	5.5	5.2	5.4
Total	100.0	100.0	100.0
N	361	442	803

The two most frequently top ranked reasons for not choosing teaching were academic in nature. The most common reason for not choosing teaching was '*wouldn't get necessary points*' – ranked as most important by 21 per cent, with slightly more girls (23 per cent) than boys (18 per cent) giving it as a reason. There was a gender difference on the recognition of the importance of achieving an honour in higher level Irish also, with slightly more girls offering it as a reason (although the honours Irish requirement only relates to primary teaching). A reluctance to do the '*same job for 40 years*' was the third most frequently ranked top reason for not choosing teaching, at 12 per cent, with again a somewhat greater proportion of girls ranking this item highly. It is clear that the very positive perception of teaching quoted above (as permitting variety, autonomy and creativity) has not percolated very widely among these school leavers.

As regards the most frequently second ranked reason for those not choosing teaching, lack of '*honours Irish*' was the most common for both genders, followed by '*I feel I would be doing the same job for 40 years*'. '*I would like more opportunities for advancement*' was the most commonly third ranked reason for both boys and girls who were not choosing teaching, followed *by* '*I feel I would be doing the same job for 40 years*'. There was one gender difference in these third ranked responses with more girls opting for '*I would like more opportunities for advancement*'.

The reasons given for choosing and not choosing teaching are interesting in that they show a considerable divide between the sexes. Girls' interest in teaching seemed to stem from an engagement with children and the mechanics of teaching: boys seem more likely to be influenced by externals (*job conditions, teaching a worthwhile job*) which may make the job less satisfying for them. Boys seemed to be less oriented towards children or less willing to admit an interest in teaching. In contrast to some of the suppositions expressed in the popular press (especially in Britain), fear of '*false child abuse allegations*' did not feature as a reason for not choosing teaching. It was selected by only one male from the list of items arising from this question.

Under 'other' a few respondents mentioned negative impressions from parents who were teachers. 'My mother is a secondary teacher and I see the stress she is under from disruptive children.' 'My parents are both primary teachers and seem very stressed.' Others had negative feelings about the education system 'I would never willingly inflict the horror of it on children', or linked it with a dislike of the 'abuse teachers take now'. Some felt there was a sameness about the job, and that it was too much a part of their childhood world. 'I feel there are more exciting worthwhile jobs . . . as children we think we want to be teachers, but as we get older the idea of teaching becomes slightly boring.'

The most common reasons given for not choosing teaching were those that loom largest for sixth year students: grade points and academic requirements. However, if some of the other factors are aggregated, the respondents' assessment of their own personalities and a perception of the job as boring or stressful may be just as, or more, important.

In order to determine the general student attitude to different types of teaching, respondents were asked which type of teaching they would choose if they had to make the choice. This provided an indication of how students who had no intention of choosing teaching – many of whom were male – felt about the profession, which aspects would appeal and which would not.

Overall, general secondary/high school teaching (other than 'physical education' teacher) was less well perceived than either primary teaching or 'physical education' teacher. There were, however, significant gender differences. Unsurprisingly, given the rest of the findings, girls were more positively oriented to primary teaching and, to a lesser extent, to secondary teaching than were boys. Boys had a much more positive view of P.E. teaching than did girls. More than half of the males said they would opt for P.E. if they had to choose, compared to less than one fifth of the girls. Other forms of specialist teaching, such as woodwork or music, were mentioned infrequently. It is interesting that P.E. teaching, which has strong associations with sport, leisure and the formation of the young male identity, should be the most positively perceived teaching sector by males – though of course not all these young men actually aspired to being P.E. teachers. It may well have been chosen as the least 'teachery' option – some of the reasons given included: it is 'a handy job' or because 'I'm sporty'.

It is clear from the data already presented that school leavers had well established perceptions of the financial returns from teaching, vis-à-vis other occupations, and that their own assessment of the possible number of 'points' they might achieve in their final school examination was playing a part in their choice processes regarding teaching. Knowledge of the academic requirements is an essential prerequisite for entry to any course and, in particular, to primary teaching. It was, therefore, important to establish how widespread such knowledge was, and whether it was related to gender, or to decisions to apply for primary teaching. At various stages of the pilot phase of the project, informants suggested that low salary levels in teaching were a disincentive, especially to young men. It was important to gauge levels of knowledge about this dimension of primary teaching also.

The analysis of the responses of school leavers showed that less than half of the school leavers were aware of the Honours Irish requirement for entry to primary teaching, which is the chief academic prerequisite, other than the overall points level. However, almost twice as many girls as boys were aware of it. There was a greater awareness of the points level required for entry with some 57 per cent of respondents estimating the level correctly. Again, there was a significant gender difference here. Girls were much more likely than boys to estimate correctly, or to overestimate, while boys were a great deal more likely to underestimate the points level required. This may go some way to explain why fewer boys than girls saw point levels or the Honours Irish requirement as a reason for not choosing teaching. Many more of the boys were simply unaware of these requirements.

Less than half the respondents estimated the primary teacher's starting salary correctly. Most tended to overestimate it. There were no significant differences between the sexes here, although girls were a little more inclined to underestimate the starting salary. This provides little support for the theory that it is the low level of pay that is the main reason for the lower proportion of boys entering primary teaching.

As regards the choice of primary teaching, significantly more of those who intended to put primary teaching as their first degree preference were aware of the Honours Irish requirement (73 per cent, compared to 48 per cent of the others; Chi-square=16.65; df=2; p<. 000). Likewise, some 63 per cent of those intending to put primary teaching first on their degree forms correctly estimated points, while a further 25 per cent of this group overestimated them. These figures suggest that the responses of those intending to put primary teaching first on their application forms represented fairly realistic choices at the time of the survey.

School leavers' and student teachers' explanations for the fall in male teachers

As well as giving of their own perceptions and reasons for choosing or not choosing teaching, school leavers and student teachers were asked to reflect on why the number of men going into teaching was falling. Respondents were asked an open question to explore this issue.

The perception that primary teaching is a woman's job or is female dominated, or that it relates to a mother's role, was the most frequently offered explanation by both the school leavers and the student teachers for the low proportion of male entrants to primary teaching, with 42 per cent of the school leavers and 45 per cent of the student teachers offering this reason. However, these overall percentages masked very considerable gender differences. Females offered this reason much more frequently than males. Qualitative analysis of the school leaver responses indicated that this explanation was sometimes couched in terms of fear of ridicule. For example, one girl wrote: 'Males now see primary teaching as a woman's job, like staying at home and minding the children. They feel they will get laughed at if they do primary teaching.' Another girl wrote that males 'feel it embarrassing going into a place full of women . . . that it wasn't a real man's job'. Yet another said it was 'due to stereotypical work roles and men fearing to be individuals'. 'Slaggings' (teasing) from friends were occasionally mentioned.

The second most common reason given by both groups was the attraction of other careers. This response no doubt reflected the school leavers' perceptions of the job market of the late 1990s and its accompanying rewards. Again, there were marked gender differences here, as almost twice as many boys as girls suggested this. One student wrote: 'men just want to be in control of themselves and their work'. One girl wrote that primary teaching 'was not seen as a socially accepted male job – that there was no power relative to other professions'. Another girl wrote: 'Society inflicts doctors, engineering, etc. on them . . . so being a teacher would mean being a faggot'. This association of homosexuality (or the ascription of it) was mentioned occasionally – in interviews one of the guidance counsellors also referred to it.

Reasons for fewer males in primary teaching

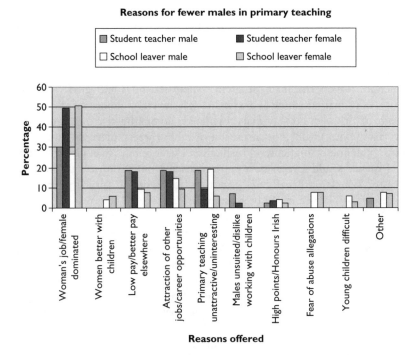

Figure 6.1 Reasons offered by school leavers and student teachers for the fall in the number of males entering primary teaching, by gender

Note: Student teachers consisted of all the males and a sample of the females.

The third most commonly offered reason by school leavers was a perception of primary teaching as unattractive – as boring, hassle, stressful or requiring too much patience. 'Young kids wreck your head and some men don't have the patience – don't want to be around kids all day'. One boy gave a reason in terms of 'hating' children himself. Another male respondent said primary teaching was 'too stressful and (males) were not caring enough. They don't have the natural caring aptitude women have.'

'Low pay' which is often given as the prime reason for fewer males in teaching came joint fourth for school leavers but was offered more frequently (and in joint second place) by student teachers. It is acknowledged, though, that there may be a 'pay' element in the attraction of other careers, as guidance counsellors mentioned in some interviews. A few school leavers mentioned inadequate pay in relation to the traditional male role of fending for a family. The proportion of school leavers offering 'low pay' as a reason was just 8 per cent. The same percentage offered the other reason ranked fourth in frequency by them – i.e. that men might be afraid of child abuse allegations, a factor not mentioned at all by student teachers in responses to this question. The perception of pay as an issue was greater among the student teachers than among school leavers, at 18 per cent, and perhaps reflected the greater salience of pay at that stage of their lives. There were no marked gender differences on this item in either survey. Among student teachers, the perception of primary teaching as an old-fashioned/low status job, from which males would be discouraged by peers, fell into fourth place with lack of interest by males falling into fifth.

For school leavers the main differences between boys and girls were: the perception of primary teaching as a woman's job, given by almost twice as high a percentage of girls as of boys; primary teaching as an unattractive career, given by twice as many boys as girls; the attraction of other careers, given by more boys than girls; high points/higher level Irish, given by more boys than girls. One boy wrote: 'I myself would love to be a primary teacher but am unable to meet the needs of the Education Board [sic]'. Another boy wrote, 'it [primary teaching] was not as accessible as it could be to someone average'. These reasons suggest that it is boys' perceptions of the job as associated with women along with the prospects (if not the reality) of unlimited change and possible excitement in other jobs which are the greatest negative influences on male school leavers choosing teaching as a profession. It is interesting that considerably more girls felt that this was the major factor discouraging boys. An essentialist view of women as 'naturally' better with children was also to be observed – and was commoner among boys than among girls. This was sometimes coupled with a view that men were also 'naturally' lacking in patience.

Among student teachers the main gender differences in the reasons given for the low proportion of men in teaching were: (i) the idea that primary teaching is perceived by men as a woman's job, with more females suggesting this; (ii) that primary teaching would be unattractive to males, offered more often by males; (iii) that males were unsuited to or would dislike working with children, offered by a higher proportion of males. In a booming economy where private enterprise is engaged in wooing the clever student, teaching may appear dull, old-fashioned and not particularly rewarding to some. One male guidance counsellor commented on the flatness of the career structure – and the predictability of the job. There is evidence here that the main inherent feature of the job, i.e. dealing with children, is perceived as off-putting to a proportion of males.

The reasons suggested for the dropping numbers of male primary teachers indicate a bias towards seeing the ideal primary teacher as female, based on an essentialist belief that a woman's nature tends to make her better with children. This belief is stronger among boys than among girls, more of whom are convinced of each sex's potential to teach at primary level. Nevertheless more girls give reasons favouring women teachers than favouring equal ability among men and women. It is hard to know if these perceptions are based on the young people's own experience of their particular teachers or on ideological beliefs.

Student teachers (but not school leavers) were also asked if they felt that the lack of males in primary teaching was problematic. Some two thirds felt that it was. Proportionately more males (78 per cent) than females (61 per cent) thought it would be a problem.

Table 6.3 Reasons offered by student teachers as to why lack of male primary teachers is a problem, by gender

Reasons	Males %	Females %	Total %
No male role models/lack of male influence	55.6	37.0	42.2
Balance/equality needed in the profession	22.2	34.8	31.3
Not a problem if teachers are good	2.8	17.4	13.3
Other	19.4	10.8	13.2
Total	100.0	100.0	100.0
N	36	92	128

Note: Student teachers consisted of all the males and a sample of the females.

Table 6.4 Student teachers' suggestions on strategies to bring about a more equal gender balance in primary teaching, by gender

Suggested strategies	Males %	Females %	Total %
Encouragement to males in school	15.4	41.1	34.7
More pay/pay to take account of family responsibilities	23.1	23.1	23.1
Targeted advertising/Recruitment	23.1	11.5	14.4
Lower points for males/interviews	19.2	12.8	14.4
Incentives/positive discrimination	11.5	5.1	6.7
Other	7.7	6.4	6.7
Total	100.0	100.0	100.0
N	26	78	104

Note: Student teachers consisted of all the males and a sample of the females.

Lack of male role models or male influence in primary teaching was the main reason offered by students for their perception of the paucity of males as problematic. This was followed by the need for balance or equality in the profession. There were marked gender differences on both of these. Males were much more likely than females to offer 'role models' as a reason, whereas proportionately more females offered the need for balance or equality. A degree of ambivalence among females on this issue was evident from the third most frequent reason – 'it's not a problem if teachers are good'. This reason was offered predominantly by females. Males, on the other hand were more likely to offer a range of 'other' reasons, such as 'becoming a female job', 'stereotyping', or other miscellaneous reasons.

Student teachers were also asked for their views on what could be done to keep a more equal gender balance in primary teaching. Their responses to this are given in Table 6.4.

Encouragement to males in schools was the most frequently offered strategy, but this was offered predominantly by women. Preferred strategies by males were more pay and targeted advertising or recruitment. These two strategies were offered by almost half the males. Males were also more disposed than females to lower entry points for males and other forms of positive discrimination.

To summarise, the predominant reason offered by student teachers for the dropping numbers of male primary entrants was the perception of primary teaching as a woman's job. Pay came second as a reason but much less frequently. More women gave 'woman's job' as a reason. These explanations mirrored those of the school leavers, although pay featured highly as a reason among student teachers. Proportionately more males than females viewed the dropping proportion of male teachers as problematic. Lack of male role models and the need for equality in the profession were the most frequently offered rationale for the problem but again there were considerable gender differences – males being more inclined to give the former, and females the latter, as an explanation. Gender differences also emerged in the strategies suggested by students to bring about greater gender balance – females favoured encouragement in schools, males favoured more pay, targeted recruitment and positive discrimination.

Student teachers' experience of initial teacher education

Student teachers were asked to give some information on their experience of initial teacher education. The issues explored were the subject options taken, their reactions to teaching practice and whether they participated in part-time work. Analysis of subject choices showed a tendency for the student teachers to choose fairly conservatively from the traditional core subjects and specialisms in teacher education – mathematics, Irish and history. There was a somewhat greater tendency among males to indicate that mathematics was their chosen specialism.

Students had all been on teaching practice for a period of time when the survey was administered. They were asked to reflect on this experience and to highlight the aspects that they found enjoyable, and those they found difficult.

Respondents found various aspects of their relationship with children to be the most enjoyable element of their teaching practice (Table 6.5). Other enjoyable dimensions related to successfully implementing personal teaching strategies and to aspects of the subject areas being taught. While relationships with children were the dominant aspects selected as enjoyable by these student teachers, women were markedly more likely to choose this dimension. Men were more likely than women to choose 'teaching strategies' successfully implemented, and aspects relating to 'subjects'.

Student teachers were also asked to identify the aspects of teaching practice they found difficult. The categories into which their responses fell are presented in Table 6.6.

Table 6.5 Aspects of teaching practice found enjoyable by student teachers, by gender

Enjoyable aspects of teaching practice	Males %	Females %	Total %
Aspects relating to the relationship with children	53.4	76.3	70.9
Aspects relating to student teacher's own teaching strategies	33.3	13.3	18.0
Aspects relating to subjects being taught	13.3	10.4	11.1
Total	100.0	100.0	100.0
N	45	144	189

Note: Student teachers consisted of all the males and a sample of the females.

Table 6.6 Aspects of teaching practice found difficult by student teachers, by gender

Difficult aspects of teaching practice	Males %	Females %	Total %
Paperwork and lengthy class plans	46.8	31.0	34.8
Control and discipline in classes	13.4	35.9	30.5
Inspection/Assessment of classes	4.4	9.2	8.0
Feelings of lack of confidence/competence	0.0	7.7	5.9
Lack of resources/class sizes	11.2	2.1	4.3
Miscellaneous	24.2	14.1	16.5
Total	100.0	100.0	100.0
N	45	142	187

Note: Student teachers consisted of all the males and a sample of the females.

The two most difficult aspects of teaching practice for the students related to the length of time they felt they had to spend on preparing, correcting and planning classes. This very necessary aspect of teaching had been identified earlier by both school leavers and student teachers as the least attractive element of teaching. However, it was clear that males found it to be an even more difficult part of the work than did females. Control and discipline in classes were also found to be difficult by almost a third of the student teachers. In this case proportionately more women than men found it difficult. The 'inspection' of classes by college supervisors was identified as a difficulty by 8 per cent of the students – proportionately more females than males. This figure is a testament, perhaps, to the quality of the relationship between college staff and students as it might have been expected to feature more highly in the responses.

Lack of confidence/competence was a feeling confined to the women students. Whether such feelings were warranted can only be a matter of speculation. However, it is useful to recall that, in Chapter 1, figures were presented which indicated that the level of awards was markedly higher among female than among male graduates of the colleges.

Summary

International research on the teaching career had indicated that interpersonal possibilities of working with children and a sense of service were attractors into teaching. These proved to be important factors in respondents' decision-making. The reasons given for choosing and not choosing teaching showed considerable division between the sexes. Student teachers were asked their reasons for choosing primary teaching as a career. Child-focused reasons were those most frequently offered for the choice of primary teaching, although these were offered proportionately more frequently by women. Many more women had had experience of working with children before going to college. A liking for young children was the most frequently cited reason for choosing primary rather than second level teaching – again more frequently cited by women students. Two thirds of the sample could see themselves in primary teaching in twenty years' time, with somewhat more women than men having this long-term commitment. Enjoyment of the job was the most frequently given reason for staying, while 'wanting a break' was the most frequently envisaged reason for moving on.

School cultures, the hidden curriculum, and the socialisation of males and females into masculine and feminine forms of educational ethos have been found to be important elements of the formation of gender identity. In due course, this affects the perceptions of young people of appropriate subject choices, and roles for themselves and others. When asked to give their rationale for the low proportion of men in primary teaching, the most frequently offered explanation by both boys and girls was that it is a woman's job; women are better with children. However, girls more often offered this reason, whereas boys highlighted much more frequently than did girls other reasons such as primary teaching being boring or stressful, or other careers being more attractive.

Student teacher respondents found various aspects of their relationship with children to be the most enjoyable element of their teaching practice. Other enjoyable dimensions related to successfully implementing personal teaching strategies and to aspects of the subject areas being taught. The two most difficult aspects of teaching practice for the students related to the length of time they felt they had to spend on preparing, correcting and planning classes. These were the factors that had been identified by both school leavers and student teachers as aspects of the role which would be off-putting. Student teachers' initial experience of teaching provided them with a more realistic view of the profession and a deeper understanding of the factors which attract men and women, or otherwise. The views of experienced teachers and teacher educators are also important and these are presented in Chapter 7.

The views of experienced professionals

Experienced teachers and teacher educators play important roles in the formation of professional identities and the socialisation of pupils and student teachers into male and female cultures. This chapter presents the results of interviews with three groups of experienced professionals. The views of guidance counsellors are first set out; these are followed by those of senior college managers/administrators (all of whom were, or had been, academics teaching in their institutions). Finally the views of a group of experienced male teachers are presented. This was part of the triangulated research methodology on which this study is based. This triangulation made use of documentary research, quantitative data-gathering and qualitative methods.

The guidance counsellors, senior college managers/administrators involved with the school leavers and student teachers, as well as a group of experienced male teachers were key informants. In the case of guidance counsellors, this was because of their roles in providing advice and information to school leavers; because of college managers/administrators' insights deriving from their experience of administering the third level initial teacher education system; and because of the insights deriving from working as primary/elementary teachers in the case of the experienced male teachers. Semi-structured interviews were carried out during the course of visits by the researchers to the schools and the colleges, while a focus group interview was conducted with the male teachers.

The initial motivations and subsequent career experience of professionals shape their own self-perceptions and may colour the way they advise pupils and student teachers. One of the best known sociological analyses of the views of experienced teachers is one conducted in French-speaking Switzerland, with a focus on the teachers' perceptions of their career at various stages of their lives. This classified respondents' initial motivations for teaching into the categories of 'active' (e.g. contact with young people and love of the subject), 'material' (job conditions, security, etc.) and 'passive' (natural inclination) motivations (Huberman and Grounauer, 1991: 109–37). 'Active' motives, similar to the motives classified as 'intrinsic' in this study, had accounted for two thirds of these Swiss teachers' reasons for entering teaching. There were some significant differences in the initial motivations of men and women. The men's responses showed a configuration which was strongly affected by material and passive motivations, especially among those in the high school group. Women and the middle school group tended to cite motives which identified teaching as a calling.

Huberman and Grounauer argued that the initial motivation of teachers will have consequences for their working lives and for teaching as a profession. They suggested that 'active motivations are related to the absence of a loss of impetus, to the presence of a second phase of rejuvenation, stabilisation and pedagogical mastery' (ibid.: 124). These themes and motivations emerge from the interviews with the three groups of professionals interviewed. Teachers and teacher educators are important players in the way the profession is perceived by pupils and student teachers.

Guidance counsellors

Interest in and take-up of teaching

Of the sixteen second level schools in the survey, twelve were entitled to an ex-quota guidance counsellor on the basis of pupil numbers (i.e. with 500 or more pupils). However, all of the schools had some member of staff who performed the guidance counsellor role. One school (a fee-paying boys school) had two staff performing this role. In this school both individuals were involved in the interviews. However, the data derived were treated as a unit as there was a very high level of agreement in the responses of the two individuals. Guidance counsellors were asked to assess the level of interest in and take-up of primary and second level teaching among their pupils over the previous five years. Because teacher education for second level schools is mainly conducted on the consecutive model (i.e. where students first do an arts, science, commerce or other relevant degree, followed by professional education on a postgraduate teacher education programme), guidance counsellors were much less certain of the numbers from their schools who had considered second level teaching, or who had in fact taken it up over the previous five years. However, as initial primary/elementary teacher education is conducted on the concurrent model, with the majority of entrants transferring directly from schools to undergraduate teacher education courses, guidance counsellors were much clearer on the numbers interested in primary teaching and entering the colleges of education.

There were some interesting variations in the responses according to the different types of school. Guidance counsellors in the three girls secondary schools attested to the greatest evidence of interest among their pupils. These guidance counsellors suggested that, over the previous five years, interest in primary teaching had been expressed by 43 girls, with approximately 15 having taken up places. Together in the survey year, these three schools had a total pupil population of 1,944 girls. However, one school had a strong tradition of girls going into primary teaching as it had had some 12 girls who had entered the primary colleges in the five-year period. By contrast, guidance counsellors in the boys secondary schools gave evidence of very little interest in primary education among their pupils. In the two boys secondary schools in this survey, with a total of 976 pupils in the year of the survey, guidance counsellors claimed to have had interested enquiries from just one boy and to have had no primary school entrant at all over the previous five years.

According to the guidance counsellors' responses, there was greater interest in the coeducational schools – three of which were located in predominantly rural areas. Four of these schools had a total pupil population of 1,228 boys and 928 girls in the year of the survey. In these four schools, guidance counsellors had had interested inquiries about primary teaching from approximately 30 boys and 31 girls over the previous 5 years, and approximately 6 boys and 7 girls had actually gone into primary teaching. In a further three (which together had some 1,009 boys and 754 girls in the year of the survey) guidance counsellors were less sure of the numbers who had expressed an interest in primary teaching. Nevertheless they estimated that, in the five-year period in question, they had had approximately 2 boys and 9 girls transferring to primary colleges. However, of these, the 2 boys and 5 of the girls came from a Gaelscoil (an Irish language medium school), which clearly gave a great deal of encouragement to its pupils to go into teaching. The remaining three coeducational schools (with total pupil populations of 1,133 boys and 1,063 girls) had experiences of interest from approximately 12 girls and 5 boys over the five-year period. Approximately 1 girl and 1 boy entered primary teaching from these schools.

On the basis of the estimates of the guidance counsellors relating to the five-year period prior to the survey, the schools most likely to have had pupils go on to primary/elementary teaching were: the Irish medium school, girls secondary schools, and rural coeducational schools. The least disposed to primary teaching (i.e. who had no primary entrants at all) were boys' secondary schools.

Advice given by guidance counsellors

All of the guidance counsellors who had inquiries about primary teaching claimed to have given positive guidance about primary teaching as a career, although some said their advice varied according to the pupil. Guidance counsellors from the girls secondary schools said their advice revolved mainly around the course requirements. One put a heavy emphasis on the benefits of pupils obtaining some work experience in primary schools during mid-term or Easter holidays. There was little difference in the approach taken by guidance counsellors in the coeducational secondary schools, with encouragement and information on the nature of the work, and college requirements predominating. This advice also predominated in community and vocational schools. All of the guidance counsellors in coeducational schools said they made no particular distinction in their advice to boys and girls.

Suitability of teaching for men and women

All of the guidance counsellors interviewed saw both primary and second level teaching as equally suited to men and to women. More than half of them suggested the need for role models for boys or for the necessity for gender balance in the profession as a rationale for their answer.

Female guidance counsellor, coeducational secondary school
> I think boys have a kind of caring side as well that wants to help people develop. But as well as that I . . . well I suppose . . . I mean probably going off at a slight tangent I think the way that society is going . . . if we look for example at the primary school across the road here . . . one of the things that the teacher will tell you across there . . . in [the school] here we have a boys national school and a girls national school. But some students would now have gone through the whole primary school system and a large part of the secondary school system with no male role model, and if they come from a single parent family there has been no significant male in their life at all. Which I think is a major lack in their upbringing really you know. That they don't have some sort of a male role model somewhere along the way.

Female guidance counsellor, coeducational secondary school
> There's a tremendous need for balance, especially in coeducational schools – even in administration – and in the staff room.

Male guidance counsellor, coeducational vocational school
> Women do it just as well, though it pains me to say it.

Male guidance counsellor, boys secondary school
> Well if I put it this way, I would prefer to see a primary school representative of society, in which case you have men and women.

Some of the complexities of developing an interest among boys in primary teaching are evident in the quote below. The following responses are from two guidance counsellors in a boys' secondary school who, while believing that primary and secondary teaching are equally suitable for boys and for girls went on to say the following:

Female guidance counsellor, boys secondary school
> There are some young men who would genuinely like to be involved in teaching at primary or in second level but they see it as something that doesn't guarantee them, you know, a particular quality of life or even in terms of their social status or even, you know, the kind of money they would get. It gets a very negative reputation in terms of money.

Male guidance counsellor, boys secondary school

> What the boys would say here is that they would look out at the car park and they would see the cars that the teachers drive, they would compare and contrast those with the cars that the parents in the school would drive and they would see a vast difference both in size and age and condition.

Guidance counsellors thus evidenced a strong belief that both primary and second level teaching is equally suited to boys and girls – primarily on the grounds of the need for male role models, and for balance in the profession. However, teachers in a school with boys from higher income backgrounds suggested that awareness among pupils of income differentials between teaching and other professional careers was a deterrent.

Most important values for school leavers when choosing a career

Guidance counsellors placed a very heavy emphasis on the importance of job satisfaction or personal satisfaction as the most important priority for young people when choosing a career. All of them (bar one person who felt that intrinsic, extrinsic and altruistic motivations were all equally important) emphasised the need for personal satisfaction. Nevertheless one person felt that money was a bigger motivator for boys, while another felt that for girls altruistic factors rated higher, with caring underdeveloped in boys.

Female guidance counsellor, girls secondary school

> What's important for them? . . . first of all it comes back to their own sense of self . . . and their sense of self-worth which puts them in a position then to realistically look at . . . right what am I suited to? For example, do I want to work with young kids, do I want to work with older kids. But from their own secure kind of understanding of themselves and sense of self-worth as well, but I would come across a lot really . . . of students wanting some . . . areas that would have a very high profile in society like law or medicine or whatever, just for the only reason that this is what is highly favoured by parents or by society or that students perceive it that way and that for a student can put them really on the wrong road in terms of what is right for them. So looking behind their actual reasons for choosing.

Male guidance counsellor, coeducational secondary school

> Well I strongly go with the intrinsic. I give them always an interest test, I know I do aptitude tests . . . but if you like what you do you will be good at it, and it will also be good for your kids and family you know. So I think more intrinsically, liking what you do. So I say to them keep all the areas open and apply say to the CAO/CAS [and to what] used to be post-Leaving Cert. Courses and apprenticeships, so keeping all the doors open because that's the

way . . . I think that's the best thing to do and apply for everything and then many of them will come back . . . I always come back the last week in August and I have some of them here who might get an offer of 2 or 3 and they are wondering what to do even then you know.

Female guidance counsellor, coeducational community school
Absolute job fulfilment. I talk about that . . . and that it is going to affect everything else about them. Your job should be a part of your day.

Thus, a strong orientation was evident on the part of guidance counsellors towards intrinsic, and perhaps somewhat individualistic, values in their advice to young people when choosing a career.

Perceptions of selected careers

During the interview, guidance counsellors were asked to evaluate the same list of occupations that were included in the second level questionnaire in order to gauge their perceptions of them. The dimensions explored were the same as for the school leavers – i.e. which would offer the greatest job satisfaction, were most suited to men, would offer the greatest financial reward or prestige, were most suited to women, or were of greatest social benefit.

In marked contrast to the pupils, more than two thirds (11) of the guidance counsellors selected some form of teaching as offering the greatest job satisfaction. Indeed, six of the sixteen counsellors specifically mentioned second level teaching. One person was reluctant to choose any of the careers and one each selected doctor, television producer, computer programmer and social worker.

Female guidance counsellor, coeducational community school
The funny thing is, they [the pupils] know . . . you know they say, 'you're really happy in your job aren't you?' They know, and I couldn't come in, in September, if I wasn't and I am honest with them, I am totally honest . . . that's not to say that there are not days when I am wishing I was doing something else!

As regards the question of whether men were more suited to any of the careers listed, the majority of the guidance counsellors (10) were reluctant to select any of the occupations, preferring to suggest that men were equally suited to all of them. Six did highlight a career – five chose engineering and one accountancy. Thus insofar as there was a stereotyped view among this minority it was highly concentrated along the traditional lines observable among school leavers. However, even where this was the case it was sometimes tempered by the guidance counsellor's own reflections, or by a feeling of somehow trying to push back the tide of young people's own stereotypical views in subject choices:

Female guidance counsellor, coeducational secondary school

I honestly couldn't . . . I think maybe in the engineering area, em . . . I know I have a friend here in town who is a woman engineer and she comes in and talks to the students sometimes and she is a very capable assertive kind of woman. And she would say that she has had to be more assertive and be quite assertive and be quite strong in her job more so than men, particularly when she is out on building sites and things like that. People don't tend to take her as seriously as they would . . . a man. So I suppose that kind of thing might make engineering more difficult for women. It's the one that I find I have to actually consciously say to the lads here – 'because you are doing physics and because you are doing honours maths does not automatically mean that engineering is the work for you', and I have to consciously say to them about other options . . . and they say 'well what can I do? I have physics and I have chemistry and maths and maybe technical graphics and what else can I do?' And I have to actually explain to them that there are huge wide options available to them. But at the same time I can think of three, I think, past pupils who were very bright who went into engineering against, I won't say against my advice, but even though I was saying (to them) I think you should look at something else. And one particular guy he started off in first year he got first class honours in his first year exams, he got second class honours in his second year exams and by third he was deciding whether he would drop out or whether he wouldn't drop out and gradually the college actually cajoled him into . . . he came to his degree, didn't do his project – basically failed his degree but the college kind of supported him in doing it and he got a pass degree. And all the time he was thinking he should have been doing something like primary school teaching. Both his parents were primary school teachers and . . . but even at that, when this graduate [postgraduate entrance to primary teaching education] came up he still didn't go for it.

Guidance counsellors were asked to identify the occupations offering the greatest financial rewards. Most of their responses were evenly split between accountants and computer programmers as getting most financial reward (six in each case). This contrasted with the perceptions of the school leavers who were more inclined to see doctors and lawyers as most highly paid.

As regards the occupations carrying the most prestige, guidance counsellors were fairly traditional. More than half (9) chose doctor and a further three chose lawyer. No one selected either form of teaching.

When it came to selecting the occupation best suited to women the majority of the guidance counsellors were again reluctant to select any particular one. Most (11) suggested that all were equally suitable. Two people selected social worker, and one of each chose primary teacher, doctor and social worker – all caring professions. Where occupations were deemed suitable for women the rationale was primarily in terms of the other pressures on women's lives.

Male guidance counsellor, coeducational secondary school
> I'd say the least (suitable) is probably doctor which is not answering your question. I think, given the fact that women are lumbered with what women are lumbered with, those (jobs) with most regular hours would be the most suited – plus primary and secondary teacher and possibly social worker, engineer, computer programmer. It is not answering your question very specifically now, but I think the ability to organise time is obviously a prime thing.

With regard to the occupation of most social benefit, a majority of the guidance counsellors (10) selected teaching, with five specifically mentioning primary teaching. A further three chose social work and one chose doctor. Two people felt that all of the occupations were of social benefit.

Female guidance counsellor, coeducational community school
> Primary teaching is [of most social benefit] actually, because you have such a young little sap in front of you. I'd love it. A huge human bond of some sort takes place there [in primary school] that must be magic really knowing . . .

Male guidance counsellor, coeducational vocational school
> [Of most social benefit] Primary teaching. I would yeah. Because that is where your young people start off, their ideas are formulated.

To summarise, guidance counsellors' perceptions of the nine careers selected were somewhat in contrast to those of the school leavers and even of the college students, insofar as most saw some form of teaching as offering greatest job satisfaction. Just a quarter of the guidance counsellors selected another career. The majority of the counsellors felt that both men and women were equally suitable for all of the occupations listed. Even for those who selected particular occupations as more suited to men or to women, their views were somewhat qualified. The two careers perceived as having the greatest financial rewards were accountant and computer programmer. Doctors and lawyers were perceived as having highest prestige. Secondary/high school, followed by primary/elementary teaching, was chosen by a majority as of greatest social benefit.

Aspects of primary teaching that would attract or put off

When asked to identify the aspects of primary teaching that would attract people or put them off, there was greater agreement among the guidance counsellors regarding the attractive than the unattractive elements. In terms of attractiveness, over half of the counsellors mentioned the children themselves, or their openness and receptivity at the primary level age. The hours and/or holidays were also mentioned by more than half of the respondents. The value of primary education to society and the ability to shape young people in the future were also mentioned by more than a third of the guidance counsellors.

Female guidance counsellor, girls' secondary school
> There is great fulfilment in seeing children grow and develop – you feel you're doing something worthwhile in life.

Male guidance counsellor, coeducational secondary school
> [Attractive] about primary teaching? Well again I suppose the fact that . . . like in a sense you have an opportunity to help shape the next generation. Maybe the fact that they are young and a little more innocent still, so imaginatively they are more open. When they get into teenage years they are less communicative than they are then, but there is more imaginative qualities still open for children or younger children anyway. I have great admiration for primary teachers, I don't think I could do it myself.

Female guidance counsellor, coeducational secondary school
> The innocence of young children. There's a great authenticity and originality from youngsters. They're 'with you' – not rebelling. There's creativity. You're free to beautify your own classroom. There's freedom – the group is yours.

The factors mentioned as unattractive were more diverse. Three people mentioned the curriculum – either its basic quality or its presumed lack of variety, or indeed the requirement to teach all subjects (including Irish and religion). Two people mentioned the Honours Irish requirement at entry. Two people mentioned large classes and/or lack of resources. Two people mentioned difficulties associated with the denominational character of primary teacher education, especially for minority religions or for unbelievers. Other issues raised ranged from the lack of contact with other adults, to dealing with parents, stress in the job, and the fact that primary teaching is perceived as a woman's job.

Female guidance counsellor, coeducational community school
> [Things about primary teaching that would put off]
> Everything! The awfulness of the set-up – each teacher in a classroom on their own all day long; in a rural school, one male principal dominating all the females, and being in there for ever . . .

Female guidance counsellor, coeducational secondary school
> Finances. Also the perception that 'it's a woman's job'. In this school, even some of the boys who went on to do primary teaching wouldn't have said they were going to in front of the group. Many people were surprised when they got their offers.

Male guidance counsellor, coeducational vocational community college
> I think the publicity at the moment about class sizes. Anyone who is kind of interested in what's happening, I think that would put a lot of people off, the responsibility, the lack of resources, the lack . . . how difficult it is for a primary

teacher to get basic resources. I'm involved on a parents association for a primary school myself and I am even shocked at how difficult it is that we have to fund-raise to get art materials for a teacher, I think it's scandalous.

To sum up, the attractive qualities of primary teaching were seen as the children themselves, the ability to shape and influence the future through them, and the hours and holidays which are part of the conditions of work. Off-putting aspects included the primary curriculum itself, the Honours Irish requirement at entry, large classes and lack of resources.

Aspects of second level teaching that would attract or put off

There were somewhat greater levels of agreement among the guidance counsellors about what was attractive and unattractive at second level. While people often named more than one factor, the two aspects of second level teaching deemed most attractive were the young people/teenagers themselves and teacher's ability to have a more adult relationship with them (by 10 respondents) and the nature and variety of subjects in the curriculum (by 10 individuals). Job satisfaction was mentioned by two people and a further two mentioned holidays.

Female guidance counsellor, girls secondary school
About secondary teaching I think actually working with students from 12 to 17. I think that it is one of the attractions and also just the changes that are taking place in teaching and that the changes that will continue to take place. I think that this is also very attractive.

Male guidance counsellor, coeducational secondary school
I would certainly . . . when I started, I don't know whether it is the same now for a lot of us . . . I suppose the idea of having a wide range of students that you come in contact with . . . there is great mobility within the school for teaching subjects. You are not stuck with the subjects you had in your primary degree . . . and in fact some people . . . some are experts ironically on other subjects you know and it allows for that. Now some criticise that, but there is flexibility. Also the idea of curriculum development, certainly myself now I would have been humanities, I would have brought that in here with another guy and pastoral care I sort of have . . . I co-ordinate pastoral care here, so the social side.

Male guidance counsellor, coeducational vocational community college
Again I think any kind of teaching is a challenge. It is different [at second level] obviously because you are dealing with a different area . . . a different age group . . . it's going to be . . . the job's going to be quite different . . . I think there are some exciting things in second level which people have an

option of getting involved in, (like) Transition Year, Health Education, new areas like that, Personal Development. I think those are very good opportunities for students but for teachers they are challenging as well, and in that sense it is very rewarding as well.

As regards the aspects of second level teaching that guidance counsellors perceived as unattractive or off-putting, there was a fairly high level of agreement on the dominant ones. Discipline problems and lack of pupil motivation were mentioned by over half (10) of the respondents. Lack of permanent positions for many young teachers was mentioned by three people. Issues relating to pay were mentioned by two people, with the 'flat profession' (i.e. 'flat' career structure) mentioned by a further one. Social problems spilling over into the school was mentioned by two individuals and the 'public flak' received by teachers by one person.

Female guidance counsellor, coeducational secondary school
> The discipline – what teachers have to cope with in classrooms, especially for young teachers. You need to use a bit of 'psychology'. There's a growth in dysfunctional families.

Male guidance counsellor, coeducational vocational school
> I suppose the change in attitudes in young people over the past number of years. The discipline problems that have come in . . . not necessarily through the school but through the whole society, the home environment, the whole society.

Male guidance counsellor, coeducational vocational community college
> I would say in some cases things like discipline and apathy from some students which can make a job very difficult for a young teacher. I think the difficulties they see as well that secondary teachers are finding it very difficult to get jobs and it's not encouraging for a young intelligent 18 year old . . . it's not . . . when they see a person out of college six years with an honours degree and an honours H. Dip it's not very encouraging to go into it, when they can go to an Institute of Technology for two, three, four years and be much better off . . . more security.

In sum, the dominant factors about second level seen as attractive by respondents were dealing with, and having a more adult relationship with teenagers than would be possible with younger children, and the nature and variety of the second level curriculum. The dominant aspects found unattractive concern discipline problems, or social problems spilling into the classroom, with a smaller number identifying the lack of permanent jobs as unattractive.

Is primary teaching an appropriate career for high achieving boys and girls?

Although all of the guidance counsellors had said that primary teaching was a career equally suited to both men and women, when asked if primary teaching was an appropriate career choice for *high achieving* boys and girls some interesting variations emerged. While a sizeable majority (14) felt it was an appropriate choice for high achieving girls, just half (8) thought it appropriate for high achieving boys. The underlying reasons for negativity related mainly to promotion prospects and presumed boredom.

Female guidance counsellor, coeducational community school
(Is primary teaching an appropriate career choice for high achieving boys?) Definitely not! . . . (laughter) Shocking isn't it. Total prejudice isn't it? (Why?) Well the highest you'd get would be Principal and even that after many years . . . a good 10 years anyway . . . If you went into business, accountancy, computers very quickly in your twenties you could be earning serious amounts of money, be part of a dynamic young team, jet-setting around the world instead of locked away in the classroom. You might say you're forming children's minds but lots of people can form children's minds . . . They would be bored . . . Some might use the job to earn money and use the rest of their time to do all sorts of interesting and creative things . . .

Female guidance counsellor, girls secondary school
No, there would be boredom after a while – they are likely to have their sights set on a prestige career which would be held in more esteem in society. Such as a doctor or lawyer or TV producer – one who hangs out with someone like Neil Jordan.

Male guidance counsellor, boys secondary school
Very often if they figure out they are going to get 480 points they feel they have to do something that requires 480 points or if they get 550 points they feel that they must do medicine . . . If they are capable of getting 550 points, instead of choosing a career from the point of view that they would like to do it. But if you are an ambitious high achiever, certainly, and you were looking at the job and the financial rewards at the end of it, you *wouldn't waste your time becoming a primary teacher* . . . That's the way they would look at it you know.

Female guidance counsellor, girls secondary school
(Is primary teaching an appropriate career choice for high achieving girls?) Really high flyers are not choosing teaching though they did in the past. I feel a lot of people who really want teaching miss it by a small margin (because of the points) and these are people who would have been superb primary teachers.

Some of the guidance counsellors were very positive about high achieving boys and girls going into primary teaching, while others viewed it as depending on the person.

Female guidance counsellor, coeducational secondary school
> (Is primary teaching an appropriate career choice for high achieving boys?) Yes. They're very fulfilled. There are opportunities to be involved in sport, with youth, in community work. The extra-curricular work is very important.

Male guidance counsellor, coeducational vocational school
> Yeah, yeah I would see it as appropriate . . . again . . . it's . . . again I would see it appropriate as not so much for the high achiever or low achiever as the suitable person.

To summarise, although all of the guidance counsellors suggested that primary teaching is equally suitable as a career for men and women, when pressed as to its appropriateness for *high achievers* just half felt it appropriate for high achieving boys, while 14 of the 16 felt it appropriate for high achieving girls. Reasons given related mainly to promotion prospects and presumed boredom in primary teaching on the part of high achieving males.

Do men or women make better teachers?

When asked who make better teachers at primary and second level, the majority of the guidance counsellors (11 for second level, 12 for primary) felt that men and women were equally good as primary or second level teachers. Of those, at primary level two people felt that women were better with infants because of their caring qualities. Five individuals were unsure whether men or women were better and thought that it depended on the person at second level, with four feeling that way about primary teaching.

Female guidance counsellor, coeducational community school
> It's now an urban society . . . You want really cool guys – not guys who pretend to be cool – but genuinely cool guys in a soap opera (as role models) to get people to do Science and boys to do Primary teaching.

(This person was also very definite that primary teaching was not appropriate for high achieving boys)

Female guidance counsellor, girls secondary school
> I worry about the profession becoming female dominated. I think women get walked on (as happened in nursing). [In industrial disputes] women cave in. They care a lot too – too much – they don't like disruption, and they will accept less money. A man who is the only breadwinner will fight more. The

unions have contributed to making teaching as good as it is today. Otherwise Ireland would be like other countries where there is less respect for teachers. I was amazed by the attitude of friends from America where the idea of being a teacher was almost laughable. No self-respecting person would take it on as a career. They are poorly paid and poorly taught – it's only reasonable in the private sector and even there the pay is not good. In England I feel teachers are also badly paid and treated. Teaching in Ireland is still better – not as good as in the past but still a positive option.

Female guidance counsellor, coeducational secondary school
I think probably women are more in touch with the general fact of the care and needs of others. But I would say that if you have men who are in touch with that then they definitely would make great teachers.

Male guidance counsellor, coeducational vocational community college
I suppose because of my own contact with a primary school and getting an insight into it from a parent's point of view but also being on a committee – Parents Association, I suppose I have learnt a bit more this year than I would have known and again because in this school . . . there are very few males teaching in the school and as a parent I think it's . . . you know I have come to see how important a job it is and how important the caring is, certainly from my own experience the female teachers have been exceptionally good and I am not sure how many males would be as conscientious . . . I think the maternal instinct in the female teachers I have seen dealing with infants and senior infants has been tremendous and I am not sure how many males could fill that role as well. Now I think in the older classes I think it would be different.

In sum, the majority of the guidance counsellors felt that men and women made equally good teachers at primary or second level, in that it depended on the individual. Two people felt that women would be better with infants. Overall, guidance counsellors were very positive about primary teaching as a career and indeed about second level teaching also. Just a quarter selected a career other than teaching as offering greater job satisfaction. They were gender egalitarian in their views on the suitability and capability of men and women in primary teaching. There was just one exception to this gender egalitarian and positive approach. When asked about the appropriateness of primary teaching as a career choice for high achieving boys and girls most thought it appropriate for girls but only half thought primary teaching appropriate for high achieving boys. In the surveys of school leavers and student teachers it was apparent that the principal influence on school leavers' and students' career choices was that of their parents. Nevertheless, guidance counsellors still play an important role. The points requirement for entry to colleges of education is relatively high, and the distribution of points among the student teachers surveyed indicated that a substantial minority would have qualified for most of the so-called 'high prestige' courses. It would appear therefore to be important, if the proportion of male entrants is to be increased, that high achieving boys are actively encouraged to consider primary teaching as a serious and attractive option.

Senior college managers/administrators

On each visit to collect data at the colleges of education, interviews were held with college administrators. These interviews were conducted as semi-structured interviews. All of the five most senior college administrators were available for interview during the time of the survey.

All of the five colleges of education have been coeducational since the early 1970s. Until that time, apart from three smaller colleges nowadays attached to one of the universities, there were two major colleges of education for women and one major college for men. As one senior administrator put it, the colleges recruited separately and this structure automatically resulted in approximately one third of all applicants being male. Figures from the early 1970s show an initial rapid drop in the proportion of male entrants to primary teaching, followed by a continuous decline, after the colleges of education became coeducational and introduced common entrance requirements (Drudy, 2004). This proportional decline continued in spite of the closure of one of the larger, formerly female, colleges in the mid-1980s. One of the first colleges to go coeducational was a women's college in the west of the country. This college took the initiative as a result of a belief among college personnel that there were many young men in the western region who might be attracted to primary teaching but who would be unable to travel out of the region to avail of training. Other colleges soon followed suit and became coeducational institutions. All of the senior staff interviewed, and who were on the college staffs at the time, attested that the move to admit the opposite sex was greatly welcomed by staff and students.

In the 1990s (1993) a further major change took place at point of entry to the primary/elementary colleges of education. This was the move from selection by interview as well as by academic prerequisites, to admission by academic results only, processed by the Central Applications Office. At the time of the change there was a good deal of public debate and speculation on the question of the potential effects of this move on the calibre of entrants. All of the college personnel interviewed said that they could detect no discernible effect as a result of the move away from entrance interviews. The quality of student, they felt, remained very good. This is reflected, it was suggested, in the proportions of graduates who get honours. It was also pointed out that, even with the entrance interview, there were always a small number of failures. One college administrator pointed out that, on average, they had been interviewing over 1,000 applicants and yet, on average, could only point to 14 or 15 who were definitely 'unsuitable' for teaching. One person felt that female students are very focused and tend to be more mature.

In general, the colleges felt that female students perform better on both the academic and teaching practice elements of the course (this is confirmed by analysis of aggregate data submitted by the colleges to the Higher Education Authority – Drudy, 2004). Nevertheless, administrators confirmed that there were some very good, or outstanding, male students in each cohort. A couple of administrators suggested that male students showed much greater differentiation than female ones: the good ones were outstanding, but there were a few who had considerable difficulties in terms of motivation and discipline. Female students tended to be more consistent.

There was a general perception among the college administrators that the primary reasons for the low proportion of male entrants were related to the following:

(i)   poorer salary levels in comparison to other graduate occupations;
(ii) more limited career structures than in other professions;
(iii) the counter-attraction of other occupations/professions;
(iv) the perception of primary teaching as a female occupation.

All of them felt that the low proportion of male entrants was problematic. All tended to couch the problem in terms of the lack of male 'role models' for boys in primary schools. One person suggested that young boys take a great pride in being friends with an adult, that there can be real 'bonding' of the best kind. The teacher is a most influential figure.

All felt that something should be done to effect an equal balance in primary teaching and suggested a number of strategies. These were:

(i)   Raise the salary of primary teachers;
(ii)   Increase promotional prospects through reform of the career structure;
(iii) Continue in-career development opportunities (leading to Masters degrees etc.);
(iv)   Encourage single-sex boys schools to recommend primary teaching to their pupils as a serious career choice;
(v)   Develop a sense of service among second level pupils;
(vi)   Promote primary teaching in careers exhibitions;
(vii) Department of Education and Science should produce promotional booklet for primary teaching, in consultation with the colleges of education and the INTO;
(viii) Department of Education and Science should produce a video also in consultation with the colleges and the Union. This should show men as well as women as primary teachers.

To summarise, senior college of education managers/administrators were keenly aware of the degree of gender disparities at entry to colleges, which were a matter of great concern to them. They mainly conceived the problem in terms of the need for male 'role models' in schools. Even among those students already in the colleges, a performance gap was identified between the average levels of achievement of male and female student teachers on the academic and teaching practice elements of the course. All of the administrators felt that there was a need for a number of strategies to address the gender imbalance in primary teaching. These included strategies to address salary levels, promotion, pupil attitude and careers information, and promotional materials.

Experienced male primary teachers

A small-scale focus group study of a cohort of experienced male primary teachers was carried out in order to provide an additional dimension to the views of the professionals on the issue. The focus group interview was conducted with seven mid-career primary/elementary teachers. These men were aged 35–40 at the time of the interview.

With regard to their own entry into the profession of primary teaching, a rural–urban divide was evident, even within this small group of experienced male teachers. Accounts of their own entry to teaching suggested that the male teachers from rural backgrounds felt there was a general perception within their own community that this was a high status career choice. On the other hand, the men from the urban areas had an impression of swimming against the tide in their choice of primary teaching, particularly in the context of boys secondary schools.

Participants were first of all asked their reasons for entering teaching – what had attracted them into the profession. Three teachers stated that they had been encouraged to enter teaching when they were in post-primary school.

Teacher 1
It was definitely seen as the thing to aim for.

Teacher 2
Relative to other jobs that were available, say to the top end of the class, it was seen to have prospects and it was seen to have status.

Teacher 3
In the school I went to it was drummed into us, it was seen as the secure pensionable job, high status, and like it was up there. It was one of the things to be in . . . at that age, you didn't question it. There were only a few choices, if you didn't get X you got Y. If somebody had asked me what I wanted to be, I wouldn't have said I'm going to be a teacher.

The three teachers above all came from rural areas, and it was decided to ask the remaining teachers if their experience had been different in post-primary school. Two of the group had attended secondary school in Dublin and their responses were quite different.

Teacher 4
My situation was different. I was in a private secondary school in Dublin. Most people aspired to careers in science and medicine, and it was unheard of to go into primary teaching.

Teacher 5
Where I went to secondary school there was a male career guidance teacher. Male secondary teachers didn't value primary teaching, and that was definitely so in his case.

At this point, two other teachers had comments to add on career guidance (or the lack of it) during their years of post-primary education. Both felt quite strongly that a range of options was never presented to them. The general experience seemed to be one of 'drifting' into teaching, and the researcher asked if any of the participants had selected teaching for positive reasons:

Teacher 1
It wasn't until I was teaching two or three years myself that I realised I wanted to be a teacher, that I liked teaching.

Teacher 6
I went into teaching with no expectations. I didn't actually enjoy it until I got a few years experience.

None of the interviewees identified any intrinsic attractors but one teacher referred to extrinsic factors, such as free tuition and accommodation at the colleges of education (in general, undergraduate third level education was not free during this time).

Participants were asked to compare their initial perceptions of teaching as a career with their personal experiences in the job to date. The suggested areas for comparison were job satisfaction, image, status and career structure.

Teacher 3
There's very little vertical movement in teaching – I obviously didn't think of that when I went into it first.

Teacher 7
I think status has deteriorated rapidly over the past ten years. We have less respect, we're the subject of chat shows and generally a lot more vulnerable as a group.

Teacher 2
The idea of a career structure didn't enter into it in the early days, but when you saw people getting on in other jobs – either through ambition or inherent

promotional structures – it got to you . . . There doesn't appear to be the prospect of change within teaching.

Teacher 6
There needs to be a career structure – not necessarily a competitive structure – but more opportunity for career development. I think that people of our age, with ten to twenty years in the classroom, have ideas, have experience, yet that expertise can only really be applied in your own classroom.

The group were then asked if they felt that the working conditions of teachers had changed to any significant level since they began their careers. On the one hand, it was generally felt that social conditions had changed, and that added pressure was put on schools and teachers to deal with the new conditions. On the other hand, two teachers (who worked in schools serving areas designated as 'disadvantaged') spoke about the low pupil–teacher ratios and other conditions that had improved in recent times. As one teacher put it, there were new problems, but there was now much greater scope for solutions.

At this point Teacher 1 returned to the issue of career structure:

It's a dangerous job in a way, to put in a career structure, because you are working with young children: if you have a cut-throat career ladder system the children will suffer – but I firmly believe that there should be specialisms in areas like sport and music.

This teacher felt that areas of specialism, rather than an overly vertical career structure, would attract more men into teaching. Teacher 3 stated that he didn't wish to appear too negative by his initial statements, and he identified a number of improvements in working conditions for teachers over the past couple of years.

The issue of gender had been raised earlier by Teacher 1 when he suggested that curriculum specialisation in the primary school might attract more men. He also stated:

Generally, I believe that women are better at handling young children. Maybe they have more patience with the children.

In relation to the comparison of primary and post-primary teaching as suitable careers for men, most interviewees felt that there was little or no difference in terms of suitability, but they believed that the general public view was different from their own: namely, that post-primary teaching was more suitable for men and that it enjoyed a higher status.

Teacher 1
I don't feel any inferiority to secondary teachers if I'm teaching the 9–12 age group.

Teacher 2
I don't feel at all inferior to second level teachers. It's at least of equal importance if not of greater importance to be dealing with younger children. I would regard secondary teachers as having more privileges in regard to resources and staffing. I would have to say though that, when you are not involved in teaching, you would attach a higher status to secondary than to primary.

Teacher 7
There's some perception among male primary teachers that teaching 6th has a higher status than teaching infants, but we know it's ten times more difficult. The perception is the opposite: we're child-minders, they are little babies, and there's nothing more to it. The perception is still out there – primary teachers as a group have lower status than their secondary colleagues.

The main differences between men and women teachers were identified in positive terms. The participants reported that parents were usually pleased if their child had a male teacher. On this point they also felt that the presence of male teachers was important in schools.

Teacher 1
It's important for the children – boys and girls – to have male role models because we go about things in different ways.

The issue of child abuse and the possibility of suspicion of male teachers was explored. Teacher 1 believed that men are suspected more often of sexual abuse than are women, whereas women have to work harder to maintain discipline. None of the other interviewees expressed any opinion on this issue.

Participants were asked about issues of control – did they feel they had control and autonomy in their professional work, comparing teaching to the medical and legal professions? The researcher referred to the hierarchical relationships that are sometimes institutionalised in education. For most of the group this was not an issue in their lives, but for Teacher 5 it was quite different. He stated that he resented certain conditions of his work such as the obligation to 'sign on' each day and the insufficient time allowed for coffee breaks and lunch breaks. He elaborated somewhat on what he perceived to be a lack of recognition for qualifications and experience:

Many teachers go out and gain extra qualifications but they're not recognised or acknowledged in their own work situation. We have a tradition where people who do extra and above, they're not rewarded . . .

Teacher 5 went on to state that there were many teachers like himself in large schools who had been teaching for more than fifteen years and had not been promoted above the entry grade of teaching assistant. He also discussed the social and personal impact of working in a predominantly female staff:

> One thing that has annoyed me since I began teaching: I expected that there would be more of a social aspect to it, but the fact that, being a male in all female staff who have been there for twenty years, there's no new people coming in – it's the same people year after year – I think that's not healthy. None of the male kids in the school would aspire to live or to work like that.

Teacher 6 stated that he did not share this type of experience, and he felt that it would depend on the particular environment of each school. However, Teacher 3, who himself came from a mixed staff, agreed with Teacher 5 about the 'social and professional impact of stagnation on school staffs'. Teacher 7 felt that extra-curricular activities could help to offset such feelings of stagnation:

> Taking kids out for games, in many ways this has been a safety valve, because you establish different relationships and interests, and because of that maybe, you value yourself, the kids value you more highly.

Teacher 3 reflected some of the views expressed above by Teacher 5 about the lack of mobility in teaching. However, he agreed with Teacher 7 regarding the positive benefits of relating to children in extra-curricular settings. In his case it was with music. Teacher 2 summed up this part of the discussion thus:

> I think it's a very natural thing to look for affirmation in all walks of life, but the structure isn't really there for those working in education.

In response to the question of why so few men now take up primary/elementary teaching, the views of participants are illustrated by the quotations below.

Teacher 3
Salary and status

Teacher 5
The holidays and hours appeal more to mothers.

Teacher 3
Also, in the past couple of years Honours Irish classes have become predominantly female.

Teacher 2
When we were at that age we felt obliged to get jobs that were permanent and pensionable. Those who have started work in the last five or six years – an awful lot of work is based on short-term contracts.

Teacher 7
The perception has become more female-oriented, especially with younger kids. Male students – young men – are more influenced by that perception.

Interviewer
And is that perception worse now than when you entered ten to twenty years ago?

Most of the group
Yes

Teacher 7
And there are more opportunities nowadays also . . . Teaching doesn't offer enough attractions for the young male.

Teacher 5
It's not solely teaching: all the caring professions have changed in this way.

Teacher 3
The joy of a past-pupil telling me he's in Trinity doesn't really compare with having a company car (said half-jokingly).

Teacher 5
Business is promoted in secondary school – say with 'start your own company' – and those entrepreneurial values are emphasised. What's being done about teaching?

Teacher 7 agreed with this position, stating that junior business schemes for 5th and 6th class pupils were in place in his own school:

After this experience God is the marketplace – everyone wants to become a business person or manager.

Teacher 7 asked how many of the group present would encourage their sons, real or hypothetical, to choose teaching as a career. Most participants said that they would adopt a neutral position, neither encouraging nor discouraging their sons in choosing teaching as a career. Also, it was generally felt that the choice should not be made for family reasons, but rather on the relative merits of that career. The options would have to be clear, and one participant said that he would wish his son to have some 'time out' before entering third level education, as opposed to entering any career naively. However, Teacher 4 was less than neutral on this question:

If one of my two sons came home and said they wanted to be a teacher, I'd be very pleased with myself. In the end we're there for the kids, it's the reason why we're there. It's very hard to quantify that: they don't have to be doing degrees in Trinity. You get a kick out of doing it, it's very hard to explain. Like, the money's not great or the status, and you turn on the radio to hear M. . . . F. . . . (a radio presenter) complaining. But I wouldn't change it for anything. If the kids said to me they were anxious to teach, I'd be very proud.

In summary, with regard to their own entry into the profession of primary teaching, a rural–urban divide was evident, even within this small group. Accounts of their own entry to teaching suggested that the male teachers from rural backgrounds felt there was a general perception within their own community that this was a high status career choice. The men from the urban areas had an impression of swimming against the tide in their choice of primary teaching, particularly in the context of boys secondary schools. There was a strong perception of a poor career structure and a lack of mobility in primary teaching among these male teachers – something they had not been fully aware of when they entered the profession. Apart from this, there was a generally positive view that there had been improvements in teachers' working conditions in recent years. There was some evidence of a perception among these teachers that women were better with very young children and that they had more patience. However, this view did not emerge strongly from the study. There was a somewhat stronger feeling that the public at large perceived working with older children as more prestigious than working with younger children. Some concern was expressed that there might be more suspicion of men because of fears of child abuse, but this was not a strong feature of the study. There was greater support for the notion that the media are biased against teachers. There was also support for the value of involvement in extra-curricular work, and that a degree of subject specialisation at primary school might make it more attractive to males. The reasons offered for the low proportion of men entering teaching were as follows: lower salary and status; holidays and hours appealing more to mothers; more females taking Honours Irish and hence being eligible; an increase in the number of short-term contracts at the start of the career; the impression of the profession as increasingly feminised; a wider choice of careers for school leavers; the promotion of business in secondary schools and lack of promotion of primary teaching. The reasons offered by these experienced teachers for the low proportion of males entering primary teaching very much reflected the views of the school leavers, student teachers, guidance counsellors and college administrators.

Summary

The initial motivations and subsequent career experience of professionals colour the way they, in turn, advise pupils and student teachers. In this study of guidance counsellors, college administrators and experienced teachers there was a generally positive view of the teaching role, although it was also perceived as having a poor career and pay structure. While the teachers interviewed all expressed gender-egalitarian views with regard to the suitability of men and women to teaching, there was evidence of some hesitancy with regard to the appropriateness of primary teaching for academically high achieving males. The view that women are better with very young children was also evident in the responses. Guidance counsellors, administrators and experienced male teachers were concerned with the gender imbalance in teaching and the explanations they offered for the falling numbers of men in the classroom did not differ greatly from those of the school leavers and student teachers.

Chapter 8

Conclusion: can more men be attracted to the classroom?

The quality of the teaching workforce is of central concern to policy makers around the world. In this regard, the decline of the proportion of males in teaching has been highlighted as an issue of disquiet. In most developed countries women are numerically and proportionately dominant in first and second level teaching (although not in management). At the outset of this volume on gender and teaching the question was raised – to what extent is this a problem?

Public discourse has focused on a number of issues. The first of these relates to academic underachievement among boys in second level schools. The research reviewed here suggests that factors affecting boys' levels of achievement are complex. They include, very crucially, factors such as social class and locality. It is much less clear that teacher gender plays any significant role.

The second, perhaps related, issue identified by commentators in the media and elsewhere related to gender differences in teacher competence. Data on the awards of the most recent graduates of primary and second level teacher education courses in Ireland (the case-study country) indicated that women, on the whole, obtain higher awards than men, especially on primary teaching courses. In this sense, then, increasing proportions of women entering the profession should have a positive, rather than a negative, impact on levels of competence.

Public debate has also suggested that the status of teaching as a profession has declined. The reasons for any changes in the status of teaching are complex, and it is difficult to be precise or definite about the effects of feminisation on this. Insofar as lower rates of pay and/or status in teaching (in comparison to other all-graduate professions) are related to female dominance, they perhaps raise more questions about the position of women in society than about teaching itself.

There are some issues in respect of which increasing levels of feminisation at point of entry to teaching could be problematic. The first is the issue of equality in the labour market. It is undesirable from this perspective that any occupation, be it engineering or primary teaching, is unduly dominated by one gender or the other. The second matter of concern lies in the area of the socialisation of pupils. There is some evidence that both male and female pupils benefit from a representation of both genders on a school staff, although more research is required on this. A further problem is that of the hidden curriculum of schooling. What are pupils learning about male–female power relationships if the teaching profession, and its management structures, are highly gender-differentiated?

Notwithstanding debates concerning whether teaching is a 'profession' (by whatever definition), or rates of pay, or status, there is no doubt that in a society increasingly dependent on the knowledge industry, and one where citizenship and equality are so greatly affected by education, the role of the teacher is a crucial one. The teacher plays a pivotal role in the areas of both the formal and the hidden curriculum. Teaching has been, and will undoubtedly continue to be, an important professional career path for women, one in which they have distinguished themselves extremely well. It has also been an important career for men, one in which they too have been very distinguished.

This book explored a number of themes relating to the choice of teaching as a career. It examined the existing balance of women and men in the teaching profession internationally; the patterns at entry to teaching; and, finally, some of the questions that are raised by these trends. The analysis of international trends formed an essential background to the study of gender differences in choice of teaching as a career. The questions raised concerning men, women and teaching were explored by means of research among school leavers, student teachers and experienced educational professionals. Ireland is the site in which these issues were explored. While entry to teaching in Ireland demonstrates patterns that have a social and historical specificity, given Ireland's specific location as a country that has, in policy terms, embraced the global changes of late modernity, it is argued that the trends observable in this study of gender differences in choice of teaching in Ireland may be interpreted as an 'ideal type' in terms of the structuring of the profession.

Men, women and teaching

International research makes a clear distinction between 'sex' and 'gender'. This can best be summarised by using 'sex' to refer to the most basic physiological differences between women and men. 'Gender', on the other hand, refers to the culturally specific patterns of behaviour, which may be attached to the sexes. It is, thus, culturally determined and highly variable. Cultural definitions and perceptions of 'gender-appropriate' behaviour patterns, choices and occupations are fundamental to understanding male/female differences at entry to teaching.

The 'feminisation of teaching' refers to the processes by which teaching became a mostly female occupation. A number of factors which have contributed to this development have been identified, namely, the economic policy of education administrators, beliefs about the nature of women, and patriarchal control. These factors, it has been argued, have been less influential in rural areas than in indus-
⁻ʼlised, urban areas.

ᵗhe past twenty years, most empirical qualitative work on gender,
ᵢₑctivity and schooling have studied girls rather than boys. It has
ₐt future research could be employed to understand more about

the experience of boys in education, especially with regard to the gendered subjectivity of boys, an area which might reveal more variation than had been heretofore assumed.

Research on the social construction of masculinity within schools suggests that the whole area of masculinity and education is a problematic one. First of all, the relation between the two is complex in that, although education systems have been subject to tight patriarchal control, there is a tendency for some masculine identities to be formed in varying degrees of opposition to that authority. Second, there may be conflict and struggle in the definitions of various masculinities, and a whole range of problems ensues from this divergence. There are obvious difficulties for those who do not identify with 'hegemonic' masculinities. This would suggest that male entry into highly feminised occupations might be a difficult choice for young men.

Existing patterns suggest that the feminisation of teaching involves a number of conditions: a high proportion of women in the teaching profession; a strengthened feminine interpretation of the specific professional activity; a reduction in social prestige of the teaching profession due to the high number of women employed in it; and/or a domestic ideology. The first of these is clearly observable in Ireland, especially in primary teaching. The remainder were explored in this research via the perceptions of school leavers, student teachers and experienced education professionals.

Previous research identified the tendency towards differentiated career paths within the teaching profession according to gender, particularly with regard to senior management positions in schools. This last factor has obvious implications for males within the profession, which at face value could be considered to be advantageous for them and perhaps attractive to them at the point of decision-making about career choices. Whether this is indeed a significant factor for males choosing teaching was also explored in this research.

Previous research also suggested that men's interest in female-dominated fields is, in general, less usual than women's interest in male-dominated fields. Although there are perceptible patterns, practices and ideologies in various careers, the structural configurations of gender differences vary from job to job, as do individual, subjective experiences of masculinity or femininity. The perception of particular occupations as female-dominated, and the associated perceptions (both negative and positive) of the minority of men who work in them, may have implications for school leavers' perceptions and decision-making. Previous studies on men in teaching suggest that there are conflicts and contradictions in their role. A good deal of these are focused on being male in what is perceived to be a female profession.

Nevertheless, it was recognised that the operation of difference is, to a large extent, mediated by wider socialising factors and by ideological constraints. The relative advantage that girls might have with regard to the entry requirements of initial teacher education does not, in itself, explain why so few boys consider primary teaching as a career option. Recent patterns of similarity in subject choice may also be a cause for concern, insofar as, increasingly, arts and humanities subjects appear to be valued less by boys and girls alike, and the decline in their status at school may reflect a wider societal reappraisal of educational aspirations. Curricular choice is just one part of the structural socialisation that takes place in any school. Ideologies that sustain beliefs about such differences are also central. These issues provided the backdrop for the survey of schools leavers, student teachers and professionals and of their perceptions of teaching.

Perceptions and choice of teaching

The study of school leavers, student teachers and professionals looked in particular at why the number of young men choosing primary teaching as a career has fallen so dramatically. The objectives of the survey of school leavers were: to look at their course and career choices; the motivation and influences behind those choices; their perceptions of different jobs; their attitudes to teaching as a career for men and women. Also included was basic demographic information on parents' education and occupations, and on students' academic level. A further facet was the debate to be gleaned from interviews with guidance counsellors in the schools selected. The objectives of the study of student teachers were to obtain information on their backgrounds and academic achievements, their reasons for choosing primary teaching, and their attitudes to and perceptions of teaching. Information was also to be sought from senior college administrators on their perceptions of the key issues pertaining to primary teaching as a career. In addition a focus group study of a small group of experienced male primary/elementary school teachers was conducted.

The research instruments were developed with reference to similar work done elsewhere – especially in the United States, Britain, Switzerland and Northern Ireland. There was also consultation with personnel from the colleges of education and from the teacher unions, as well as pilot studies with school pupils and student teachers.

A total of 1,049 respondents gave valid returns to the school leaver survey, of whom 40 per cent were male and 60 per cent female. These pupils were distributed throughout the different school types in 16 Irish second level/high schools selected for study. All of the students were in the final year of school and all had indicated that they intended to apply for a third level place, a prerequisite for inclusion in the survey. The analysis showed that the girls' academic performance was significantly higher than that of boys, mirroring overall patterning in pupil examinations as a whole. From the point of view of entry to primary teaching, the pool of suitably qualified boys is smaller than the equivalent pool of girls. In addition, higher level Irish is a requirement for entry to initial teacher education colleges in Ireland, but less than half of all of the pupils surveyed intended to take it in their final examinations. Boys were significantly less likely than girls to take higher level Irish. Thus the pool of qualified male applicants was reduced even further among these school leavers.

It was evident that a certain amount of critical assessment of their own chances had already taken place among the students themselves. Those who indicated that they would put primary/elementary teaching as their *first* preference (just over 6 per cent of all students, almost all girls) had grade point averages in the two top bands, and were taking a higher than average number of honours subjects for Leaving Certificate. The proportion of those who intended to put primary teaching as one of their top university/college choices was 17 per cent, of whom 15 per cent were males and 85 per cent females.

Examination of first preference course choices for all areas of study showed major gender differences in most fields. Male choices were significantly more often directed to technology, computers and commerce, female choices to humanities, primary teaching, nursing, social science, medical and dentistry. In short, many course choices seemed to be gender stereotyped, with boys choosing from a narrower range of courses. Responses to the questions on career choices, as opposed to university/college choices, revealed understandably lower levels of certainty. The gender differences observable in choice of university/college courses, were also evident in relation to choice of career. The data showed that the split between technical and caring professions to some extent coincided with the gender divide. Altogether 13 per cent of the sample expressed an interest in some form of teaching (i.e. at first or second level) as a career – six per cent in primary teaching, five per cent in second level teaching and just a small proportion in specialist teaching such as P.E. and materials technology. Significantly more girls were attracted to teaching of whichever type.

Some 87 per cent of respondents reported having had career guidance, and most found it useful. However, parents emerged as the most influential for course and career decision-making. 'Guidance counsellor' was judged most influential by just over a fifth of boys, but by a significantly lower proportion of girls. Thus guidance counsellors appeared to play an important, but not a primary role in course and career choice.

The attitudes or orientations of students towards work were assessed using a measure of the things highly valued by them when they were thinking about a career. Three different types of attitude/orientation to work were identified – 'intrinsic' (high value on job satisfaction, fulfilment, creativity); 'extrinsic' (high value on pay, prestige, job conditions); 'altruistic' (high value attached to caring, 'making a difference', or to children). Overall, intrinsic values were most highly valued, followed by extrinsic, and finally by altruistic values. There were significant gender differences. Girls attached greater importance to intrinsic and altruistic values; boys to extrinsic. The findings suggest that, while intrinsic factors are usually most important for both girls and boys in choice of career, ancillary reasons are different for each sex, with girls rating altruistic factors higher and boys tending to value extrinsic ones. People choosing primary teaching (and they were mainly girls) attached most importance to intrinsic values and were also significantly more likely than other respondents to have attached high importance to altruistic values. They attached less importance than others to extrinsic values.

Students' perceptions of primary and second level teaching were established, with statistically significant gender differences evident here and in students' perceptions of other careers listed. Both sexes thought that the job of medical doctor would offer most job satisfaction. In relation to other career satisfaction, girls were most likely to see social worker and primary teacher as offering most satisfaction, boys to offer engineer, computer programmer and television producer. 'Secondary teacher' ranked poorly in relation to primary teaching on this dimension. Students had very stereotyped views on the careers suited to men and women – engineering for men, primary teaching followed by social work for women. School leavers' perceptions on the careers offering greater financial returns were almost evenly split between doctor and lawyer, while the caring professions practically vanished from the chart. The role of medical doctor was also seen as having the highest prestige and of being the career of most benefit to society. Other caring professions, social work and primary teaching, came second and third as being of most benefit to society. Intending primary teachers were most likely to see their chosen career as the one of most social benefit. A broader group who had given some consideration to teaching also ranked primary teaching somewhat higher. However, no such difference was to be seen in relation to second level teaching. The lack of high ranking of second level teaching on all of the variables was notable. For these school leavers it would seem to be held in a good deal lower regard than primary teaching. Another factor worthy of note was the level of unanimity and conservatism among the school leavers' perceptions – for example, engineering for boys, perceptions of high level of pay, prestige and social benefit attaching to the older professions, especially medicine and law. However, primary teaching appears to be a respected profession even among those not choosing it. As regards how enjoyable the different careers might be, primary teaching was ranked in the top three for enjoyment, only slightly behind TV producer and at the same level as engineer. There were significant gender differences here also. Girls had higher positive perceptions about primary teaching than boys did. Boys had better perceptions of engineering. The career which appeared least enjoyable to students was that of second level teacher. It was rated lowest as regards level of enjoyment. Gender differences were apparent here also – boys' perceptions of second level teaching were significantly less positive than girls. Boys were less likely to rate teaching, or indeed other caring occupations, as enjoyable.

Location (i.e. whether urban or rural) was significantly related to choice of teaching. Those choosing primary teaching were most likely to be attending a community school and least likely to be at a boys single-sex school (nobody from a boys single-sex school intended to give a first preference to primary teaching). Those who had seriously considered any type of teaching (including primary) were most likely to be at a coeducational secondary school, in a rural area, or from a cluster of schools in the most rural region of Ireland. The least likely to have considered teaching (any type) were from boys single-sex schools, or from the most urbanised regions of Ireland.

The reasons given for choosing and not choosing teaching showed considerable division between the sexes. Girls' interest in teaching seemed to stem from an engagement with children and the mechanics of teaching. Boys seemed more influenced by externals such as job conditions. Boys seemed to be less oriented towards children or less willing to admit to an interest in teaching. The most common reasons given for not choosing teaching were those that loom largest for sixth year students: points and course requirements (i.e. higher level Irish). In spite of the fact that the points level and the higher level Irish requirement were offered more frequently than other reasons as factors in not choosing teaching, the data showed that less than half of the sample were aware of this requirement. However, almost twice as many girls as boys were aware of it. Girls were also significantly more likely than boys to estimate the points requirements for initial teacher education courses correctly. Less than half of the students had estimated a primary teacher's starting salary correctly. Most tended to overestimate it. People choosing primary teaching tended to be aware of the requirements. This suggested that the responses of those intending to put primary teaching first on their university/ college forms represented fairly realistic choices.

The influence of 'significant others' in the students' decision-making in relation to primary teaching was explored. Students were asked how they felt others would react if they chose primary teaching as a career. In general students felt that parents would be more positive than any other group (including teachers and guidance counsellors), and that mothers would be more positive than fathers. Girls felt much more often than boys that others in their lives would be positive about primary teaching as a choice for them. Although just over a tenth of the students felt there would be a negative reaction from their peer group to such a choice, boys were a great deal more likely (over seven times as likely) to feel this as were girls. Young men, undoubtedly, perceived there would be relatively less support for them from significant others for a decision to go into primary teaching. A young woman, on the other hand, was likely to perceive herself as having the support of almost everyone.

When the leavers' perceptions of a selection of aspects of primary teaching were explored it emerged that extrinsic features were the most attractive to the vast majority of the students – the short day, long holidays and job security. There were significant gender differences with regard to other aspects perceived as attractive. These reflected the greater altruistic/other directed orientation of girls, which has been observed earlier. The aspects of primary teaching perceived as most off-putting were intrinsic ones – after-school planning and correcting, classroom management and discipline, and upholding the religious ethos of the schools. Significant gender differences were found here too – girls found these aspects less off-putting than boys, as did those intending to put primary teaching as a choice. Girls were more oriented to the needs of children – again reflecting the more marked orientation towards children observed earlier.

Leavers' views of primary teaching, as compared to second level teaching, were rather stereotyped. Almost half thought that primary teaching was best suited to women. Significantly more boys held this view. Girls were much more likely to think that men and women were equally suited to it. Far more of the leavers thought second level teaching was equally suited to men and women, although there were, again, gender differences. There was greater gender stereotyping of primary teaching than of second level teaching, with boys more likely to have stereotyped views than girls. Just over half of the school leavers thought women made better primary school teachers, while, on the other hand, nearly two thirds thought men and women would be equally good at second level. The main reasons that women were thought to be better teachers at primary level were rather stereotyped – i.e. students suggested that they were more patient, motherly or caring, or simply 'better with young children'.

Gender differences were apparent here also, with more girls having egalitarian views. When asked to give their rationale for the low proportion of men in primary teaching the most frequently offered explanation by both boys and girls was that it is a woman's job; women are better with children. However, girls significantly more often offered this reason, whereas boys highlighted much more frequently than did girls other reasons such as primary teaching being boring or stressful, or other careers being more attractive. Issues that might have been expected to play a much greater part (on the basis of media coverage of them) in the respondents' explanation of the low proportion of male entrants to primary teaching (such as the level of pay or allegations about male child abuse) did not feature highly.

The attitudes of the school leavers to five dimensions of teaching were explored: the nature of teaching, its status, women in teaching, men in teaching and gender equality in primary teaching. It would appear from the findings that boys were less engaged with the issues relating to primary teaching than were girls. They were less inclined to have strong feelings about any of the issues explored. While their dominant view of primary teaching was egalitarian in gender terms (albeit significantly less so than that of the girls), they were also a great deal more likely to agree with a statement on male control than were girls, but were less likely to agree that boys need male teachers as role models. They also were less likely to see primary teaching as a job with a lot of interest and variety. Girls appeared to find the issues under examination of much greater salience, and to have a significantly greater orientation towards equality and caring.

The strongest feelings about the various dimensions of teaching were expressed in the responses of the students who intended to put primary teaching as their first preference on their CAO application forms. They were the group who felt most strongly that being a good primary teacher depends on personality and training, not gender. They also felt most strongly that there is a lot of interest and variety in primary teaching, and that teachers perform a service of moral value to society. The wider group who expressed a preference for any type of teaching (including primary but also second level) had very similar views to those prioritising primary teaching. This wider group differed in just one noteworthy respect – they appeared to be less focused on the intrinsic aspects of teaching.

With regard to the influence of social class background on academic achievement, the research showed that pupils from the professional, employer and managerial social classes were a great deal more likely than others to have had Junior Certificate grade point averages in the highest achievement band, and were less likely to have scored in the two lowest bands. However, while social class background had an impact on academic performance, it had little overall impact on preference for teaching among the school leavers, or for selection of primary teaching at third level. However, when the question of the influence of having *teachers* within the family circle was specifically examined, it was found that respondents who had teachers as family members were significantly more likely than others to have given some consideration to teaching as a career. They were also significantly more likely to have declared an intention to put primary teaching as their first preference on their university/college application forms. It would appear that exposure to teaching within the family gives a very positive orientation to students towards the profession, in spite of whatever complaints they might also hear about teaching and its conditions. Given the high points level required for entry to primary teaching, there may be a form of 'double effect' at work here. First, teachers as an occupational grouping fall within Social Classes 1 and 2 (the professional, employer and managerial grouping) which are more likely to achieve higher levels of academic performance in public examinations. They are thus more likely to be candidates for a third level course in the first place. Second, exposure to teaching at home provides a positive orientation to the profession.

A survey was conducted among second year student teachers in the five primary colleges of education in Ireland. Questionnaires were completed by 457 students – 46 males and 411 females. Thus, 90 per cent of the students surveyed in the colleges of education were female. The vast majority had entered the colleges directly from school although, at 12 per cent, the proportion of mature entrants was twice the national average for third level at the time of the survey. As regards place of origin of the student teachers the more rural regions of Ireland were over-represented. Fully half of the student teachers were from rural areas, with less than a third of the proportion that would have been expected from large urban areas, given the population distribution in the country as a whole. An even greater proportion of the male students were from rural areas. There was a disproportionate representation of students from middle-class and farming backgrounds. In addition, over 60 per cent of the students had a near relative who was a teacher.

The student teachers in the colleges of education had been high academic performers at Leaving Certificate. Indeed, a substantial minority had points levels which would have qualified them for entry to most courses in the university system, including the so-called 'high prestige' courses. The differences between males and females on points level were not large, although male performance was somewhat lower. There were, however, significantly more males with grades lower than 'B' in honours Irish.

When student teachers were asked what had been their first preference when applying to university/college, a total of 84 per cent of male and 93 per cent of female first preferences were for courses leading to the caring professions (including primary teaching). This suggests a high orientation towards caring by this group, with an even greater orientation by females than males. In this sense it reflects the patterns observable among the school leaver cohort. As was the case with the school leavers, parents had by far the greatest influence on students' decision-making. It would appear that, in retrospect, student teachers evaluated guidance counsellors as having had very little influence on their decision-making. However, more than a quarter of males found the more general category of 'teacher' to have been influential. Overall gender differences in students' perceptions of the reaction of others to their decision to take up primary teaching as a career confirmed the finding from the school leaver survey that young men get much less positive reinforcement and support for this career choice then do girls. In this context it is likely that many young men found it difficult to make such a 'non-traditional' choice.

The career-related attitudes of the student teachers were explored. In comparison to the school leavers' average scores on the scales, both male and female students were more strongly oriented to altruistic values than were second level pupils. This was particularly marked in the case of the female student teachers. The student teachers were less oriented towards intrinsic values, and particularly towards extrinsic values, than were school leavers. This stronger orientation towards caring among the student teachers confirms the linkages between caring and primary teaching already observed in this study. The data also suggested that males studying to be primary teachers were most markedly different from other males in relation to their attitudes to caring. Indeed, males going into primary teaching were much less oriented towards factors like pay and prestige, and much more oriented towards caring and towards others than were males in general.

The perceptions of the same range of careers as had been explored with school leavers were explored with student teachers. They ranked primary teaching, followed by doctor, as offering the greatest job satisfaction. Similar to the school leavers, they were rather stereotyped in their perceptions of careers which were most suitable for men and for women – engineering for men, primary teaching and social work for women. Doctors, lawyers and computer programmers were perceived as having highest levels of pay, while primary and second level teaching were not mentioned at all. Doctors were viewed as having the highest prestige, although primary teaching was ranked in the top three by more than half of the students, and by just over one fifth of second level respondents. Doctors and primary teachers were viewed by the third level students as being jobs of most social benefit. Primary teaching was included in the top three rankings by almost all student teachers and by almost half of the school leavers. Not surprisingly, primary student teachers were very positive (if somewhat stereotyped) in their perceptions of primary teaching as a career – apart from the pay dimension. Second level teaching was far less positively ranked. It was perceived least often of all the careers, apart from accountancy, as offering the most job satisfaction. Students also perceived second level teaching as having lower prestige, and being of less social benefit than primary teaching. The student teachers, as might be expected, were more positively disposed towards teaching than were the school leaver respondents. This more positive orientation was accounted for primarily by females and by a more positive orientation to primary teaching rather than to secondary teaching.

Although they were highly oriented to intrinsic and altruistic values, the aspects of primary teaching identified by the student teachers as most attractive were extrinsic factors – the short day and good holidays; job security and availability; a respected position in the community. School leavers had also seen most of these factors as the most attractive. However, two other factors were also seen as very attractive by the student teachers: making a difference to people's lives and personal fulfilment – an 'altruistic' factor and an 'intrinsic' one. The aspects of primary teaching identified by student teachers as most off-putting were after-school planning and correcting; having responsibility for managing and disciplining up to 30 pupils; and upholding the school's religious ethos by preparing children for church events. These three were also identified by school leavers as most off-putting. However, student teachers found two of these three even more off-putting than did the school leavers. It would seem that experience of these two integral aspects of the primary teacher's job rendered them even less attractive, as the student teachers would already have had exposure to these aspects during teaching practice. In the case of only one of the fifteen aspects of primary teaching was there a gender difference. Females were significantly more inclined than males to view involvement with children's day-to-day needs as attractive.

On the issues of which gender was most suited to, and better at, primary teaching student teachers were rather less stereotyped in their views than school leavers. Their view of male/female suitability and competence in second level teaching were much more comparable to those of the school leavers. This would suggest that exposure to the professional demands of primary teaching and greater knowledge about it served to reduce the stereotyping. It can be seen from the student teachers' responses to the twenty-one items on attitudes to teaching that there was more agreement with the gender egalitarian statements and on those relating to the nature and status of teaching, than there was with those which related to stereotypical roles and perceptions of men and women in teaching. Where stereotypical responses were espoused this was significantly more likely among men than among women. However, both male and female student teachers expressed high levels of agreement with the suggestion that it is important for children to see men in caring roles.

Compared to the attitudes to teaching among the school leavers, there was greater agreement among student teachers that primary teaching is a demanding and exhausting job but also that there is a lot of interest and variety in it. Scores on these two items had been shown to differ significantly between school leavers choosing primary teaching and others. There was greater agreement among student teachers of both genders than among school leavers that teachers perform a service of moral value to society, and that they are able to influence children for the good. These two items had also given rise to significant differences among pupils selecting primary teaching and those selecting other courses. On the whole, student teachers were rather less stereotyped than the school leavers in their views on women in teaching, as measured by their average scores. Male student teachers were less inclined than male school leavers to endorse stereotyped views on men in teaching. As regards the two statements presenting egalitarian views on gender equality in education, levels of agreement among student teachers were higher than among school pupils as a whole. However, among school leavers these too had been significantly related to choice of teaching, with greater agreement among those selecting primary teaching than among others.

Student teachers were asked their reasons for choosing primary teaching as a career. Child-focused reasons were those most frequently offered for the choice of primary teaching, although these were offered proportionately more frequently by women. Many more women had had experience of working with children before college. A liking for young children was the most frequently cited reason for choosing primary rather than second level teaching – again more frequently cited by women students. Two thirds of the sample could see themselves in primary teaching in twenty years' time, with somewhat more women than men having this kind of commitment. Enjoyment of the job was the most frequently given reason for staying while wanting a break was the most frequently envisaged reason for moving on.

Interviews were conducted with guidance counsellors in the sample schools, with senior college of education administrators and with a small focus group of experienced male primary teachers. Overall guidance counsellors were very positive about primary teaching as a career and indeed about second level teaching also. Just a quarter selected a career other than teaching as offering greater job satisfaction. They were gender egalitarian in their views on the suitability and capability of men and women in primary teaching. There was just one exception to this gender egalitarian and positive approach. When asked about the appropriateness of primary teaching as a career choice for high achieving boys and girls most thought it appropriate for girls but only half thought primary teaching appropriate for high achieving boys. Although it was found that parents were the principal influence on school leavers' and students' career choices, guidance counsellors still play an important role. The points requirement for entry to colleges of education is relatively high, and the distribution of points among students already in teacher education indicated that a substantial minority of the student teachers surveyed would have qualified for most of the so-called 'high prestige' courses. It would appear, therefore, to be important, if the proportion of male entrants were to be increased, that high achieving boys are actively encouraged to consider primary teaching as a serious and attractive option.

The college of education administrators interviewed were keenly aware of the degree of gender disparities at entry to the colleges. These were a matter of great concern to them. They mainly conceived the problem in terms of the need for male 'role models' in schools. Even among those students already in the colleges, a performance gap was identified between the average levels of achievement of male and female student teachers on the academic and teaching practice elements of the course. All of the administrators felt that there was a need for a number of strategies to address the gender imbalance in primary teaching. These included strategies to address salary levels, promotion, pupil attitude and careers information, and promotional materials.

The reasons which emerged from the small focus-group study of experienced male primary teachers as accounting for the low proportion of men entering teaching were as follows: lower salary and status than some other professional occupations; the holidays and hours of primary/elementary teaching appealing more to mothers; more females taking Honours Irish and thus eligible for entry to initial teacher education; an increase in the number of short term contracts at the start of the career; the impression of the profession as increasingly feminised; a wider choice of careers for school leavers; promotion of business in secondary schools and lack of promotion of primary teaching.

Men and the classroom – an unresolvable dilemma?

Arising from this study of international research of school leavers, guidance counsellors, third level students and college administrators, and male primary teachers, a number of implications emerge. The findings of the case study in Ireland clearly demonstrate the complexity of the problem of attracting more men into teaching, but especially into primary/elementary teaching. There are complex economic, historical, cultural and sociological factors at play. The changing patterns of entry to teaching are associated with changes in the economy, in the industrial structure and in the occupational structure. Ireland is currently experiencing processes that have been experienced in many other countries a decade and, in some instances, a number of decades ago. In addition, to a significant degree one is dealing not only with professional issues but with the social construction of masculinity and femininity. To some extent, attempts to change these processes could be described as attempts to change the course of history.

The analysis here implies that the feminisation of teaching is a historical and economic process as much as it is a social, psychological or educational one. Research on the history and sociology of teaching indicates that the gender composition of the teaching force at primary and at second level is influenced by the level of economic development and degree of urbanisation of regions and countries, by the economic policies pursued by state administrators, especially educational administrators, by beliefs about the nature of women and men, and by patriarchal control. The historical patterns identified, and statistics presented on gender and teaching from around the world over the last quarter of the twentieth century, indicate that the proportion of women in teaching at primary and at second level could be used as a referent for the economic development and level of urbanisation of a society or region. Personal choices made by women and men to select, or not to select, teaching as a career are mediated by the level of economic and industrial development, of occupational diversity, and of the broad patterns of gender differentiation in occupations in a society.

These choices are also affected by the extent and nature of patriarchy in a society at any given epoch, or in any given location, and the degree to which males have higher status than females or to which male dominated occupations have higher status than female dominated ones. It must also be recognised that, where patriarchal values are the dominant values in a society, women will have internalised them to a very significant degree and will be active agents in the socialisation of others, and particularly of the young, in such dominant values. This is illustrated in our research by the identification by primary college student teachers of parents (but especially mothers) and teachers (who are predominantly female) as being most influential in their choice of a career.

Patterns of choice or lack of choice of teaching as a profession are linked to the social construction of masculinity and femininity. Research indicates, and this is evident in these findings, that the feminisation of teaching is a cumulative historical and social process. The manner in which the feminisation of teaching has occurred involves subtle patterns of socialisation in Western cultures. The review of research points out that, in many Western societies, there has been an ideological link between women's domestic roles and their commitment to teaching. This 'domestic ideology' proposes that women are 'naturally' more disposed towards nurture than are men. This is particularly reflected in the perceived association between the nurturing role of women and their assumed greater suitability for teaching very young children. This was officially reflected by the state as early as the beginning of the twentieth century in Ireland in the official exclusion of men from the teaching of infants. This bar continued for a considerable portion of the first part of the century in Ireland and is currently reflected in the low proportions of men in early and infant education. It is reflected in findings by Irish researchers among school-goers in the 1980s that part-time work is considered to be compatible with the perceived responsibilities of married women.

The domestic ideology which provides cultural support for the notion that women's careers should be compatible with homemaking responsibilities, while weakening somewhat over the last couple of decades, is still strong. It was evident in a number of ways in the findings in this study – e.g. in the perception of school leavers and, albeit to a lesser extent, student teachers, that women were best suited to the career of primary teaching, and, in the views of some of the guidance counsellors that women made better primary teachers because of their caring qualities. No such ideology exists to provide a connection between men's careers and homemaking/parental responsibilities. Indeed, both student teachers and school leavers surveyed in this study gave, in very similar proportions, as by far their most frequent explanation for the low proportion of men in primary teaching the perception that it is a woman's job.

Schools play an extremely important part in the formation of gender identities. When considering the social construction of gender identities in school, factors such as educational organisation and policy, social class and locality are strong intervening variables. Compulsory schooling and higher retention rates in recent years may result for some boys (in particular, but not exclusively, working-class boys) in the formation of a male counter-culture in which school figures as a place for 'sissies' and girls.

The research examined the third level choices of school leavers across the range of school types in the Irish second level system. Subject provision and allocation varies between school types and might be expected to influence career choices. Research on the Irish school system shows that school ethos also varies. In the schools in this project there was little variation between school leavers from each school type in the choice of primary teaching, with one exception: nobody from a boys secondary school chose primary teaching as a career – nor could guidance counsellors recall anyone who had made such a choice in recent years. Boys secondary schools would appear to most strongly incorporate a 'masculinist' ethos. This means that, in formulating educational and policy responses to the issue, the value systems of schools must be addressed, particularly of boys schools. Nevertheless, the mechanisms of the wider society must also be included in any assessment of the problem. The research here suggests that to address the feminisation of teaching (or indeed any other profession), there must be a focus on the socialisation of boys, not only in schools but in the wider society. This is particularly illustrated by two of the findings here: the lower scores of the male school leavers on the measures of academic performance and the lower scores of males on the measures relating to caring, or other-directedness. Both of these were significantly related to choice of teaching but both are rooted, not only in schooling, but in more general patterns of male socialisation. The somewhat poorer academic performance of boys, reflected in this research (and in public examination results), and the fact that fewer take up Honours Irish at Leaving Certificate (which is a compulsory requirement for entry to primary teaching) are two factors associated with boys' schooling and wider patterns of male socialisation which are very directly related to male entry to primary teaching as they reduce the pool of suitably qualified boys.

Research into the social construction of masculinity suggests that it may be more accurate and useful to conceptualise the issue in terms of a number of 'ideal types', or categories, of masculine identity. The research review in this study suggests that, in Western societies, the earliest stages of the formation of masculine identity involve processes which result in the association of a masculine identity with patterns of behaviour that are 'not feminine'. For some men, such processes may also involve the denigration of the 'feminine'. The research also indicates that, while in most societies there is a 'hegemonic', or socially dominant, form of masculinity, at any one time this may also co-exist with other definitions and forms of masculinity some of which may be in opposition to the hegemonic form, some complicit with it. It is also suggested that, in rapidly changing post-modern societies, schools and educational institutions are places where gender identities, but especially masculine identities, are constantly being negotiated, tested and constructed.

Research has also indicated that different learning cultures may emerge in the different subject areas which support either masculine interests (e.g. in physical sciences, engineering or technology) or feminine interests (e.g. arts and humanities). It is in this situation, and within the context of a highly feminised teaching profession, that male educational and occupational choices are being made. It would appear that, in patriarchal societies, as the proportion of women in an occupation increases, entry to occupations which are highly feminised, or which are in the process of becoming so, becomes an increasingly difficult choice for men. This is borne out by the findings of this research in a number of different ways – by the analysis of the patterns of male and female entrance to the professions, by the much lower proportion of boys than girls among the school leavers who were actively considering primary teaching as a career, by the low proportion of male student teachers in the colleges of education, and by the highly differentiated perceptions of females and males among the school leavers and students concerning the levels of support they would receive from families, and especially from peers, in the choice of a primary teaching career.

The findings on career orientations mirror findings of research conducted among established teachers in the US and elsewhere in Europe. The patterns of differentiated gender socialisation outlined above result in different overall orientations to work and careers among boys and girls, and proved to be a differentiating factor between those school leavers who were seriously considering a teaching career and those who were not. The majority of the school leavers and college students ranked intrinsic factors most highly when considering future careers. This was to be expected among this cohort as, by definition, they were either anticipating entry to higher education, or were already in it, and were thus contemplating middle-class careers where such rewards are available. It was the second most highly ranked orientation of those examined which was the strongest discriminator between boys and girls and between those considering, or not considering, teaching. That is, in common with findings elsewhere, both girls in general, and those girls and boys considering teaching, were more oriented to caring and to service than were others. There are implications here also for the socialisation of both girls and boys in the wider society, and for their education in schools. In the Irish second level school system which is still, in comparison to other countries, highly gender differentiated, there is evidence that girls schools put a great deal more emphasis on caring than do boys schools. The implications of the research here are that, if society wishes to substantially increase the proportions of young men entering primary teaching, schools, parents and all agencies of socialisation (including the media and the state) are going to have to place a very substantially greater emphasis on the centrality of caring as a core social value and one which is as relevant to men as it is to women.

Debates on the feminisation of teaching suggest that it may involve a number of characteristics. The most obvious of these is an increasingly high proportion of women in the teaching profession but also, arguably, a strengthened feminine interpretation of the specific professional activity accompanied, perhaps, by a reduction in social prestige of the teaching profession due to the higher number of women employed in it. Research in other countries has suggested that there is a conflict between the prior gender socialisation of men and the roles that are required as teachers. It is suggested in this volume that this affects the social construction of their career preferences and choices (and, indeed, female choices). Gender socialisation may also affect the way in which those *who do* enter the profession experience it. For example, among the student teachers surveyed for this research, the tasks considered most irksome by males were paperwork and preparing class plans, while control and discipline issues were much more predominant in female responses. On the other hand, with regard to the aspects of teaching practice found most enjoyable, the core aspect of primary teaching, i.e. the relationship with children, proved much less enjoyable for male students than for female students.

The role and status of the teaching profession is central to the issues examined in this research. It has been pointed out earlier that, given the development of the educational knowledge base, the fact that teaching in Ireland is now an all-graduate profession, the nature of teacher involvement in curriculum and policy development, the growth and importance of continuing in-career education for teachers, and the predicted involvement of teachers in the regulation of the profession and of the professional affairs of teachers through representation on the proposed Teaching Council, it is reasonable to conclude that, in Ireland at any rate, teaching is a profession in any sense of the term. However, the international literature and the industrial relations difficulties experienced among Irish second level teachers in the early 2000s illustrate that, relative to the older established professions, teachers are still subject to much control, and this level of control may continue to undermine the professional status of teachers that is envisaged in the *Teaching Council Act*.

The issue of control is closely related to gender and to the feminisation of schooling, and the hierarchical relation between teachers and administrators is also gendered. The feminisation of teaching does not refer solely to gender imbalance; it describes also the processes by which male and female teachers have been made to conform to the pervasive constraints of educational systems and environments. Among the school leavers, although primary/elementary teaching was lower ranked in terms of prestige than were the older professions, it nevertheless received rankings in the middle range of the professions examined. Second level/high school teaching, however, received much lower ranking. While this may reflect wider attitudes to the different types of teaching, research elsewhere suggests that it may reflect the age and stage of the respondents who were in the early post-adolescent stage and still at school under the discipline and constraints of study for, arguably, the most major examination of their lives. However, the perception of second level teaching as carrying lower prestige was evident among the responses of primary student teachers also. These findings would imply that if Irish society wishes to sustain the high calibre of, albeit mainly female, entrants to the profession that it has been able to take for granted in the last quarter of the twentieth century and before, then a concerted effort will need to be made by the state and the education system.

In the period following the fieldwork for this study there has been a slight fall in the number of first preferences for primary teaching but a rise in the number of postgraduate applicants for places on Higher Diploma in Education courses (the initial teacher education programme for most second level teaching). The proportion of men entering primary teaching has risen somewhat but the trend is still one of overall decline. This research study began by raising the question of whether the low proportion of men entering teaching is, in fact, a serious social problem. The findings do not directly answer this question as the research objectives focus mainly on explaining the low proportion of men entering teaching rather than examining its impact. Based on the review of the literature and global figures on teaching, this is an almost universal phenomenon as economies develop, as urbanisation occurs, and as women become more incorporated into the formal economy. There are important issues to be raised in terms of gender equality and the hidden curriculum of education. Given the centrality of teaching to personal, social and economic development, the impact of the feminisation of teaching is an important area for future research so that policy may be based on substantive data rather than taken-for-granted assumptions or ideology.

Recommendations

As argued above, the feminisation of primary teaching is an almost universal global phenomenon, resulting from profound historical, economic, social, cultural and political processes. The effects of this pattern of feminisation on pupil development and educational achievement, particularly that of boys, is largely speculative and under-researched. Whether the reversal of this trend should be a national priority would itself require considerable debate, research and further analysis. It has been argued above that there were three issues in respect of which increasing levels of feminisation at point of entry to teaching could be problematic for a society. The first is the issue of equality in the labour market. The second matter of concern lies in the area of the socialisation of pupils, although this requires further research. The third problem is that of the hidden curriculum of schooling, and the unintended pupil learning from occupational hierachies may be observed in the educational system.

It is difficult to see how any society could bring about an immediate reversal of the trends outlined in this volume. They are firmly rooted in issues related to economic development, urbanisation, the position of women in society, cultural definitions of masculinity, the centrality and value of children and childcare. These processes are also linked to the relative importance of values such as caring in comparison to other values such as competitive individualism. They are related to the socio-economic organisation of the occupational structure and work practices

– including whether family friendly structures extend vertically as well as horizontally throughout the occupational structure, and whether they are availed of equally by males and females. They are also related to patterns of gender socialisation and to the relative strength of what is described in this report as a 'domestic ideology' for women. In other words, if the patterns of feminisation of teaching evident in Ireland and in so many other countries were to be reversed, it would require very radical social change and a re-orientation of many social and economic values and practices. To highlight this is in no way to suggest that it should not be attempted. Indeed, such radical social transformation could improve the quality of life in society as a whole.

If it is considered desirable to increase significantly the proportion of men entering teaching, a number of strategies are possible, based on the research findings in this report. These include long-term strategies for social change which could bring about major reversals, as well as short-term strategies which could be effected quickly and which could be expected to bring about some increases in male entry to teaching. The key recommendation is that policy makers, legislators, administrators and educators should adopt and emphasise caring as a core human value, one which is as central for boys and men as it is for girls and women; they should include and vindicate this core value in all policy documents, regulations, strategies and laws and provide implementation, monitoring and reward systems to reflect the centrality of caring in all social, economic, political and cultural institutions. Children, childcare and child protection should be put at the centre of state policy. Gender equality should be prioritised to ensure that women and men are equally valued and represented on public bodies, at all levels of the labour market, in social welfare policies and in domestic and caring roles. Schools should take proactive steps to improve male performance in education, particularly in public examinations and should actively promote a sense of service as a central human value and inculcate it among all of their pupils, but particularly among males. Teachers and guidance counsellors should emphasise to male pupils the attractions of careers which involve working with children and point out their suitability to high achievers, male as well as female. A publicity and awareness-raising campaign on the value of teaching and its suitability to men as well as women should be mounted (as has been done in some countries, for example the United Kingdom). This campaign should be directed to both boys and girls, but in a particular way to boys second level schools. Parents and families should emphasise the importance of male participation in family life and childcare and should see men as having equal responsibilities as well as rights in this regard, and should mirror this in their everyday practices – i.e. they should develop a 'domestic ideology' which is appropriate to men as well as women. Men's role in family life should be reflected in, and facilitated by, labour market and social welfare policies and by employers. In short, what is required is a significant shift away from patriarchal social, cultural and economic structures.

Nevertheless, a number of specific strategies and policy interventions can be recommended. These are based on the research findings in this report. They include long-term strategies for social change which could bring about major reversals, as well as short-term strategies which could be effected quickly and which could be expected to bring about some increases in male entry to primary teaching but not at the level of significance of the increases that might be expected through the greater long-term changes recommended. In each case, the agencies which would have primary responsibility for implementation are indicated.

Policy makers, legislators and administrators

Long-term strategies

- All policy makers, legislators and administrators should adopt and emphasise caring as a core human value, one which is as central for boys and men as it is for girls and women; they should include and vindicate this core value in all policy documents, regulations, strategies and laws and provide implementation, monitoring and reward systems to reflect the centrality of caring in all social, economic, political and cultural institutions
- All policy makers, legislators and administrators should put children, childcare and child protection at the centre of state policy
- All policy makers, legislators and administrators should prioritise gender equality and ensure that women and men are equally valued and represented on public bodies, at all levels of the labour market, in social welfare policies and in domestic and caring roles

Short-term strategies

- Policy makers, legislators and administrators should ensure that teaching (both primary/elementary and secondary/high school) has conditions at entry, and a pay and career structure that is as attractive as those pertaining in other professions with equivalent educational requirements at entry
- Policy makers, legislators and administrators should support a major public service broadcasting initiative to stage an annual prize-giving event, with a high profile publicity campaign to celebrate teaching
- Ministries of education should mount a publicity and awareness-raising campaign on the value of teaching and its suitability to men as well as women and direct this campaign to both boys and girls, but in a particular way to boys secondary schools; this campaign should make full use of all available media – including careers exhibitions, videos, booklets, etc.
- Ministries of education should examine ways in which to increase the level of mobility among teaching staff, without prejudice to job security and promotional prospects

Schools

Long-term strategies

- Schools should take proactive steps to improve male performance in education, particularly in public examinations
- Schools should take proactive steps to increase the proportion of boys participating in the senior cycles of school systems and taking honours subjects across the curriculum
- Schools should take proactive steps to increase the proportion of boys taking any mandatory requirements for teaching within their state

Short-term strategies

- Schools should very actively promote a sense of service as a central human value and inculcate it among all of their pupils, with particular reference to males
- All teachers (and especially those in boys secondary schools) should emphasise the attractions of teaching (and especially primary/elementary teaching) as a career suitable to high achievers, male as well as female

Guidance counsellors

Short-term strategies

- Guidance counsellors should emphasise to male pupils the attractions of careers which involve working with children
- Guidance counsellors should put more emphasis on teaching (especially primary/elementary teaching) as an attractive option for boys, particularly high achieving boys
- Guidance counsellors should raise awareness among parents of the attractions of teaching (especially primary/elementary teaching), particularly for high achieving boys
- Professional associations of guidance counsellors should mount a publicity and awareness-raising campaign among their members, to mirror that mounted by the ministries of education, on the value of teaching (especially primary/elementary teaching) and its suitability to men as well as women and direct this campaign to both boys and girls, but in a particular way to boys secondary schools; this campaign should make full use of all available media – including careers exhibitions, videos, booklets, etc.

Teacher Unions

Short-term strategies

- Teacher unions should mount a publicity and awareness-raising campaign, to mirror those of the ministries of education and professional associations of guidance counsellors' campaigns, on the value of teaching (especially primary/elementary teaching) and its suitability to men as well as women and direct this campaign to both boys and girls, but in a particular way to boys secondary schools; this campaign should make full use of all available media – including careers exhibitions, videos, booklets, etc.

Colleges of education and universities

Long-term strategies

- Colleges of education and universities should undertake research to assess the impact, if any, on pupil development and learning resulting from the increasing feminisation of teaching, and of the effect on the culture of teaching and learning, and on employment conditions, of the pattern of feminisation

Short-term strategies

- Colleges of education and universities should hold open days and target boys and boys schools in particular
- Colleges of education and universities should mount a publicity and awareness-raising campaign, to mirror those of the ministries of education, professional associations of guidance counsellors and teacher union campaigns, on the value of teaching (especially primary/elementary teaching) and its suitability to men as well as women and direct this campaign to both boys and girls, but in a particular way to boys' secondary schools; this campaign should make full use of all available media – including careers exhibitions, videos, booklets, etc.

Parents and families

Long-term strategies

- Parents and families should emphasise the importance of male participation in family life and childcare and should see men as having equal responsibilities as well as rights in this regard, and should mirror this in their everyday practices – i.e. they should develop a 'domestic ideology' which is appropriate to men as well as women

Short-term strategies

- Parents and families should emphasise that teaching (especially primary/elementary teaching) is an attractive option for boys, particularly high achieving boys and should actively support the choice of teaching (especially primary/elementary teaching) as a career among any male family members who are considering that choice

Tables

Appendix 1, Table 1: Females as a percentage of the teaching profession at different education levels worldwide, 1970–1997

Region	Females as % primary teachers 1970	Females as % primary teachers 1997	% Inc/Dec female primary teachers 1970–97	% Inc/Dec total primary teachers 1970–97	Females as % second level teachers 1970	Females as % second level teachers 1997	% Inc/Dec female second level teachers 1970–97	% Inc/Dec total second level teachers 1970–97	% Inc/Dec total third level teachers 1970–97
Europe	70	83	+14	–3	52	62	+115	+81	+169
America	82	79	+59	+66	47	51	+61	+46	+129
Asia	36	48	+136	+77	30	42	+339	+213	+277
Oceania	63	72	+49	+72	43	52	+195	+145	+313
Latin America & Caribbean	81	77	+142	+155	49	47	+128	+138	+399
Africa	36	45	+403	+250	31	35	+684	+604	+572
Developed countries	73	82	+11	–1	49	58	+96	+64	+126
Developing countries	40	52	+169	+108	31	41	+342	+237	+360
Least developed countries	21	35	+380	+195	22	30	+468	+312	+375
World total	52	58	+88	68	41	48	+177	+139	+193
N	7.694m	14.447m	6.783m	10.051m	3.970m	10.977m	7.007m	13.373m	4.138m

Source: Table calculated from figures provided by UNESCO (2001); *World Education Report*, <http://www.unesco.org/> (accessed 17 January 2002)

Note: Figures on females as a percentage of third level teachers not available.

Appendix 1, Table 2: Attitudes of school leavers and student teachers relating to primary teaching, by gender, first choice of primary teaching (university), and whether teaching (any type) a preference

Attitudes towards the nature of teaching	School Leavers		School Leavers		School Leavers		Student Teachers	
	Males	Females	Primary teaching	Other choice	Any type teaching	Other choice	Males	Females
Primary teaching is a demanding and exhausting job	2.41*	2.10*	1.96*	2.23*	2.14	2.25	1.67	1.55
There is a lot of interest and variety in primary teaching	2.73**	2.36**	1.68**	2.57**	2.00**	2.64**	2.25**	1.75**
Younger children are easier to manage than teenagers	2.61	2.75	2.40	2.72	2.85	2.66	2.53	2.66
Attitudes Towards the Status of Primary Teaching								
Teachers perform a service of moral value to society	2.19	2.14	1.74**	2.07**	1.85*	2.24*	1.84	1.86
Teachers have less status in society today than they had in the past	2.29	2.31	2.54	2.27	2.36	2.29	2.00	2.26
Jobs in which women are in the majority are less well paid than those with more men	2.72	2.62	2.75	2.63	2.72	2.65	2.29	2.43
Primary teachers able to influence children for the good	2.16*	2.04*	1.70**	2.08**	1.83**	2.16**	1.91	1.87
Attitudes to Women in Primary Teaching								
Women teachers have more patience with children than men have	2.33**	2.88**	2.86	2.64	2.90**	2.60**	3.42	3.53
Women are better than men at managing young children	2.39**	3.03**	3.00	2.74	2.95**	2.73*	3.16	3.47
Primary teaching is an extension of the mother's role	2.72	2.69	2.54	2.70	2.66	2.71	3.24	3.02

continued

Appendix 1, Table 2: continued

Attitudes towards the nature of teaching	School Leavers		School Leavers		School Leavers		Student Teachers	
	Males	Females	Primary teaching	Other choice	Any type teaching	Other choice	Males	Females
Primary teaching is a good career for a woman who has children of her own	2.65	2.77	2.54	2.73	2.68	2.74	2.58	2.40
Because primary teaching is seen as a woman's profession it doesn't attract men	2.71	2.80	3.04*	2.71*	2.94*	2.72*	2.09	2.20
Attitudes to Men in Primary Teaching								
Men are more suited to secondary teaching	2.71**	3.62**	3.72**	3.24**	3.43*	3.21*	2.80**	3.80**
It is important for children to see men in caring roles	2.49*	2.00**	1.96*	2.20*	1.92**	2.27**	1.89	1.79
Boys need male teachers as role models	2.85**	3.26**	3.32	3.09	3.18	3.08	1.98**	3.03**
Male teachers are more likely to come up against false child abuse allegations	2.28**	2.76**	3.11**	2.52**	2.74*	2.53*	2.30**	2.95**
Male teachers are better at organising sporting and other activities	2.28**	3.64**	3.88**	3.07**	3.54**	2.99**	2.76**	3.96**
Children have more respect for male teachers	2.83**	3.75**	3.89**	3.38**	3.68**	3.31**	3.09**	3.75**
Male teachers are better at controlling older pupils	2.08**	3.34**	3.36**	2.81**	3.14**	2.76**	2.71**	3.56**
Attitudes to Gender Equality in Primary Teaching								
Men and women are equally capable of teaching primary school children	2.56**	2.06**	1.81**	2.51**	1.98**	2.33**	1.67	1.51
Being a good primary teacher depends on personality and training, not gender	2.01**	1.38**	1.16**	1.65**	1.35**	1.70**	1.47	1.29

Note: 't' test significance between means is indicated as follows:
*p<.01 – p<.05; **p<.000 – p<.001 (see Appendix 2 for discussion of the 't' test).

Appendix I, Table 3: Decision-making on teaching, by respondents' social class background and parental education

| | Social Class Background | | | | | | Parental Education | | | | | |
| | Classes 1 and 2 | | Classes 3 and 4 | | Classes 5 and 6 | | 3rd Level Degree/Diploma | | At end of Senior Cycle | | At or before end of Junior Cycle | |
Decision-making	Father %	Mother* %	Father %	Mother* %	Father %	Mother* %	Father %	Mother %	Father %	Mother %	Father %	Mother %
Primary Teaching 1st preference	7.3	9.1	6.5	6.8	10.6	0.0	5.9	7.1	8.3	6.3	6.3	6.6
Other course 1st preference	92.7	90.9	93.5	93.2	89.4	100.0	94.1	92.9	91.7	93.7	93.7	93.4
Teaching ever considered as a career choice	19.8	26.4	22.5	21.0	21.4	10.1	19.9	22.4	20.2	19.2	20.7	19.6
Teaching never considered as a career choice	80.3	73.6	77.5	79.0	78.6	89.9	80.1	77.6	79.8	80.8	79.3	80.4

* Only mothers working outside the home, with classifiable occupations, are included in this figure.

A methodological note

Introduction

The empirical part of this study surveys patterns of entry to the teaching profession. Given that primary/elementary school teaching is the most gendered sector of the profession, the study looks in particular at why the number of young men choosing primary teaching as a career has fallen so dramatically. In Ireland, over the last twenty-five years, the percentage of males in the primary teaching force has dropped from just under 30 per cent to just over 20 per cent. For entrants to colleges of education the drop is more marked. Ninety per cent of entrants to the primary colleges of education in 2003 were females.

The study used a triangulated research methodology. This made use of documentary research, quantitative data-gathering and qualitative methods. An extensive review of the existing research literature was conducted, as well as analysis of official statistics. The quantitative element consisted of two surveys – one conducted among second level school leavers, the other at third level among student teachers undertaking initial teacher education for primary/elementary teaching. The qualitative research consisted of interviews with the guidance counsellors in the schools selected for the survey, interviews with senior managers/administrators in the third level colleges, and a focus group interview with experienced male teachers. The objectives of the second level survey were to look at the course and career choices of a cohort of school leavers. The objectives also included the examination of the motivation and influences behind those choices, the perceptions that school leavers have of different jobs and their attitudes to teaching, both at primary and secondary level, as a career for men and women. Also to be included were basic demographic information on parents' education and occupations, and on the levels of students' academic performance. A further objective was to ascertain the views of guidance counsellors on primary/elementary teaching in particular, as this is the most gendered area of teaching. At third level the objectives were to obtain information on the background and academic achievements of student teachers, their reasons for choosing primary teaching, and their attitudes towards and perceptions of teaching. Information was also sought from senior college administrators on their perceptions of the key issues pertaining to primary teaching as a career. Finally, the objective of the focus group interview with male teachers was to record the views of experienced male teachers with regard to the issues under scrutiny.

The questionnaires for school leavers and student teachers were developed over a period of several months in 1998, through discussion among members of the research team with reference to similar work cited in the review of previous research on gender and teaching, particularly Lortie (1975), Huberman *et al.* (1991) and a recent Northern Ireland study (Johnston *et al.*, 1998). There was also consultation with personnel from the colleges of education and from the teacher unions. In the first phase of the pilot study, the questionnaire for school leavers was piloted with Leaving Certificate pupils about to enter sixth year in three schools in the Dublin area. In a second phase of the pilot study, in September 1998, the questionnaire was tested again in a coeducational Community College and final adjustments made. A similar piloting process took place with question- naires distributed at colleges of education, in November 1998. The third level questionnaire was piloted with a cohort of student teachers on a postgraduate course in initial teacher education. As before, the questionnaires were coded using SPSS and adjustments made as required by the results. They were then analysed in full. The questionnaires and interview schedules are available from the main author of this study (Professor Sheelagh Drudy, Education Department, University College Dublin), on request.

Samples

The team was aware that, with the resources available, a full-scale national sample of schools was not a possibility. Nevertheless, it was important that the schools chosen for the study would be as representative as possible. Therefore it was decided that the use of a form of proportionate cluster sampling would be appropriate. The target population in the school leaver study was school leavers who intended to apply to universities, colleges of education and other third level institutions in 1999.[1] The first task was to ensure that the schools selected would, as far as possible, reflect the national distribution of schools. This procedure resulted in sixteen schools selected from five regional clusters consisting of the Dublin metropolitan area and each of the four provinces, Leinster (excluding Dublin), Munster, Connacht and Ulster. The number and type of schools selected were roughly proportionate to the number and type of schools in the counties selected. The final sample of 16 second-level schools throughout the country, comprised:

- nine secondary schools (three boys, three girls, and three coeducational)
- three community schools (coeducational)
- two community colleges and two vocational schools (all coeducational).

Of these 16 schools one was fee-paying, one was under Protestant management, the remaining denominational schools were under Catholic management, one was an all Irish language medium community college, and one was a boarding school.

In the end, the schools selected in the final sample were typical in a number of key characteristics of the post-primary school stock.[2] The main shortcomings are that smaller schools were less well represented in the sample than among post-primary schools at national level, and that the community sector is over-represented. Bearing in mind that the number of schools selected is small, and that there was no attempt to make the sample statistically representative of the total 763 second level schools in the system, the analysis of school leaver data does not use any weighting procedures. The methods used in sampling and selecting the schools however, and the patterning of the responses, convinced the researchers, and an adviser to the team in the Statistics Section in the Department of Education and Science, that the schools and pupils were typical, if not statistically representative, of schools and school leavers as a whole in Ireland.

For the student teacher survey, in consultation with the college administrations, the team was advised that the most feasible method of administration of the questionnaire in the five primary colleges of education was to distribute it to all of one year-group. The year-group selected was the 1998–99 second years. This group was chosen because, by the time of the survey, they could be assumed to have settled in to their course and to be familiar with the issues being explored in the questionnaire, while not being unduly burdened with the pressure of examinations. A total of 457 questionnaires was returned (of which 10 per cent were from males and 90 per cent from females). Questionnaires were administered to 457 people present in the colleges on the days of the survey. This number represented some 81 per cent of those who accepted places in the colleges of education the previous year. Because of drop-outs over the course of the intervening eighteen months, the 457 thus represent a high proportion of the total second year cohort in all of the colleges.

Key variables for all of the 457 student teachers were coded, inputted and analysed. For some of the attitudinal variables it was decided to draw a stratified random sample of the 411 female students for analysis, while analysing attitudinal data for all of the 46 males, who formed just 10 per cent of the total. A proportionate random sample of the returns from 150 females was drawn, stratified by area of origin, and attitudinal variables inputted and analysed. Therefore, primarily due to time constraints, analysis of attitudinal questions was based on 196 student teacher respondents.

Fieldwork

A letter was sent out from the Project Directors to the principals of the 16 second level schools, requesting their co-operation in the survey. A supporting letter accompanied this from the Assistant Chief Inspector at the Department of Education and Science, who had commissioned the study. All schools selected kindly agreed to facilitate the research by giving a class-period with their sixth year classes and another class-period with the guidance counsellor. It was indicated that the study was primarily interested in prospective college/university applicants (those who would be likely to have the minimum qualification for primary teaching), but that the whole sixth year cohort present on the day could complete the questionnaire if this was more convenient. Students do not apply to the Central Applications Office (the clearing house for third level applications) until the end of January of their final year at school and as such, some would still have been uncertain about their choices in the autumn. The confidentiality of the survey was emphasised.

Members of the research team travelled to each school in October and November of 1998 and delivered the questionnaires to students. Most schools gave the questionnaire to all sixth years present on the day in question. In all cases students were supervised and the questionnaires were collected immediately – for some of the attitude and perception questions it was important that there should be no conferring.

A total of 1,136 school leavers completed questionnaires. These questionnaires were checked and those indicating an intention to fill in a CAO form were numbered, while a small number whose responses indicated that it was not their intention to proceed to third level was eliminated (n = 87). The final total of valid questionnaires was 1,049, i.e. 92 per cent of those returned.

In the survey of the third level colleges, fieldwork was carried out with second year students in the five primary colleges of education during the months of January and February 1999. In each college a self-completion questionnaire was given to all of the second year students present on the days of the surveys, 457 student teachers in all. Detailed interviews were also conducted with college Presidents and with a number of other members of the college administration. In addition, a small focus-group study of a cohort of experienced male elementary teachers was conducted. Focus-group studies involve semi-structured interviews, normally within a narrow time frame. The organisational framework of this focus group study was developed by adapting some of the strategies outlined in Kreuger (1988).

Coding and analysis

A code-book was prepared for each of the two questionnaires. The responses were coded and entered on a database using SPSS 8.0 for Windows. The second level questionnaire comprised 37 questions resulting in some 150 variables, with extra variables added through re-coding. Most of the variables were coded numerically, while answers to the open questions were first coded as 'string' variables and later re-coded in categories which were developed according to the respondents' replies. The coding of the second level questionnaires was done between November 1998 and February 1999. Coding of the third level questionnaires was carried out between March and May 1999.

Statistics used

The principal methods of presentation used in the analysis are graphs, bar-charts, tables and cross-tabulations. Missing values were excluded from the analyses. Cross-tabulation or contingency table analysis is the most commonly used analytical method in social and educational studies. This displays the distribution of cases by their position on two or more variables. These joint frequency distributions can be statistically analysed by tests of significance. One of the most commonly used tests in the analysis is the Chi-square test, which may be used to determine the difference between two or more independent groups. The Chi-square test is only used where the conditions are appropriate – i.e. where the data refer to a sample and where no cell contains expected values of less than 5. In common with other tests of significance, the Chi-square is a formal procedure for making a decision on whether a set of variables under scrutiny are related or unrelated in a population, on the basis of knowledge obtained from a sample of that population. By itself the Chi-square test helps only to decide whether the variables are related or unrelated. It does not tell how strongly they are related. The simplest way to do this, as Blalock (1972) points out, is to report the differences in terms of percentages. This procedure is used most frequently in the analysis.

Where the measurement of attitude and perception involved the scaling of items, the forms of data presentation which seemed most appropriate were measures of central tendency and dispersion. Of the three measures of central tendency (the mean, the median and the mode) the mean was selected as it uses more information than the other two, in that exact scores are used in computing it (Blalock, 1972: 68). The mean is generally a more stable measurement than the median, for example, and it has been suggested that 'when in doubt, use the mean in preference to the median' (ibid: 69). The standard deviation is used as a measure of dispersion. The greater the spread around the mean, the larger the standard deviation. To test for statistical significance in the differences between means, use was made of 't' tests and analysis of variance. The properties of the Normal Distribution can be used to calculate confidence intervals for means and to carry out tests of significance in means when a large sample ('n'>60) is involved. The 't' test is robust so that even if the distributions are only 'vaguely' normal the 't' test[3] is still likely to be valid (Hinton, 1995: 81).

Where the number of independent samples amounts to three or more, significance in variation between the means is measured through the use of analysis of variance (ANOVA). Like the 't' distribution, each of the distributions in analysis of variance has a 'degree of freedom', which is the same as the number in the sample minus 1. In ANOVA values for the 'F' ratio are presented. ANOVA tests the null hypothesis that two or more population means are equal. A ratio of two variance estimates is computed and thus the 'F' distribution is determined by two degrees-of-freedom values (ibid.: 375). It was decided that differences between means would be accepted as statistically significant when $p<.05$ or better.

Bibliography

Acker, S. (1989) (ed.) *Teachers, Gender and Careers*, London: Falmer.
—— (1994) *Gendered Education*, Buckingham: Open University Press.
Adams, A. and Tulasiewicz, W. (1995) *The Crisis in Teacher Education: a European concern?* London: Falmer.
Agnew, U., Malcolm, S. and McEwen, A. (1989) *Children and Careers in Education*, Belfast: Equal Opportunities Commission for Northern Ireland.
Akenson, D.H. (1970) *The Irish Education Experiment: the national system of education in the nineteenth century*, London: Routledge and Kegan Paul.
Allan, M. (1993) 'Male Elementary Teachers: experiences and perspectives' in C. Williams (ed.) *Doing 'Women's Work': men in nontraditional occupations*, London: Sage.
Alexander, R.J. (1984) *Primary Teaching*, London: Holt, Rinehart and Winston, quoted in S. Acker (1994) *Gendered Education*, Buckingham: Open University Press, p. 98.
Applegate, J.S. and Kaye, L.W. (1993) 'Male elder caregivers' in C. Williams (ed.) *Doing 'Women's Work': men in nontraditional occupations*, Newbury Park, CA: Sage.
Archer, E.G. and Peck, B.T. (1990) *The Teaching Profession in Europe*, Glasgow: Jordanhill College of Education, 1990.
Arnot, M., David, M. and Weiner, G. (1999) *Closing the Gender Gap*, Cambridge: Polity Press.
A.T. Kearney/*Foreign Policy* (2004) 'Measuring globalization: economic reversals, forward momentum', <http://www.foreignpolicy.com> (accessed 4 April 2004).
Basten, C. (1997) 'A Feminised profession: women in the teaching profession', *Educational Studies*, 23: 55–62.
Benton DeCourse, C. and Vogtle, S. (1997) 'In a complex voice: the contradictions of male elementary teachers' career choice and professional identity', *Journal of Teacher Education*, 48: 37–46.
Berry, B. *et al.* (1989). 'Recruiting the next generation of teachers: conversations with high school sophomores', *Research Report 08–005*, Washington, DC: Office of Educational Research and Improvement, January, 1989.
Biklen, S.K. and D. Pollard (eds) (1993) *Gender and Education: ninety-second yearbook of the national society for the study of education*, Chicago: University of Chicago Press.
Blalock, H. (1972) *Social Statistics*, New York: McGraw Hill.
Bourdieu, P. and Passeron, J-C. (1977) *Reproduction in Education, Society and Culture*, London: Sage.
Brabeck, M. and Weisberger, K. (1989) 'College students' perceptions of men and

women choosing teaching and management', *Sex Roles: A Journal of Research*, 21: 841–57.

Bradley, H. (1993) 'Across the great divide: the entry of men into "women's jobs"' in C. Williams (ed.) *Doing 'Women's Work': men in nontraditional occupations*, Newbury Park, CA: Sage.

Breen, R. (1986) *Subject Availability and Student Performance in the Senior Cycle of Irish Post-Primary Schools*, Dublin: Economic and Social Research Institute.

Britzman, D.P. (1993) 'Beyond role models: gender and multicultural education' in S.K. Biklen and D. Pollard (eds) *Gender and Education: ninety-second yearbook of the national society for the study of education*, Chicago: University of Chicago Press, pp 25–42.

Brookhart, S.M. and Loadman, W.E. (1996) 'Characteristics of male elementary teachers in the U.S.A. at teacher education program entry and exit', *Teaching and Teacher Education*, 12: 197–210.

Burke, A. (1992) *Oideas 39: Teaching: Retrospect and Prospect*, Dublin: Department of Education.

—— (1996) 'A professional vision of teaching: implications for teachers and teacher educators', *Irish Educational Studies*, 16: 127–43.

Burnstyn, J.N. (1993) 'Who benefits and who suffers: gender and education at the dawn of the age of information technology' in S.K. Biklen and D. Pollard (eds) *Gender and Education: ninety-second yearbook of the national society for the study of education*, Chicago: University of Chicago Press, pp 107–25.

Bushweller, K. (1994) 'Turning our backs on boys', *American School Board Journal*, 181: 20–5.

Byrne, E.M. (1978) *Women and Education*, London: Tavistock.

Campbell, P.B. and Greenberg, S. (1993) 'Equity issues in educational research methods' in S.K. Biklen and D. Pollard (eds) *Gender and Education: ninety-second yearbook of the national society for the study of education*, Chicago: University of Chicago Press, pp 64–89.

Central Applications Office (2001) *Board of Directors' Report 2001*, <http://www.cao.ie> (accessed 30 March 2004).

Central Statistics Office (1996) *Census of Population of Ireland – Classification of Occupations*, Dublin: CSO.

—— (1997) *Census of Population of Ireland – Population by Area*, Dublin: CSO.

—— (2005) 'Persons in employment (1988–1997) (thousands) by year, sex, broad economic sector and region', http://www.cso.ie/px/pxeirestat/database/eirestat/Labour%20Force.asp

Clancy, P. (1988) *Who Goes to College?: a second national survey of participation in higher education*, Dublin: Higher Education Authority.

—— (1995a) *Access to College: patterns of continuity and change*, Dublin: Higher Education Authority.

—— (1995b) 'Education in the Republic of Ireland: the project of modernity?' in P. Clancy, S. Drudy, K. Lynch and L. O'Dowd (eds) *Irish Society: Sociological Perspectives*, Dublin: Institute of Public Administration.

Clancy, P., Drudy, S., Lynch, K. and O'Dowd, L. (1995) *Irish Society: sociological perspectives*, Dublin: Institute of Public Administration.

Connell, R.W. (1995) *Masculinity*, Sydney: Allen and Unwin.

Coolahan, J. (1981), *Irish Education: history and structure*, Dublin: Institute of Public Administration.

Cullen, M. (ed.) (1987) *Girls Don't Do Honours: Irish women in education in the 19th and 20th centuries*, Dublin: Women's Education Bureau.

Delamont, S. (1980) *The Sociology of Women*, London: Allen & Unwin.

Department of Education and Science (2000) *Statistical Report, 1998/99*, Dublin: Stationery Office.

Drudy, S. (1981) 'School-leavers in transition', unpublished thesis, University of Cambridge.

—— (1991) 'The classification of social class in sociological research', *British Journal of Sociology*, 42: 21–41.

—— (1995) 'Class, society, and the "declassed"' in P. Clancy, S. Drudy, K. Lynch and L. O'Dowd (eds), *Irish Society: sociological perspectives*, Dublin: Institute of Public Administration.

—— (1996) 'Gender Differences in Participation and Achievement in the Physical Sciences and Mathematics' in E. Befring (ed.), *Teacher Education for Equality*, Oslo: Oslo College.

—— (1998) 'Gender Differences in Participation in Mathematics and Science: implications for school organisation and guidance', *Journal of the Institute of Guidance Counselors*, 22: 5–11.

—— (2001) 'The teaching profession in Ireland: its role and current challenges' *Studies*, 90: 363–75.

—— (2004) 'Gender and initial teacher education in a changing context: patterns of entrance and awards', Paper presented to the Annual Conference of the Educational Studies Association of Ireland, National University of Ireland, Maynooth, April 1–3.

Drudy, S. and Lynch, K. (1993) *Schools and Society in Ireland*, Dublin: Gill and Macmillan.

Drudy, S. and Ui Chathain, M. (1999) *Gender Equality in Classroom Interaction*, Maynooth: Department of Education, N.U.I. Maynooth.

Eccles, J. and Bryan, J. (1994) 'Adolescence: critical crossroad in the path of gender-role development' in M. R. Stevenson (ed.), *Gender Roles Through the Life Span*, Muncie, IN: Ball State University.

Edmonds, S., Sharp, C. and Benefield, P. (2002) *Recruitment to and Retention on Initial Teacher Training: a systematic review*, National Foundation for Educational Research: <http://www.nfer.ac.uk/research/project_sumtemp.asp?theID=TSR> (17 October 2003).

Elwood, J. and Carlisle, K. (2003) *Examining Gender: gender and achievement in the junior and leaving certificate examinations, 2000/2001*, Dublin: National Council for Curriculum and Assessment.

Epstein, D., Elwood, J., Hey, V. and Maw, J. (eds) (1998) *Failing Boys?: issues in gender and achievement*, Buckingham/Philadelphia: Open University Press.

Etzioni, A. (ed.) (1969) *The Semi-Professions and their Organization*, New York: The Free Press.

European Commission (1997) *Key Data on Education in the European Union*, Luxembourg: Office for Official Publications of the European Communities.

Evans, H. (1993) 'The choice of teaching as a career', *Social and Economic Studies* 42: 225–42.

Freidus, H. (1990) 'The call of the sirens? the influence of gender in the decision to choose teaching as a career', Paper presented at the Annual Meeting of the American Educational Research association (Boston, MA, April 17–20, 1990).

—— (1992) 'Men in a women's world: a study of male second career teachers in elementary schools', Paper presented at the Annual Meeting of the American Educational Research Association (San Francisco, CA, April 20–24, 1992).

Frieze, I. and Olson, J. (1994) 'Understanding the characteristics and experiences of women in male- and female-dominated fields', in M.R. Stevenson (ed.) *Gender Roles Through the Life Span*, Muncie, Indiana: Ball State University.

Gaskell, J. (1992) *Gender Matters from School to Work*, Milton Keynes: Open University Press.

Ginzberg, E., Ginzberg, S., Aelrad, S. and Herma, J. (1951) *Occupational Choice: an approach to general theory*, New York: Columbia University Press.

Goldthorpe, J. (1980) *Social Mobility and Class Structure in Modern Britain*, Oxford: Clarendon Press.

Government of Ireland (1992) *Education for a Changing World: green paper on education*, Dublin: the Stationery Office.

—— (1995) *Charting Our Education Future: white paper on education*, Dublin: the Stationery Office.

—— (1997) *Universities Act, 1997*, Dublin: the Stationery Office.

—— (1998a) *Education Act, 1998*, Dublin: the Stationery Office.

—— (1998b) *Adult Education in an Era of Lifelong Learning: green paper on adult education*, Dublin: the Stationery Office.

—— (1999) *Ready to Learn: white paper on early education*, Dublin: the Stationery Office.

—— (2000a) *Learning for Life: white paper on adult education*, Dublin: the Stationery Office.

—— (2000b) *Education and Welfare Act, 2000*, Dublin: the Stationery Office.

—— (2000c) *Equal Status Act , 2000*, Dublin: the Stationery Office.

—— (2001) *Teaching Council Act, 2001*, Dublin: the Stationery Office.

Greaney, V., Burke, A. and McCann, J. (1987) 'Entrants to primary teacher education in Ireland', *European Journal of Teacher Education*, 10: 127–39.

Green, J. and Weaver, R. (1992) 'Who aspires to teach? a descriptive study of preservice teachers', *Contemporary Education*, 63: 234–9.

Griffin, G. (1997) 'Teaching as a gendered experience', *Journal of Teacher Education*, 48: 7–18.

Han, You-Kyung, (1994) 'The impact of teacher's salary upon attraction and retention of individuals in teaching: evidence from NLS-72', Paper presented at the Annual Meeting of the American Educational Research Association (New Orleans, LA, April 4–8, 1994).

Hannan, D., Smyth, E., McCullagh, J., O'Leary, R. and McMahon, D. (1996) *Coeducation and Gender Equality: exam performance, stress and personal development*, Dublin: Oak Tree Press.

Hannan, D., Breen, R., Murray, B., Hardiman, N., Watson, D. and O'Higgins, K. (1983) *Schooling and Sex Roles: sex differences in subject provision and student choice in Irish post-primary schools*, Dublin: The Economic and Social Research Institute.

Hansot, E. (1993) 'Historical and contemporary views of gender and education' in Biklen, S.K. and Pollard, D. (eds) *Gender and Education: ninety-second yearbook of the national society for the study of education*, Chicago: University of Chicago Press, pp 12–24.

Harrington, J. and Harrington, S. (1995) 'The effect of gender and age on PPST performance in an urban teacher education programme', *Education*, 116: 142–4.

Hinton, P. (1995) *Statistics Explained*, London and New York: Routledge.

House of Commons Education and Employment Committee (1997–98) *Teacher Recruitment: What Can Be Done?* (Volume I), London: The Stationery Office.

Huberman, M., Grounauer, M-M. and Marti, J. (1991) *The Lives of Teachers*, trans. J. Neufel, London: Cassell.

Huberman, M. and Grounauer, M-M. (1991) 'Teachers' motivations and satisfactions' in M. Huberman, M-M. Grounauer and J. Marti *The Lives of Teachers*, trans. J. Neufel, London: Cassell.

Hutchinson, G. and Johnson, B. (1993–94) 'Teaching as a career; examining high school students' perspectives', *Action in Teacher Education*, 15: 61–7.

Irish National Teachers' Organisation (1995) *Educating Teachers: Reform and Renewal*, Dublin: INTO.

Jacobs, J.A. (1993) 'Men in female-dominated fields', in C. Williams (ed.) *Doing 'Women's Work': men in nontraditional occupations*, London: Sage.

Johnson, T. (1972) *Professions and Power*, London: Macmillan.

—— (1977) 'The Professions in the Class Structure' in R. Seare (ed.) *Industrial Society: class, cleavage and control*, London: Allen and Unwin.

Johnston, J., McKeown, E. and McEwen, A. (1998) *Primary Concerns: gender factors in choosing primary school teaching* (Report funded by the Equal Opportunities Commission for Northern Ireland), Belfast: Graduate School of Education, The Queen's University.

Kelleghan, T., Fontes, P., O'Toole, C. and Egan, O. (1985) *Gender Inequalities in Primary-School Teaching*, Dublin: Educational Company of Ireland.

Kelly, P. (1989) 'Teacher status: what students think about the profession', Paper presented at the Annual Meeting of the Association of Teacher Educators (St Louis, MI, February 18–22, 1989).

Kelly, S. (1970) *Teaching in the City: a study of the role of the primary school teacher*, Dublin: Gill and Macmillan.

Kemper, R. and Mangieri, J. (1987) 'America's future teaching force: predictions and recommendations', *Phi Delta Kappan*, 68: 393–5.

King, J.R. (1994) 'Uncommon caring: primary males and implicit judgments', Position Paper, ERIC No: ED375086, Clearing House No. SPO35448.

Kreuger, R.A. (1988) *Focus Groups: a practical guide for applied research*, Newbury Park, CA: Sage Publications.

Lacey, C. (1994) 'The professional socialization of teachers' in *The International Encyclopaedia of Education*, 2nd edition, 10: 6122–7.

Laemers, M. and Ruijs, A. (1996) 'Statistical portrait', *Context: European Education Magazine, 12*, Brussels: Secretariat CONCORDE.

Lightbody, P., Siann, G., Tait, L. and Walsh, D. (1997) 'A fulfilling career? factors which influence women's choice of profession', *Educational Studies*, 23: 25–37.

Lortie, D.C. (1975) *Schoolteacher: a sociological study*, Chicago: University of Chicago Press.

—— (1989) *The Hidden Curriculum: reproduction in education: an appraisal*, London: Falmer.

Lynch, K. (1997) 'A profile of mature students in higher education and an analysis of equality issues', in R. Morris (ed.) *Mature Students in Higher Education*, Cork: Higher Education Equality Unit.

Lynch, K. (1999) *Equality in Education*, Dublin: Gill and Macmillan.

Lynch, K. (1994) 'Women teach and men manage: why men dominate senior posts in Irish education', in *Women for Leadership in Education*, Conference of Religious in Ireland, Dublin: Milltown Park.

Mac an Ghaill, M. (1994) *The Making of Men: masculinities, sexualities and schooling*, Buckingham, Philadelphia: Open University Press.

Mack, F.R.P. and Jackson, T.E. (1990) 'High school student attitudes about teacher education as a career choice: comparison by ethnic/racial group', Paper presented at the Annual Meeting of the Association of Teacher Educators (Las Vegas, Nevada, February 5–8, 1990).

—— (1993) 'Teacher education as a career choice of Hispanic high school seniors', Technical Report, Missouri: Grand Rapids Public Schools.

Mahony, P., Hextall, I. and Menter, I. (2004) 'Threshold assessment and performance management: modernizing or masculinizing teaching in England?' *Gender and Education*, 16, 2: 131–49.

Mancus, D.S. (1992) 'Influence of male teachers on elementary school children's stereotyping of teacher competence', *Sex Roles: a journal of research*, 24: 109–28.

Marso, R. and Pigge, F. (1994) 'Personal and family characteristics associated with reasons given by teacher candidates for becoming teachers in the 1990s: implications for the recruitment of teachers', Paper presented at the Annual Conference of the Midwestern Educational Research Association, Chicago, IL, October 12–15, 1994.

—— (1997) 'Teacher recruitment effectiveness: a comparative study of the affective attributes of teacher candidates of the 1980s and the 1990s', *Teacher Education Quarterly*, 27: 83–91.

Martin, M. and Hickey, B. (1993) *The 1991 Leaving Certificate Examination: a review of the results*, Dublin: National Council for Curriculum Assessment.

Measor, L. and Sykes, P. (1992) *Gender and Schools*, London: Cassell.

Miller, J. (1992) *More Has Meant Women: The feminisation of schooling*, London: University of London Institute of Education/The Tufnell Press.

—— (1996) *School for Women*, London: Virago.

Miller, Janet. (1986) 'Women as teachers: enlarging conversations on issues of gender and self concept', *Journal of Curriculum and Research*, 1: 111–21.

—— (1993) 'Constructions of curriculum and gender', in S.K. Biklen and D. Pollard (eds) *Gender and Education: ninety-second yearbook of the national society for the study of education*, Chicago: University of Chicago Press.

Mills, M. and Lingard, B. (1997) 'Masculinity politics, myths and boys' schooling: a review essay', *British Journal of Educational Studies*, 45: 276–92.

Mills, R. and Mills, R. (1996) 'Adolescents' attitudes toward female gender roles: implications for education', *Adolescence*, 31: 741–45.

Morales, C. (1994) 'Education majors: why teaching as a profession?', *Education*, 114: 340–342.

Morgan, V. and Lynch, K. (1995) 'Gender and education: North and South', in P. Clancy, S. Drudy, K. Lynch and L. O'Dowd *Irish Society: sociological perspectives*, Dublin: Institute of Public Administration, pp 529–62.

Morren, S. (1970) 'The occupational aspirations and migratory decisions of Galway Gaeltacht school leavers', unpublished thesis, University College Galway.

Newby, D., Smith, G., Newby, R. and Miller, D. (1995) 'The relationship between high school students' perceptions of teaching as a career and selected background characteristics: implications for attracting students of color to teaching', *Urban Review*, 27: 235–49.

Oakley, A. (1972) *Sex, Gender and Society*, London: Maurice Temple Smith Ltd.

O'Connell, F. (1993) 'Male/female imbalance in primary teaching: an analysis of recruitment statistics', *Oideas*, 41: 138–47.

O'Connor, P. (1998) *Emerging Voices: women in contemporary Irish society*, Dublin: Institute of Public Administration.

O'Hearn, D. (1999) 'Tigers and transnational corporations: pathways from the periphery?' in R. Munck and D. O'Hearn (eds) *Critical Development Theory*, London and New York: Zed Books, pp 113–134.

Oppler, S. *et al.* (1992) 'Career interests of academically talented seventh graders', Paper presented at the Annual Meeting of the American Educational Research Association (Atlanta, GA, April 12–16, 1992).

O'Sullivan, D. (1980) 'Teachers' views on the effects of the home', *Educational Research*, 22: 138–42.

Organisation for Economic Co-operation and Development (1991) *Reviews of Education: Ireland*, Paris: OECD, Centre for Educational Research and Innovation.

—— (2003a) *Education at a Glance*, Paris: OECD, Centre for Educational Research and Innovation.

—— (2003b) 'Attracting, developing and retaining effective teachers', *Update December 2003*, <http://www.oecd.org> (accessed 20 January 2004).

—— (2004) 'The quality of the teaching workforce', *Policy Brief*, <http://www.oecd. org> (accessed 21 April 2004).

OFSTED (2003) *Boys' Achievement in Secondary Schools*, HMI 1659, Office for Standards in Education: <http://www.ofsted.gov.uk/publications/index.cfm?fuseaction=pubs. displayfile&id=3316&type=pdf> (accessed 21 April 2004)

Page, J. and Page, F. (1984) 'High school seniors' perceptions of teaching as a career opportunity', Paper presented at the Annual Meeting of the Association of Teacher Educators (New Orleans, LA, January 28–1 February, 1984).

Parsons, T. (1959) 'The school class as a social system: some of its functions in American society', *Harvard Educational Review*, 29: 297–318.

Penn, H. (1997) *Childcare as a Gendered Occupation*, London: Social Science Research Unit, Institute of Education, University of London.

Perry, C. and Quaglia, R. (1997) 'Perceptions of teaching caring: questions and impli- cations for teacher education', *Teacher Education Quarterly*, 24: 75–81.

Peters Behrens, D. (1997) 'Pathways to service: a phenomenological exploration of career related values among selected preservice teachers', *Teacher Education Quarterly* 24: 21–33.

Peterson, S. (1992) 'Teachers of tomorrow academy report', Technical Report, Arkansas: Pulaski County Special School District.

Quinn, J. (1982) 'Twenty years a-teaching – a look at the class of '61', *An Múinteoir Náisiúnta*, 26: 13–17.

Ramsden, M. (1988) 'Big boys don't cry' in Flora Macleod (ed.) *Perspectives 38: Gender and Education*, Exeter: School of Education, University of Exeter.

Raphael Reed, L. (1998) '"Zero tolerance": gender performance and school failure' in D. Epstein, J. Elwood, V. Hay and J. Maw (eds) *Failing Boys?: issues in gender and achievement*, Buckingham/Philadelphia: Open University Press.

Reid, I. and Caudwell, J. (1997) 'Why did secondary PGCE students choose teaching as a career?', *Research in Education*, 58: 46–58.

Richardson, J.T.E. and King, E. (1991) 'Gender differences in the experience of higher education', *Educational Psychology: an international journal of experimental educational psychology*, 11: 363–82.

Riddell, S.I. (1992) *Gender and the Politics of the Curriculum*, London: Routledge.

Robinson, B. and Huffman, G. (1982) 'Recruiting prospective male primary teachers into teacher education programs', *Reading Improvement*, 19: 164–8.

Rose, D. and Birkelund, G.E. (1991) 'Social class, gender and occupational segregation', Occasional Papers of the ESRC, Research Centre on Micro-social Change, Occasional Paper 1, Colchester: University of Essex.

Seifert, K. (1973) 'Some problems of men in child care center work', *Child Welfare*, 52: 167–71.

Serow, R. (1993) 'Why teach? altruism and career choice among nontraditional recruits to teaching', *Journal of Research and Development in Education*, 26: 197–204.

Shachar, R. (1996) 'Teacher training and the promotion of gender equality: a case study of Israeli society' in M. L. Kearney and A. Holden Ronning (eds) *Women and the University Curriculum*, London: Jessica Kingsley; Paris: UNESCO.

Shiel, G., Cosgrove, J., Sofroniou, N. and Kelly, A. (2001) *Ready for Life?: the literacy achievements of Irish 15-year-olds with comparative international data*, Dublin: Educational Research Centre.

Siltanen, J. (1994) *Locating Gender: occupational segregation, wages and domestic responsibilities*, London: University College London Press.

Skelton, A. (1993) 'On becoming a male primary teacher: the informal culture of students and the construction of hegemonic masculinity', *Gender and Education*, 5: 289–303.

Smedley, S. (1997) 'Men on the margins: male student primary teachers', *Changing English 4*, London: Institute of Education, University of London.

—— (1998) 'Perspectives on male student primary teachers', *Changing English 5*, London: Institute of Education, University of London.

Smyth, E. (1999) *Do Schools Differ?*, Dublin: ESRI.

Stevenson, M.R. (1994) (ed.) *Gender Roles Through the Life Span*, Muncie, IN: Ball State University.

Su, Zhixin (1997) 'Teaching as a profession and as a career: minority candidates' perspectives', *Teaching and Teacher Education*, 13: 325–40.

Super, D.E. (1968) *'Work Values Inventory'*, Teachers College, Columbia University (Copyright 1968), New York: Houghton Mifflin Company.

Teacher Training Agency (1998) 'Teaching comes tops with sixth formers', Press release TTA 65/98, 14 March 1998, <http://www.coi.gov.uk/coi/depts/GTT/coi8974d.ok> (accessed 17 October 2003).

—— (2003) *QTS Skills Tests in Numeracy and Literacy (February – September 2001): Report on National Results Data*, <http://www.useyourheadteach.gov.uk> (accessed 15 March 2004).

The Irish Times (1999) *Education and Living*, Dublin: The Irish Times.

Thomas, K. (1990) *Gender and Subject in Higher Education*, Buckingham: The Society for Research into Higher Education and Oxford University Press.

Tong, R. (1992) *Feminist Thought: a comprehensive introduction*, London: Routledge.

Tyack, D. and Strober, M. (1981) 'Jobs and gender: a history of the structuring of educational employment by sex', in R.O. Carlson and P.A. Schmuck (eds) *Educational Policy and Management*, New York, London: Academic Press Inc.

UNESCO (2001) *United Nations Educational, Scientific and Cultural Organisation World Education Report*, <http://www.unesco.org> (accessed 17 January 2002).

—— (2003) United Nations Educational, Scientific and Cultural Organisation world education indicators 'percentage of female teachers in the school years 1998–1999, 1999–2000, 2000–2001', <http://www.uis.unesco.org/ev.php?ID=5264_201&ID2 =DO_TOPIC> (accessed 20 September 2003).

Virginia Journal of Education (1993) 'Men in the classroom', *Virginia Journal of Education*, 86: 6–11.

Warren, L. (1997) 'The career structure of women in education', *Irish Educational Studies*, 16: 69–84.

Wharton, A. (1994) 'Men's and women's responses to segregated work' in M.R. Stevenson (ed.) *Gender Roles Through the Life Span*, Muncie, IN: Ball State University.

Wiersma, W. (1995) *Research Methods in Education: an introduction*, Sixth Edition, Boston: Allyn and Bacon.

Williams, C.L. (1993) (ed.) *Doing 'Women's Work': men in nontraditional occupations*, Newbury Park, CA: Sage.

—— (1995) *Still a Man's World: men who do women's work*, Berkeley, CA: University of California Press.

Williams, L.S. and Villemez, W.J. (1993) 'Seekers and finders: male entry and exit in female-dominated jobs' in C.L. Williams (ed.) *Doing 'Women's Work': men in nontraditional occupations*, Newbury Park, CA: Sage.

Wong, R.E. (1994) 'The relationship between interest in teaching as a career choice and perceptions of school/classroom environment of 7th and 8th grade students', Paper presented at the annual meeting of the American Educational Research Association. (New Orleans, LA, April 4–8, 1994).

Wylie, C. (2000) 'Trends in feminization of the teaching profession in OECD countries 1980–95', *Working Papers*, Geneva: International Labour Office, http://www.ilo.org /public/english/dialogue/sector/sectors/educat/publ.htm (accessed 17 October 2003).

Yates, L. (1993) 'Feminism and Australian state policy: some questions for the 1990s' in M. Arnot and K. Weiler (eds) *Feminism and Social Justice in Education*, London: Falmer.

—— (1997) 'Gender equity and the boys debate: what sort of challenge is it?', *British Journal of Sociology of Education*, 18: 337–47.

Notes

Chapter 1

1   See for example report of the OECD on Ireland (1991) the Green Paper, *Education for a Changing World* (1992), the White Paper, *Charting Our Education Future* (1995), *Ready to Learn*, the White Paper on Early Education (1999), the Green and White Papers on Adult Education (1998 and 2000) and the *Universities Act, 1997*, the *Education Act, 1998*, the *Education and Welfare Act, 2000* and the *Teaching Council Act, 2001*.

2   For example, the categories of socio-economic class and ethnic groups.

Chapter 2

1   The term 'hegemonic masculinity' is used to describe the socially dominant form of masculinity in any given period.

2   For an account of the methodology of this study, see Appendix Two.

3   It should be noted that these are broad typologies. A more accurate breakdown of schools into those whose pupil populations are predominantly 'rural' or 'urban' according to the population size of pupil's domestic residence was beyond the scope of this study. It is likely that some of the urban schools could have pupils from rural areas, as studies have found that a significant proportion of students attend schools other than their nearest one (e.g. Lynch, 1999).

4   It was decided that the distributions on selected key variables for all respondents would be coded and analysed. For the attitudinal variables it was decided to code and analyse the responses of all of the male respondents (46) as they formed just 10 per cent of the total. However, for the coding and analysis of the attitudinal variables it was decided to draw a proportionate random sample of 150 of the 411 female respondents, stratified by area of origin (see Appendix Two). In the analysis and tables it is clearly indicated whether all respondents, or a sample, were involved.

5   Teacher education is provided by education departments in the seven universities, or by colleges of education affiliated to one or other of the universities. Teacher education for the primary/elementary school sector is mainly provided on the concurrent model and consists of three or four year programmes provided by colleges of education attached to the universities. Students apply for places on these courses through a central applications system used to process all higher education applications, run by the Central Applications Office (CAO). With a number of exceptions, teacher education for post-primary teachers (for students aged 12–18) is provided on the consecutive model. Teaching is a regulated profession and the number of places on teacher education courses is limited by the Higher Education Authority, in

collaboration with the Department of Education and Science. Students specialise in their chosen areas of study (Arts/Humanities, Business, Science, etc.) to Bachelors degree level for a period of three or four years, depending on the university or programme of study. This is followed by a one-year, post-graduate, teacher education programme – the Higher Diploma in Education – which is the professional qualification for recognised second level teachers.

6 Responses were coded as an open question (i.e. as an open variable from which codes are derived) then recoded using the 15 categories from the Central Applications Office System and three others: secondary teaching, trades and army/police force.

Chapter 3

1 'Objective probabilities' are those which can be gauged through the use of statistical measurement. Thus, with regard to occupational or career choice, the objective probabilities of males or females choosing particular occupations are influenced by the existing structural patterns of male and female employment (Bourdieu and Passeron, 1977).

Chapter 4

1 Maintenance grants for students are normally available only to students from lower income families.
2 It was not considered practical or appropriate to seek the examination results for the respondents directly from the schools or Department of Education and Science. Information on individual pupils is covered by data protection legislation.
3 *Table 4.3a Junior Certificate Grade Point Average: Scoring Method*

Table 4.3a Junior Certificate Grade Point Average: scoring method

Grade level	A	B	C	D	E	F
Higher	12	11	10	9	8	7
Ordinary	9	8	7	6	5	4
Foundation	6	5	4	3	2	1

Source: Martin and Hickey, 1993: 7

Chapter 5

1 Because one of the objectives was to compare school leavers with student teachers, the 'concomitant' part of the scale was not tested on the third level cohort.
2 A score ranging from 0 through 1. The closer the score is to 1 the greater the reliability of the measure.

Chapter 6

1 Their study does report on some differences between single-sex and coeducational schools, and on some positive and negative effects of coeducation for both sexes.
2 R. J. Alexander (1984). *Primary Teaching*, London: Holt, Rinehart and Winston. Quoted in Acker (1994: 98).
3 As regards the reasons for choosing teaching, there were 227 responses from school

leavers, more than answered 'yes'. It is possible that some respondents who had not considered teaching answered this part of the question despite the instructions.

Appendix 2

1   On the advice of school principals, this meant that senior cycle students who were on an alternative senior cycle programme (the Leaving Certificate Applied Programme) which does not provide eligibility for university/college entry were not included, nor were those who had indicated clearly to their schools that they did not intend to apply for a third level place.
2   Invaluable advice was given by Ms Mary Dunne of the Statistics Section in the Department of Education and Science.
3   The 't' distribution is, in fact, many distributions, each of which has a 'degree of freedom', or 'df', which is the same as the number in the sample minus 1. Like the normal distribution, the 't' distributions are symmetrical, and bell-shaped. As the degrees of freedom increase, the 't' distributions become more and more like the normal (Wiersma, 1995). The 't' test is appropriate for the testing of differences in means where there are two independent samples.

Index

Page references that include tables or figures are given in **bold**.